The Corporation
and the Constitution

The Corporation
and the Constitution

Henry N. Butler
and
Larry E. Ribstein

The AEI Press

Publisher for the American Enterprise Institute
WASHINGTON, D.C.

1995

Library of Congress Cataloging-in-Publication Data

Butler, Henry N.
    The corporation and the Constitution / Henry N. Butler and Larry
E. Ribstein.
      p. cm.
    Includes bibliographical references.
    ISBN 0-8447-3864-6 (alk. paper).—ISBN 0-8447-3865-4 (pbk. :
alk. paper)
      1. Corporation law—United States. 2. Corporate governance—Law
and legislation—United States. 3. Corporations—Political
activity—Law and legislation—United States. 4. Liberty of
contract—United States. 5. Corporations—United States—State
supervision. I. Ribstein, Larry E. II. Title.
KF1418.B88   1995
346.73'066—dc20
[347.30666]   94-26919
                                                    CIP

ISBN 0-8447-3864-6 (alk. paper)
ISBN 0-8447-3865-4 (pbk.: alk. paper)

The AEI Press
Publisher for the American Enterprise Institute
1150 17th Street, N.W., Washington, D.C. 20036

Distributed in Europe, the Middle East, Africa, and selected territories
outside the United States by Eurospan. For more information, contact
Eurospan, 3 Henrietta Street, London WC2E 8LU, England.

Printed in the United States of America

Contents

Preface

Much of the business activity in this country is conducted through corporations. Not surprisingly, corporate wealth is often the target of interest groups and regulators. Regulation may come in many different forms, including restrictions on competition, price controls (as indicated by the recent attack on drug prices), protection of labor unions, increasing corporate taxes, limiting corporations' roles in political debate, or ensuring nonshareholder groups a voice in corporate control. It follows that constitutional protection of corporations' business activities and of corporations' ability to participate in political debate is crucial to this country's productivity. Yet courts often minimize the constitutional rights of corporate firms by assigning these rights to an artificial, government-created entity and then holding that government should have broad power to limit the rights of their creations. Even courts that properly view the corporation as a private arrangement see it as one needing special state protection.

The inadequacy of constitutional protection of the corporation is most glaring in the area of corporate governance. Corporate governance, which refers to the economic and legal dimensions of the relationship between shareholders and managers, has been a concern of economists at least since the days of Adam Smith, and a major policy concern of legal commentators since Adolph A. Berle and Gardiner C. Means's influential book on the "separation of ownership and control."[1] The fundamental question in corporate governance is, How should shareholders be protected from managerial misbehavior? This raises numerous issues: Can shareholders protect themselves? Do managers have to have incentives to behave? Can government regulators (legislators and courts) protect shareholders? Do regulators have the incentives to protect shareholders? And, finally, do shareholders need constitutional protection from corporate regulators?

The thesis of this book is that legal and constitutional treatment of the corporation are not attuned to the economic and business reality of the corporation because many legal scholars, judges, and justices apply an outmoded understanding of the nature of the corporation in attempting to "regulate" or "control" the relationship between shareholders and managers. Contractarians view the corporation as a set of private contractual relationships among providers of capital and services. The obvious implication of this characterization is that the contracting parties should be free to adopt whatever contract terms they deem to be in their mutual interest. Corporate regulators, conversely, argue either that the corporation is not a contract at all or that it should at least be subject to more intrusive government regulation than other contracts. Instead of a regime of freedom of contract favored by the contractarians, corporate regulators usually favor mandatory legal rules—that is, regulations that cannot be contracted around—restricting the relationship between shareholders and managers. Thus, the heart of the debate is a question of freedom of contract versus government-imposed legal restrictions.

The debate is far from settled. The influential and prestigious American Law Institute (ALI) waded into a decade-long controversy between the contractarians and corporate regulators about the proper regard for freedom of contract in defining the relationship of shareholders and managers in the corporation. The controversy finally culminated in the adoption last spring of the *Principles of Corporate Governance: Analysis and Recommendations*. The ALI's deliberations featured uncharacteristic acrimony, delay, and political rhetoric.

This book seeks to correct the long misunderstanding about the corporate form of enterprise that has prevented proper application of the Constitution to the corporation. The book will articulate a contractual theory of the corporation that is based on the modern economics of the firm. It will then apply this theory to the interpretation of constitutional doctrine. Acceptance of this analysis should lead to broader constitutional protection of this important category of economic rights.

Chapter 1—"The Nature of the Corporation—Freedom of Contract versus Government Regulation"—introduces the theoretical framework that will be applied throughout the monograph. The contractual theory of the corporation states that the corporation is a set of contracts among the participants in the business, including shareholders, managers, creditors, employees, and others. The terms of the agency contract include the provisions of state law, which are regarded as a standard form that can be accepted by the parties or rejected either by drafting around the provision or by incorporating in another state. The corporate contract also specifies the extent to which the parties rely on the competitive pressures from capital, product, and managerial labor markets as well as internal incentive structures such as corporate hierarchy, boards of directors, and managerial compensation contracts to force agents to act in their shareholders' best interests. The policy implication is that private parties to the corporate contract should be free to order their affairs in whatever manner they find appropriate.

Some courts and scholars have questioned the contractual theory of the corporation on several grounds. One of these grounds is historical. A cornerstone of the corporate regulators' position is the concession theory of the corporation, which states that the corporation, rather than being a contract, is a creation, or concession, of state legislatures. This theory had its origin in the early history of the corporation, when corporations were, in fact, created by special charter. The theory has no relevance today, when corporations are freely formed by making a simple filing under general corporation laws. Nevertheless, the Supreme Court persists in citing Justice John Marshall's ancient statement, made during the special-charter era, in *Trustees of Dartmouth College v. Woodward*,[2] that the corporation is an "artificial being, existing solely in contemplation of state law." Corporate regulators assert that this view of the corporation persists today, pointing to numerous apparently mandatory provisions in state corporation law. The number of truly mandatory provisions is quite limited, however, particularly in light of the fact that a corporation can often escape these provisions simply by incorporating in another state. In any event, this argument is simply a statement about current law, not a normative argument about what the law ought to be.

Modern corporate regulators also rely on normative arguments for regulation of the corporate firm. These arguments are of two types. The first is that the corporate form is so powerful that it needs to be controlled in order to limit massive externalization of costs by corporations and wealth transfers to corporations from other groups. The second is that regulation is needed to protect corporate investors from malfeasance by remote corporate managers. As we demonstrate in chapter 1, however, these arguments are deeply flawed because they overlook or minimize the importance of well-developed financial and product markets that constrain corporate firms and their managers.

Despite the extensive literature and evidence supporting the contractual theory of the corporation, we show in the remainder of the book that the outmoded corporate regulators' position continues to inform the application of the Constitution to the corporation. We also demonstrate how application of contractual theory would change the constitutional analysis and protections of the corporate contract.

Chapter 2—"Constitutional Protection of the Corporate Contract"—discusses the application of the contract clause to the corporation. The application of the contract clause is a fundamental element of constitutional protection of the corporation. As discussed in chapter 1, powerful market forces help ensure the evolution of efficient contract terms in firms. The biggest threat to this process is that parties to the contract—particularly politically powerful corporate managers—will use the legislative process to alter contract terms. Application of the contract clause to invalidate retroactive legislative changes would prevent this from happening. An understanding of the contractual theory of the corporation shows clearly that corporations should be subject to the contract clause to the same extent as other contracts, and that there is no special justification for retroactive state interference in corporate governance arrangements.

Chapters 3 and 4 discuss two important areas in which the First Amendment relates to corporate governance. Chapter 3—"Corporate Campaign Activities"—shows that, contrary to the Supreme Court's recent decision in *Austin v. Michigan Chamber of Commerce*,[3] the political speech of for-profit corporations is entitled to the same level of protection as political speech by individuals and ideological groups. The *Austin* decision assumes that restrictions on corporate political speech are necessary to protect shareholders and the political process from managers' use of corporate resources to establish their own political power. This assumption is inconsistent with the market constraints on managers' conduct discussed in chapter 1. Moreover, even if statutory constraints are necessary, election statutes are an inappropriate way of achieving this end. It is enough to rely on the terms of the corporate contract themselves and on the contract clause, which provides the most important protection against managerial misuse of shareholder wealth to influence the political process.

Chapter 4—"Corporate Governance Speech and the First Amendment"—discusses application of the First Amendment to communications within the firm, focusing on regulation of proxy communications. We show that an important category of this speech—proxy communications—almost certainly should be characterized as political and entitled to the highest level of First Amendment protection. Moreover, even if proxy and other speech relating to corporate governance is regarded as commercial speech and therefore subject to a lower level of constitutional protection, there is still an inadequate justification for government interference. In general, the

Constitution should be applied to prevent political tinkering with control of the publicly held corporation.

Chapter 5—"Choosing Law by Contract"—discusses constitutional protection of the firm's selection of the applicable state law. Enforcement of the firm's choice of applicable law is critical to the contractual theory of the corporation because, as discussed in chapter 1, it has made possible the "race to the top"—the competition among states to develop efficient laws. Moreover, chapter 4 shows that application of the law selected by the parties to a contract has other important advantages, including promoting certainty and uniformity. This chapter can be viewed as an extension of the analysis in chapter 2: Just as the Constitution protects the parties' contract over time, so it protects the contract spatially as the firm transacts business in different states. Much of this protection is under the commerce clause, which can be interpreted as protecting the parties from state legislation that benefits locals at the expense of nonresidents. While this principle is difficult to apply generally, it strongly supports a limited rule of enforcing the parties' contractual choice of law, including the law of the state of incorporation. Our conclusion concerning the commerce clause is consistent with the Supreme Court's landmark decision in *CTS Corp. v. Dynamics Corp.*[4]

The analysis in chapter 5 presents an interesting twist on the contractual theory of the corporation. Ironically, corporations have been protected by the "internal affairs" rule precisely because they have been viewed as different from ordinary contracts. Constitutionally protecting choice of law for all contracts would ensure protection of the corporation as a contract. Moreover, securing interstate recognition for new types of firms that are now being developed, including limited liability companies and limited liability partnerships, would not only extend the race to the top broadly to all kinds of contracts, but would also enhance jurisdictional competition in corporate law. If enforcement of contractual choice of law is broadly recognized, the parties to corporate-type firms will be able to freely avoid "mandatory" corporate terms by selecting other contractual forms.

Chapter 6 offers several observations about the importance of this monograph as the first application of the Constitution to the corporation in the light of the economic theory of the firm. We believe that our monograph is a significant contribution to modern constitutional and corporate scholarship in at least two respects. First, it offers a coherent theory of applying the Constitution to the corporation. Thus, it has implications even for constitutional rights we do not discuss in detail. A second contribution of our monograph is that it forces scholars to appreciate the developments that have taken place totally outside the realm of traditional scholarly discourse on the Constitution. We show that in formulating constitutional rules it is at least as important to understand the real-world context of particular problems to which the Constitution is applied as it is to develop a global framework of constitutional analysis. Most important, accepting our theory of full constitutional protection of freedom of contract in the corporation would reduce costly government interference in corporate governance and increase the attractiveness of investing in American firms.

1

The Nature of the Corporation—Freedom of Contract versus Government Regulation

Throughout much of the history of corporate law, courts and scholars have debated the nature of the corporation and, thus, the proper role of government regulation in corporate governance.

Introduction

This chapter summarizes two fundamentally different approaches to the nature of the corporation—the contractual theory and the concession (or regulatory) theory. It is important to understand these approaches because they have significant implications for public policies toward the corporation.

The following section presents the contractual theory of the corporation.[1] In order to survive, all publicly traded corporations must take steps to minimize agency costs—the costs associated with the separation of ownership and control. Corporations employ numerous corporate governance mechanisms—market forces and contractual devices—designed to solve the corporate agency problems. These mechanisms may complement and substitute for the legal rules found in state corporation laws.

The subsequent section discusses the corporate law implications of the contractual theory. The most important implication is that courts should treat corporate governance arrangements with the same presumption of enforceability that they accord other contracts.

Last, we present the regulatory theory of the corporation and show that the historical, legal, and economic bases of the regulatory theory do not justify the regulatory implications of the theory. That section concludes by demonstrating that even if the regulatory theory were sound, many of its implications for legal rules would be ineffec-

1

tive because of problems with the passage and enforcement of mandatory rules as well as the ability of parties to avoid the rules.

In general, we do not assert that corporate governance should never be regulated. Rather, we show that because corporations are not wards of the state, and because the capital markets that discipline corporate contracts do not require more legal intervention than other markets, it follows that there is no justification for subjecting corporate arrangements to a higher level of regulation than other contracts. As we discuss throughout the book, this undercuts rationales that have been offered for limiting recognition of important constitutional rights in the corporate context.

The Contractual Theory of the Corporation

A major intellectual theme in the study of the modern corporation is the "separation of ownership and control" thesis, which was first popularized by Adolph A. Berle and Gardiner C. Means in 1932 in their famous book *The Modern Corporation and Private Property*. The basic notion is that dispersed owners of the modern corporation do not have the incentive to control corporate management—directors and officers—effectively, and that managers often act in their own interests rather than in the stockholders' interests.

Much of the Berle and Means analysis is based on their assumption that shareholders should play a major, direct role in monitoring corporate managers. This seems reasonable at first glance because, after all, the voting rules of corporations suggest that corporations are democratic institutions: shareholders elect directors and have the right to offer recommendations to be voted upon by fellow shareholders through the corporate proxy machinery. Despite these legal rights, however, the reality of the large corporation is far from democratic, because shareholders rarely have the incentive to exercise their legal rights. For many individual shareholders, dissatisfaction with the management of the corporation results in the sale of the stock. The so-called Wall Street Rule is that "rationally ignorant" shareholders sell their shares rather than become involved in the internal affairs of the corporation. Because of shareholders' apparent indifference, Berle and Means and their ideological progeny erroneously assume that directors and managers are free to operate the corporation in a manner that is not necessarily in the shareholders' best interest.

Although the analysis in this section shows that Berle and Means were wrong about the appropriate role of shareholders in corporate governance, the fundamental insight of the Berle and Means theory—

that there are costs of delegating control over financial capital to corporate managers—provides the cornerstone of the contractual theory of the corporation. The key issue is how best to minimize those costs—through contract or through regulation.

The contractual theory of the corporation is central to the arguments presented in this book. Below, we describe the fundamental problem addressed by the contractual theory—the agency costs associated with the separation of ownership and control. The next subsection states some concepts at the heart of the contractual theory. The third subsection describes the market forces and contractual constraints that minimize agency costs. The fourth subsection offers a synthesis and summary of the analysis.

Agency Costs of the "Separation of Ownership and Control." The presence of rationally ignorant shareholders presents managers of corporations with opportunities to engage in activities that are not necessarily in the shareholders' best interests. Agency costs is the name given to the costs associated with managers who are less than perfect agents of the corporation's shareholders. Agency theory, which provides the theoretical bases for the contractual theory of the corporation, suggests that agency costs are minimized by competitive forces that align managers' interests with shareholders' interests.

Before looking at the solutions to the agency costs problem, it is helpful to be more precise in the identification of some potential conflicts between managers and shareholders in the corporate firm:

• *Effort.* Both agency theory and the separation-of-ownership-and-control literature are concerned with whether entrenched managers have the incentives to maximize their efforts in pursuing the maximum rate of return for shareholders.

• *Horizon.* This conflict refers to the issue of how to encourage a manager to act in the shareholders' interests as the manager approaches retirement or prepares to leave the firm for other opportunities.

• *Risk aversion.* Entrenched managers have an incentive to avoid bankruptcy at all costs, but shareholders with diversified portfolios are risk neutral with respect to individual securities in their portfolios. In the absence of corrective governance mechanisms, managers' interests will be more closely aligned with those of bondholders than shareholders.

• *Underleveraging.* Within a certain range, the tax savings from debt and increased leverage can increase a firm's profit, but risk-averse managers may not like the increased risk associated with increased leverage and debt service demands. Once again, however, shareholders would prefer the undertaking of such risk because they specialize in bearing such risks.

• *Dividend payout problem.* Risk-averse managers may prefer to reinvest their firm's profits in the firm rather than distribute them to shareholders, even though the shareholders could put them to more productive use.

This list of conflicts between managers and shareholders is not intended to be exhaustive, but it does serve as a reference for discussing the roles of different corporate governance mechanisms that control agency costs.

A Perspective of Fundamental Concepts. The contractual theory of the firm is best understood and appreciated in light of a few fundamental concepts on which the theory is based. First, no one is forced to use the corporate form of organization: there is freedom of choice in organizational form, in the sense that investors and entrepreneurs may choose among numerous alternative organizational arrangements. Second, market forces are ubiquitous in publicly traded corporations, because efficient capital markets are constantly evaluating the impact of corporate governance arrangements. Third, it is important to trade off the inevitable costs of delegating power to agents against the benefits of doing so. In other words, it is important to distinguish between optimal and complete discipline of managers.

Choice of organizational form. Perhaps the most basic source of protection of shareholders is the existence of numerous organizational alternatives to the corporate form of business. This fundamental choice constrains the ability of corporate managers to misbehave.

Contractual protection against agency costs is not limited to devices within the corporation, but extends to choice of the corporate form of contract over types of contractual organization of economic activity. Other types of organization include economic firms[2] such as partnerships, limited liability companies, sole proprietorships and joint ventures, and nonfirm, relational contracts, such as franchises and long-term supply contracts.[3] Individuals choose among types of organization by comparing costs and benefits of forms, including the costs and benefits of delegating control to agents, so as to maximize their gains from engaging in a particular activity. Thus, we do not observe all economic activity being carried on through one type of organization. Instead, we observe millions of organizations of many types, sizes, and structures.[4]

The profusion of organizational forms can be explained best as responses to the costs and benefits of various forms in particular situations. A prominent factor in these trade-offs is the costs and benefits of particular ways of giving discretion to and monitoring agents. Monitoring costs could be sharply limited simply by dividing all enterprise into small firms that contract with each other, but this form of organization would pose formidable problems of its own. The profusion of contract types and the empirical work on the factors that determine choice of form[5] show the extent to which agency problems are being dealt with contractually. The existence of numerous organizational forms also raises serious doubts whether the government can devise a single optimal set of terms or, indeed, effectively impose these terms on firms.

The most frequently selected organizational form is the corporation—the topic of this book. After selecting the organizational form, the organizing entrepreneur must make many decisions concerning corporate governance. The more specific corporate governance mechanisms are discussed later in this chapter.

Efficient capital markets and corporate governance contracts. There can be little doubt at this stage of development about the general efficiency of the securities markets.[6] Prices of actively traded securities[7] quickly reflect at least all public information about a company.[8]

The basic mechanism of market efficiency is that information about a firm continually alters investor expectations about future returns, and hence the prices at which they will sell and buy their securities. This information reaches investors in a wide variety of ways, including voluntary and mandatory public disclosures by firms, stories in the financial media, reports by securities analysts, and disclosures of insider trades.[9] Even information that is not disclosed may be anticipatorily reflected to some extent in market prices through trades by many uninformed investors.[10]

The efficient markets hypothesis is important because it means that corporate contracts that harm investor interests will be recognized and punished by price reductions in the market. Incorporation in a state with a corporation law that facilitates managerial abuse of shareholders, for example, will result in lower share prices than would be found if the same firm were incorporated in a state with a different corporation law.[11] Thus, the efficient-capital-markets hypothesis means that securities markets are "fair" in the sense that the corporate shareholder gets what he is paying for, both in the terms of the contract and in the substantive nature of the product, including the quality of management. It also means that corporate managers will have incentives to maximize share value or risk being replaced by someone who can do a better job.[12]

The information efficiently reflected in market prices includes the terms of contracts constraining managerial discretion and the prospects that this discretion will be exercised consistently with investor interests. Any change in these contracts, and any change in or new information about the managers of such a corporation (such as their track records, reputations, and the like) will be reported in the financial media. Through the mechanisms of market efficiency, this information is reflected in market price. And because information about contract terms and managers is accurately reflected in market price, investors get what they pay for, and capital is allocated to the most efficient firms. Although the average investor is rationally ignorant of the details of corporate governance, this ignorance is of no importance regarding investment decisions as long as the efficient market operates to discount information concerning expected agency costs into securities prices.[13]

Optimal versus complete discipline of managers. The optimal amount of agency costs is not zero. Because real resources are used in reducing agency costs, it is not worthwhile to invest resources reducing agency costs unless the resulting cost reduction is greater than the value of the resources used. In this sense, even the resources devoted to controlling agency costs are properly identified as agency costs. Thus, agency costs include not only the direct costs associated with agents acting in their own interest at the expense of shareholders, but also the costs of controlling managerial agents through legal and market governance mechanisms. The use of the corporate governance mechanisms discussed in the next section merely reveals that the costs of monitoring are justified by reducing the costs of an agent's deviation from the behavior that would occur if the agent and principal were one.

As the huge body of literature on agency costs and the theory of the firm has demonstrated, delegating power to agents carries inevitable costs that are constantly traded off against benefits, as discussed above. "Play" in the contracts constraining managers should not be confused with inefficiency in the creation of these contracts. Even if markets cannot perfectly constrain acts of managers, still they can discipline the development of agency contracts, the terms of which are readily observable and reflected in market price. As discussed below in the section on corporate law, the terms of these agency contracts permit both monitoring by markets, including the corporate control and managerial employment markets, and gap-filling fiduciary duties. Thus, the parties' contracts involve deliberate choices between market and legal control of agents. In short, the presence of play in the corporate contract suggests, rather than a failure of contracting, a recognition that the least costly way of dealing with agency costs may be to allow them to be checked by incentive or monitoring devices instead of by liability rules.

Corporate Governance Mechanisms—Market Forces and Contractual Constraints on Management Conduct. Much of the economic literature on the governance of the modern corporation reflects an evolutionary view of the development and use of certain governance mechanisms.[14] In this view, the modern corporation is passing the test of time. In fact, it is not farfetched to say that the modern corporation is one of the most successful inventions in history, as evidenced by its widespread adoption and survival as a primary vehicle of capitalism over the past century. Economists, however, have only recently begun to understand the economic nature of the corporation. The contractual theory of the corporation is a synthesis of this new learning.

The contractual theory states that the corporation is a set of contracts among the participants in the business, including shareholders, managers, creditors, employees, and others.[15] The corporate contract also specifies the extent to which the parties rely on the competitive pressures from capital, product, and managerial labor markets, as well as internal incentive structures such as corporate hierarchy, boards of directors, and managerial compensation contracts, to force agents to act in their shareholders' best interests. The terms of the agency contract include the provisions of state law, which are regarded as a standard form that can be accepted by the parties or rejected, either by drafting around the provision or by incorporating in another state.[16] The policy implication is that private parties to the corporate contract should be free to order their affairs in whatever manner they find appropriate.

The contractual theory focuses on powerful market forces that encourage managers to act in shareholders' interests. In order to raise capital at the lowest possible price, managers must offer contract terms—including evidence of the existence of intrafirm incentives—that convince investors that agency costs will be minimized. This section identifies and discusses those contractual terms.

Shareholder voting rights and the market for corporate control. Berle and Means argued that the dispersion and passivity of public corporation shareholders disconnected ownership from control of assets, with potentially serious consequences for the use of corporate property.[17] A literature has developed over the past twenty years, however, establishing that the problem is not as great as was feared by Berle and Means and modern opponents of private ordering. This literature accepts the basic Berle and Means characterization of shareholders' incentives, but recognizes that other mechanisms protect shareholders. Thus, it is true that shareholders are rationally ignorant in the sense that active and informed participation in corporate affairs would involve large costs, of which an individual shareholder could capture only a small portion of the benefit.[18] But shareholders nevertheless are protected from managerial misconduct by, among other things, their right to vote for directors and on other matters, and their right to sell their shares.[19]

Shareholder voting power can be aggregated into a control bloc through purchase of shares by a bidder for control, who thereby acquires sufficient economic interest in the firm to make active monitoring worthwhile.[20] If the buyer improves the firm through displacement or other change in management, it reaps a profit as the stock price rises to reflect the improvement. This so-called market for corporate control provides an external source of control over internal corporate affairs, and it provides incumbent managers with the incentive to write optimal contracts.

Considerable evidence supports the importance of this market in protecting against mismanagement.[21] There is also evidence of the continued importance of shareholder voting rights,[22] which, in light of shareholder passivity, must be largely explicable in terms of the market for corporate control.

Although the market for corporate control is important, exclusive reliance on it to solve all the potential conflicts of interest associated with the separation of ownership and control is neither justified nor necessary. Thus, it is not a substantial criticism of the contractual theory of the corporation to argue that the market for control alone fails to achieve perfect discipline. Managerial discretion is also constrained by other market and legal mechanisms discussed elsewhere in this section, including monitoring by large owners and outside board members. While the market for corporate control is therefore properly viewed as a last resort mechanism for correcting excessive managerial discretion, it is the persistent threat of displacement through control transfers that is primarily responsible for reducing the likelihood that shareholders will be harmed by their agents. The market for corporate control provides the glue that holds together the nexus of contracts.

Corporate hierarchy, the board of directors, and the market for directors. A substantial body of influential theoretical work on corporate management recognizes the importance of the development in the 1920s of the multidivisional, or M-form of organization of large firms, replacing the unitary, or U-form of organization.[23] The M-form of organization places responsibility for long-range planning and policy on a group of managers separate from those responsible for day-to-day operations, thus facilitating coherent planning for the entire enterprise instead of factional war among subgroups. The general planning group includes the board of directors. Most important for present purposes, the planning group provides internal monitoring of managers by efficiently separating decision management (the initiation and implementation of strategic plans) and decision control (the ratification and monitoring of the strategy formulation and implementation process).[24]

The superior efficiency of the M-form of management for many large firms has been empirically validated.[25] Empirical evidence also shows that there is a systematic, although nonlinear, relationship between board composition and corporate financial performance.[26]

Executive compensation contracts and markets for managers. Executive compensation is often structured in ways that attempt to solve conflicts between investors and managers by aligning their interests, as through stock options, stock appreciation rights, phantom stock, and other mechanisms that tie compensation to market-based performance.[27] Incentives can also be aligned by rewarding managerial achievements through payments that constitute a form of "ex post settling up."[28]

Corporate managers recognize that they can improve the firm's performance by reducing agency costs. Managers compete with one another to attain the top positions in their companies, and most promotion decisions are made on the basis of an individual's productivity. Moreover, top-level managers often increase their salaries by jumping to other firms or threatening to do so. Thus, competition for managerial services, both inside and outside the corporation, encourages managers to act in shareholders' best interests.[29]

Ownership structure. Ownership structure plays an important role in corporate governance.[30] In contrast with the conventional view of residual claimants as rationally ignorant of the firm's internal affairs and exiting the firm in dissatisfaction, some owners of large blocks of shares may have so much of their wealth tied up in a firm that they cannot afford to ignore the governance of the corporation. Monitoring, or the possibility of monitoring, by large shareholders alters managerial behavior and reduces agency costs.[31] Thus, ownership structure is another of the many corporate governance mechanisms that can be utilized in controlling agency costs. Of course, in many corporations, the ownership structure is so diffuse that shareholders are truly rationally ignorant, in which case the other governance mechanisms become relatively more important.

One example of the trade-offs inherent in choice of form concerns the selection of closed versus open (sometimes referred to as public) ownership of the firm.[32] In closely held corporations and partnerships, in which all owners are generally active in managing the business, monitoring of agents is less a problem than in public companies, in which ownership is separated from control. But public ownership has many benefits. Among other things, it permits specialization of capital-raising and managerial functions and development of a public market for the firm's stock. A public market, in turn, accurately values the firm's assets, thereby facilitating value-increasing investments that may not pay off before owners expect to sell out.[33]

The choice between the more intense monitoring of agents in the closely held firm and the advantages of public ownership depends on many factors. The benefits of public ownership may outweigh the costs where decision making is sufficiently complex that monitoring and direct management cannot cheaply be combined in single individuals. Also, a firm may need larger amounts of capital than can be cheaply raised from individuals who are willing to contribute managerial services (as where, because of the risk of opportunistic conduct by contracting parties, the firm must own rather than contract for expensive assets).

Capital market competition and capital structure. Most corporations use a mixture of debt and equity financing. In a path-breaking 1958 article, Franco Modigliani and Merton Miller showed that, under a set of specified assumptions, including absence of transaction and information costs, the capital structure of a firm—that is, its selection of the combination of debt and equity financing—is irrelevant to the total value of the firm.[34] This poses a riddle: Why do we observe different capital structures across firms?

The analytical strength of the contractual theory of the corporation is demonstrated by its ability to answer the Modigliani and Miller riddle. In a landmark article, Jensen and Meckling use agency problems and monitoring of managers to identify the relevance of capital structure to the value of a firm.[35] An all-equity structure gives substantial discretion to managers to use corporate assets for their own benefit subject to the various monitoring and devices discussed in this section. Managers may, for example, directly benefit them-

10

selves at investor expense by appropriating corporate funds for personal use and by retaining earnings beyond what the company profitably can reinvest. Moreover, managers may make investments that are less risky than the shareholders would prefer because their nondiversifiable human capital and financial investments in the firm may make them more risk averse than the diversified shareholders. Equity holders would demand to be compensated for or protected from these risks.[36]

Corporate managers have an incentive to minimize the combined costs of debt and equity capital because failure to do so would make them vulnerable to takeover. In order to raise equity capital at the lowest possible cost, a corporation's managers must convince potential shareholders that agency costs will be minimized.

Bondholders also must address conflict of interest problems. A debt-heavy structure, for example, may be in the shareholders' interests from a management-monitoring standpoint, in that it constrains excess retention of earnings or excessive risk avoidance by managers.[37] Conversely, such a structure may exacerbate the equity-debt conflict, because it encourages equity holders to make highly risky investments that may produce great benefits to the equity holders if they succeed, and losses to the debt holders if they fail.[38]

The above brief discussion only scratches the surface of the complex trade-offs involved in designing capital structures and related contracts that minimize agency costs. Under the Jensen-Meckling view, different capital structures may be responses to the different types of agency problems inherent in different types of firms.[39] There is no one optimal capital structure for all corporations. The important point is that the market responds to agency problems in a more sensitive way than would be possible through mandatory legal rules.

Product market competition. Product market competition forces managers to attempt to maximize their firms' profits, because failure to do so in competitive markets often means the failure of the firm. As discussed above, managers have reason to be more risk averse than shareholders about failure of the corporation because of their nondiversifiable investments in the firm. Moreover, failure to maximize profits will be reflected in a below-average return on shareholders' investments, thus making the firm an attractive takeover target.

The role of corporate law and fiduciary duties. The corporate law of fiduciary duties, which proscribes theft and specifies standards of care and loyalty, is a governance mechanism that the contracting parties may select to minimize corporate agency costs. These duties

11

may be useful because markets do not operate without cost, and because market and incentive mechanisms may be inadequate to deal with last-period or one-time conduct when the agent rationally concludes that the benefits of a one-time misuse of discretion are worth the penalties the employment market will impose.[40] Fiduciary duties reduce the transaction and negotiating costs of reaching and adhering to optimal contracts, particularly those calling for acts over an extended period in which it is costly to anticipate and draft for every contingency.[41] Conversely, where the benefits (including certainty) of specifying duties are significant and the costs are relatively low, the parties may enter into a "fully contingent" contract, in which the parties' acts under all contingencies are specified. Alternatively, even in long-term contracts the parties may forgo legally enforceable duties in favor of the kinds of market constraints discussed elsewhere in this section.

In selecting between fiduciary duties and alternative constraints, the parties consider both the costs and the benefits of fiduciary duties, and at the margin they trade off fiduciary duties for other constraints. On the benefit side, it is relevant that the other contractual and market devices discussed in this section do not operate perfectly. Thus, the parties to corporate contracts may conclude that a judicial remedy is necessary to fill in the gap left by extrajudicial remedies. But the parties may also conclude that the costs of fiduciary duties outweigh their gap-filling benefits. Among other things, fiduciary duties shift risk to managers, who are poor risk-bearers, and expose the corporation to costly litigation.[42] Just as there are imperfect extrajudicial remedies, so there are imperfect judicial remedies. Thus, it is a fallacy to assume that merely because fiduciary duties and remedies are part of the contract in some cases that they are always so, and that shareholders should not be able to opt out of these duties.

Fiduciary duties are part of rather than separate from the parties' contract. It is irrelevant that the terms invented by courts, like clothes manufactured for potential consumers, are not explicitly bargained for and may even be contrary to what particular parties would want. If the parties can choose the terms by either accepting them or contracting around them, the result of this choice is a contract. Thus, the question is not how the terms are articulated, but how they apply to the parties.

Synthesis. Legal and market governance mechanisms, when combined in the manner most appropriate for the particular circumstances of each firm, resolve most of the conflicts between shareholders and managers. In particular, the market for corporate control provides an external monitoring mechanism that discourages shirking and encourages managers to select the optimal governance contracts for their corporation. The horizon problem is reduced by the use of stock options and pension plans. The risk-aversion and underleverage problems are ameliorated by stock options. The dividend payout problem is rationalized by capital-market competition. Managers substitute among the various governance mechanisms until the marginal net productivity of each mechanism is equal. The sophistication and the firm-by-firm variation of contractual devices that have been developed to deal with a problem provide important circumstantial evidence that markets are protecting shareholders.

The contractual theory of the corporation does not assert that agency costs are or can be reduced to zero. The reduction of agency costs through contract and reliance on market forces is not free. The market for corporate control, for example, and the other market mechanisms cannot work without costly monitoring of the agent's performance. Agency costs, however, are minimized by contracts, and these contracts are subject to effective market discipline.

The contractual theory provides a basis for understanding the appropriate roles of privately negotiated contracts and mandatory legal rules, as well as a powerful set of tools for responding to persistent calls for mandated changes in corporate governance. The corporation, and the current system of state corporate law, appears to have passed the ultimate market test, as evidenced by the fact that the corporation is the dominant form of business organization. The major lesson of the contractual theory is that the success of the large publicly traded corporation should encourage critics of the corporation to attempt to figure out what is right with the modern corporation before trying to fix it.

Freedom of Contract, Corporate Law, and the Contractual Theory

The primary emphasis of this book is the implications of the contractual theory of the corporation for greater constitutional protection of contractual aspects of the corporate governance contract. To appreciate the significance of the constitutional protections, we must first consider the implications of the contractual theory for traditional corporate law doctrine. This section extends the analysis of the contractual theory of the corporation by considering what is involved in enforcement of the corporate contract. The relevant issues concern interpretation and application of the parties' agreement and the appropriate roles of federal and state law.

Freedom of Contract in Context. It is reasonable to assume that the parties to the contracts that a firm comprises anticipate the numerous problems associated with specialization, delegation, team production, and agency relationships. Freedom of contract allows the parties to structure their relations in a manner that ameliorates most of the agency problems inherent in the large corporation. In this regard, it is useful to consider the legal nature of the corporation within the context of the contractual theory of the corporation.

Most state corporation laws are enabling in that they reflect the philosophy of freedom of contract that has guided corporation law since the first truly modern general incorporation laws were passed in the late nineteenth century. The state's corporation law specifies the terms of the contract in the absence of a specific provision varying the laws. Firms can alter most, if not all, of the terms by a specific provision in the articles of incorporation or bylaws to suit their particular needs.

This model of corporate law is consistent with the discussion in the previous section. The trade-off, or contingency, model of corporation law argues that the desirability of certain corporate law provisions is a function of the characteristics of the particular corporation under examination. This is most obvious when comparing the legal rules applicable to closely held firms with the needs of firms with widely scattered holdings. Moreover, only the contracting parties can know the particular set of corporate law rules most appropriate to their circumstances. Freedom of contract allows the corporate transactors to contract for the optimal mixture of market and legal restraints on agency costs.

The contractual model of state law is supported by the efficient-capital-markets hypothesis. The information efficiently reflected in market prices includes the statutory and case law of the firm's state of incorporation, including the terms of contracts constraining managerial discretion and the prospects that this discretion will be exercised consistently with investor interests. Any material change in these contracts, like new information reflecting on the abilities of the corporation's managers, will be reported in the financial media and reflected in market prices. In this way the stock market constrains managerial decision making in selecting the optimal corporate contract. Thus, the existence of efficient securities markets justifies clear default rules preventing managers from acting contrary to shareholders' interests, and it simultaneously permits firms to contract around those rules.

Fiduciary Duties and Freedom of Contract. Corporate law provides a standard-form contract for business organizations. Key components of the standard-form contract are the gap fillers provided by the law of fiduciary duties, including the duties of care and loyalty. Fiduciary duties and remedies, however, may impose substantial burdens, such as the distraction of executives' and attorneys' fees. Thus, the shareholders may wish to contract out of some or all fiduciary remedies, particularly where strong alternative incentive and monitoring devices are in place. The fundamentally contractual nature of fiduciary duties means that they should be subject to the same presumption in favor of private ordering that applies to other contracts.[43] The most important implication of this perspective is that parties to the corporate contract should be free to contract out of the coverage of standard-form fiduciary duties. This section considers two common ways that parties may opt out of fiduciary duties.

Opt-out (or modification) by unanimous agreement. If all of the shareholders agree to opt out of fiduciary duties by means of a provision in the charter or shareholders' agreement, it follows from the contractual theory of the corporation that such an agreement should be enforced. Moreover, investors who buy into the corporation after adoption of the provision should be deemed to consent to the arrangement.

Opt-out provisions by subunanimous vote. When most, but not all, of the shareholders decide to change the rules and adopt opt-out provisions by charter provision or other shareholder agreement, the contractual theory of the corporation suggests that the sole question concerning validity is whether the governance rules of the corporation should be interpreted to permit subunanimous consent. In general, under current corporate law, even if the statute and certificate generally permit amendment by subunanimous vote, this amendment power has not been applied to provisions concerning transferability of shares.[44] The qualification may also extend to other matters, including amendment of class voting requirements that protect limited-vote shareholders from controlling shareholders. If such a qualification applies to a provision opting out of fiduciary duties, a free contracting perspective indicates that the provision should be enforced.[45]

Statutory Modification. States often change their corporate law, such as by adopting statutory provisions that limit fiduciary duties, and purport to apply the changes to all corporations chartered under their laws. The contractual theory of the corporation suggests that some statutory modifications of the corporate contract should not be enforceable against preexisting contracts because of their retroactive

15

effect.[46] From both a private law and a constitutional perspective, the most offensive statute is one that simply changes the directors' duties for all corporations incorporated in the state.[47] In such a situation, the corporations' agent-principal problem can be exacerbated by the exercise of political power by corporate managers to rewrite agency contracts.[48] In other words, regulation, instead of increasing shareholder protection, may only replace the shareholders' contractual safeguards with the unilateral power of corporate managers working through state legislators.

Charter Amendments. Charter amendments may alter the basic relationship among the contracting parties. The charter may, for example, change voting rules or, as discussed above, limit fiduciary duties or remedies. The basic argument in this section is that markets effectively discipline corporate contract terms. The market discipline discussed to this point, however, is in the form of efficient pricing of terms. This argument superficially does not seem to apply to charter amendments that are applied to existing shareholders. The case for regulation depends critically on whether shareholders are adequately protected by their right to vote.[49]

There are substantial market constraints on shareholder voting. While the average shareholder may have little incentive to acquire information or persuade fellow shareholders to vote against wealth-decreasing amendments, large institutional holders do have such incentives, and have increasingly been exercising their prerogatives.[50] Even if such holders do not control a majority, managers may be unwilling to risk turning the vote on the amendment into a referendum on management that puts the company in "play." Because an inefficient shareholder decision will reduce corporate share prices, this provides a profit opportunity for an investor to aggregate sufficient stock to change or block the decision.

Even if there are defects in shareholder voting—such as management's ability to determine the agenda—mandatory rules are not necessarily a solution. Corporate charters, which are priced in efficient-securities markets, can prescribe general amendment procedures or prohibit certain types of amendments. If managers' manipulation of the agenda is a problem, for example, the charter, at least under a private ordering regime (the current rule requiring proposal by the board is mandatory), could permit shareholder-proposed amendments. Indeed, survival of many currently mandatory terms, despite the state competition for corporate charters, may be attributable to the amendment problem. While charter provisions limiting amendments are no more likely to operate perfectly than are any other charter provisions, this does not itself establish that mandatory rules would be any better. Courts and legislators do not have a larger arsenal of weapons against opportunistic amendments than have the parties themselves. The question is whether they are more likely to choose the correct devices. As discussed in the section on regulatory theory below, substantial evidence suggests they are not.

Opting out by Selecting the State Statute—Federal versus State Law. Corporations chartered in one state are free to operate in other states under the law of the chartering state, regardless of where they are headquartered.[51] Corporations can choose the law under which they wish to operate. It follows that even if one or more state statutes preclude opting out of fiduciary duties, the parties to a corporate contract may be able to enter into an enforceable opt-out provision, among other ways, by incorporating under a state statute that permits opt-out provisions. A widely cited 1974 article by William Cary[52] argued that states compete for incorporation business by offering terms that appeal to corporate managers. This "race to the bottom" allegedly emasculates shareholders' interests. The antidote, according to Cary, must be preemption of the competition through regulation at the federal level.

This position ignores the powerful effects of the financial markets. The same markets that discipline the selection of contract terms also discipline the selection of the state of incorporation.[53] Although managers are active in the selection of the chartering state and shareholders are passive and rationally ignorant in this process, the shareholders voluntarily contract for the application of a particular state's law through their purchase and sale of corporate shares. Share prices reflect incorporation choices, which ultimately provide incentives for managers to choose corporation statutes that take into account shareholder interests. Not only is there no race to the bottom, but it is not even clear that Delaware has "won" in any general sense, because different corporations choose different chartering states based on their needs.[54] It follows that federal regulation of corporate law may both impede the development of efficient state laws and be ill suited to many firms.

The competition for state charters does not necessarily produce state laws that perfectly protect shareholder interests. It has been argued, for example, that state law is to some extent shaped to suit the interests of lawyers who dominate the process of corporate code drafting.[55] Moreover, an important theme of this book, elaborated in chapters 2 and 5, is that there are significant constraints on the

17

effectiveness of the state chartering competition—namely, retroactive changes and limitations on the contracts that can compete. These constraints necessitate strong constitutional countermeasures under the contract and commerce clauses.[56]

Although state law may be imperfect, it is also important to consider the imperfect motivations of agents of the federal government. While federal legislators and regulators may respond to interest groups different from the ones state legislators would, the former are hardly immune to interest-group pressure. The SEC, for example, arguably protects the interests of its chief "clientele," large investment banking firms, resulting in disclosure rules that curb corporate management's monopoly on inside information.[57]

The federal-state law debate is, therefore, simply a restatement of the private ordering debate. The primacy of state law is compelled by the same arguments that justify reliance on private ordering, including the efficient functioning of the financial markets. The arguments for federal regulation are fueled by the same misconceptions regarding these markets that underlie the anticontractual position.

The Regulatory Theory of the Corporation

This section presents and offers a critique of the regulatory theory of the corporation that holds, in contrast with the contractual theory, that corporate arrangements are sufficiently different from "ordinary" contracts as to be, as they should be, subject to additional regulation by the state. The regulatory theory of the corporation is based both on the historical origins of the corporation and on an economic response to the contractual theory of the corporation.

In considering the legal bases of the regulatory theory, this analysis begins with the historical concession theory of the corporation, which holds that incorporation is a state-conferred privilege. A corollary of this concept is that mandatory regulation of corporate contracts does not need to meet the same tests of validity as does regulation of ordinary contracts. Next, serious questions are raised about the validity of that historical perspective in drawing implications for the regulation of the modern and different institution of the corporation. Then, the modern legal basis of the regulatory theory—that many terms of modern corporate law appear to be mandatory—is criticized by showing that the appearance of mandatory rules is both misleading and irrelevant.

The next subsection analyzes the economic arguments used by corporate regulators to attack the contractual theory of the corporation. As the contractual theory of corporation gained support from economists and lawyers in recent years,[58] it provoked harsh responses from numerous traditional legal scholars.[59] One indication of the influence of the contractual theory is that corporate regulators have been forced to attack the legitimacy of private ordering as well as the consistency of the economic theories supporting it. In general, the arguments questioning the contractual nature of the corporation reflect flawed analysis.

The following discussion takes a different approach to the corporate regulators' efforts to impose on private firms their views about appropriate corporate governance arrangements. For the sake of argument, it assumes that the corporate regulators have made a credible argument for the imposition of the mandatory rules of their choice. The analysis points out that mandatory rules have serious problems of their own and that the availability of numerous alternative organizational forms means that truly burdensome mandatory rules can always be avoided by contract.

In short, there should be a presumption in favor of unrestricted contracting, and corporate regulators have not met the burden of proof necessary to justify the imposition of their regulatory regime.

The Legal Bases of the Regulatory Theory. Traditional legal scholars, who are always the main adherents of the regulatory theory, rely on three observations to support the continued relevance of the regulatory theory: the historical origins of the corporation as a concession of the state, the supposed mandatory nature of current corporate law, and limited liability. This section considers and rejects these bases of the regulatory theory.

The concession theory. Under the concession theory, the corporation is viewed as coming into existence only as a result of a special concession or grant made by the government, rather than by purely private contracting. This view of the corporation was stated in the first great corporation case in this country, *Trustees of Dartmouth College v. Woodward.*[60] A corporation is an artificial being, invisible, intangible, and existing only in contemplation of law. Being the mere creature of law, it possesses only those properties that the charter of its creation confers upon it, either expressly or as incidental to its very existence. These properties are such as are supposed best calculated to effect the object for which the corporation was created.[61] Although the Court in *Dartmouth College* did view the corporation as a contract,[62] the chartering authority was deemed a party to the contract.[63] This view is in sharp contrast with contracts formed under

19

other statutory standard forms. No one, for example, views the state as a party to a private contract merely because the contract is governed by the Uniform Commercial Code. This state-as-a-party-to-the-contract view is an important predicate for the exercise of unusual state power over corporations as compared with other contracts, particularly including the state's reserved power to alter the corporation's charter at will.[64]

At the time of *Dartmouth College*, the concession theory of the corporation was supported by the fact that most corporations, like Dartmouth College itself, were government-created franchises or quasi-public institutions. Later, although the quasi-public character of corporations became less important, corporations were "created" by special legislative acts, thus preserving the image of state creation. Special chartering, however, long ago yielded to private formation under general corporation laws.[65] The fact that corporations are brought into existence by a perfunctory state filing does not justify a "state creation" view any more than does the role of obtaining a birth certificate indicate state creation of a child. Accordingly, there is no longer any justification for regarding the corporation as a concession of the state.

Yet the concession origins of the corporation continue to rule from the grave. Despite the demise of the state-creation foundation of the concession theory, the courts and commentators continue to pay lip service to the theory itself. Most important for present purposes, the Supreme Court has repeated approvingly the ancient dictum from the *Dartmouth College* case quoted above to justify infringement of corporations' constitutional rights.[66]

Mandatory provisions in modern corporate law. Prevailing judicial views and statutory provisions carry vestiges of the concession approach. Some corporate regulators suggest that the nature of the modern corporation should be inferred from observing these aspects of modern corporate law.

Despite shedding their state-creation origins, modern corporate statutes do include many apparently mandatory terms, including voting rules, fiduciary duties, and legal capital rules. Some commentators believe that the existence of mandatory terms casts doubt about the contractual nature of the corporation.[67] Even if it were true that regulators continue to assert authority over corporations, this would hardly be a normative argument for the regulatory theory.[68] Moreover, for several reasons this view of corporate law is not even an accurate characterization of current law.[69]

First, most apparently mandatory terms are so easily avoided that they are, in substance, optional. If company *A* wants to acquire company *B* but does not want *A* shareholders to vote as apparently required by the corporate statute,[70] it can accomplish the merger by establishing subsidiary *C*. Corporation *A* may even be able to avoid offering target shareholders "mandatory" appraisal rights[71] by buying *B*'s assets and liquidating it.[72] The legal capital provisions of some corporation statutes require payment of dividends out of "surplus,"[73] but permit manipulation of the surplus account.[74] These optional terms in mandatory disguise are a sign of the evolution of the corporation from state concession to private contract.

Second, some apparently mandatory fiduciary duties are implied contract provisions that supply terms the parties did explicitly bargain for, but which can be avoided by explicit terms. In *Donahue v. Rodd Electrotype Co. of New England, Inc.*,[75] for example, the Court accorded noncontrolling close corporation shareholders access to share buyouts equal to that enjoyed by controlling shareholders. In light of the limited market for close corporation stock and the difficulty of exit, recognition of such an implied duty either is consistent with actual expectations of the parties, or is an appropriate implied standard form provision that anticipates what the parties would have drafted had they focused on the situation.[76] As such, the duty does not limit opting out, but is simply part of the parties' contract.[77]

Third, corporations can opt out of even some mandatory terms simply by reincorporating in another jurisdiction. A company that finds a Model Act-type mandatory appraisal provision overly restrictive, for example, can reincorporate in Delaware. In the same way, shareholders can choose mandatory terms—perhaps as a check on the majority's opportunistic use of its amendment power. The evolution of mandatory and nonmandatory provisions can be seen as an outcome of the state competition for chartering, and therefore as an aspect of private ordering. In fact, this is the basic process involved in the evolution from special chartering and strict limitations on corporate powers to the enabling, general-incorporation approach of modern corporation law.

Fourth, the parties to a firm can opt out of terms that are mandatory for all corporations simply by choosing among different investment and organizational forms. The mandatory requirement of at least majority shareholder voting on significant corporate transactions, for example, and perhaps even heavy fiduciary duties can be avoided by disincorporating into a limited partnership.[78] Alternatively, the impact of the requirement can be drastically altered by converting equity into nonvoting debt through a leveraged buyout or other restructuring.

21

In sum, truly mandatory provisions are the exception rather than the rule in the law of business associations. Thus, the supposed prevalence of such rules cannot serve as a premise for government regulation.

Limited liability. Some commentators cite corporations' limited liability as a pretext for broad regulation of the corporate form.[79] Limited liability seems at first glance to confirm the survival of the concession theory of the corporation, because it is created by means of a filing with a state official. As discussed above, however, the state filing itself no more justifies broad regulation of corporations than a birth certificate justifies broad regulation of individuals. Moreover, limited liability itself is clearly contractual, despite its link with corporate filings.[80] Limited liability is clearly a term of the firm's contract with voluntary creditors, who can bargain both on interest rates and for contractual protection, including personal guarantees. Corporate limited liability is simply a nonrecourse contract, with the state filing merely providing notice of the limited liability term. Even limited liability to involuntary creditors should be regarded as no more than a legal consequence of the contractual relationship between the parties to the firm, just as limited liability is a consequence of extending credit to rather than becoming a member of a partnership,[81] or of entering into a franchise rather than an agent-principal relationship.[82]

Nor does corporate limited liability to involuntary creditors provide a policy justification for broad regulation of corporate governance. Although academic commentators have recently attacked tort limited liability,[83] strong evidence suggests that limited tort liability is efficient and does not give rise to significant externalities.[84] In any event, even if tort limited liability is costly, this justifies at most only measures designed to minimize these costs, such as mandatory insurance or restrictions on limited liability in particular contexts. It does not justify broad regulation of corporate governance or a refusal to extend full constitutional protection to corporations.

The Corporate Regulators' Assault on the Contractual Theory. The basic theoretical model presented in the contractual theory section powerfully supports the principle that investors and entrepreneurs should be left to their own devices in fashioning the governance arrangement that best suits their particular needs. The theoretical argument for freedom of contract is buttressed by considerable empirical support. Many corporate legal scholars, almost all of whom have been trained in the corporate regulation tradition, have resisted this approach. It is not surprising that law professors continue to put up a fight, since broad acceptance of the contractual theory would significantly depreciate the value of their human capital. In the final analysis, the fight is about the value of economic analysis.

Corporate regulators challenge the contractual theory on numerous grounds. In this subsection, we present a critique of the most prominent arguments used to attack the contractual theory. First, we consider some general—almost philosophical—objections based on concerns about whether the corporate contract is a "real" contract. Second, we address some narrow and technical objections based on the assumption that there are some fundamental problems in the workings of securities markets.

Adhesion and freedom of choice in the formation of the corporate contract. For the traditional legal scholar, it is difficult to imagine a legally enforceable contract without the clear presence of discrete bargaining stages of offer and acceptance. Because the corporate contract does not appear to include the requisite steps of contract formation, the basic existence of the corporate contract has been denied by some commentators.[85] These commentators assert that the shareholders' plight is one of burdensome terms and unfair bargains. They cannot imagine that shareholders would freely consent to such terms and corporate arrangements as in "conventional" contracts. Rather, dispersed shareholders must accept, without any direct bargaining over details or alternatives, package deals crafted by managers.

This vastly overstates the shareholders' plight. Investors are not forced to accept any particular investment. In fact, as discussed in the contractual theory section, investors are offered a formidable array of investment alternatives—including corporations with different governance structures, noncorporate investments such as limited partnerships, mutual funds, money market accounts, real estate, and simple savings accounts. If contractual volition is lacking, it is only in the sense that investors accept contractual packages rather than dickering over individual terms. But "adhesion" in the sense of an absence of individualized bargaining is a common feature in the world of contract, ranging from standardized warranties, leases, trust indentures, and employment contracts.[86]

Manufacturers and corporate managers have incentives to offer potential customers and potential shareholders terms that are beneficial and attractive. Indeed, a contracting party does not usually want to "have it [his own] way," but is often willing to accept the manufacturer's or corporation's package. Not only is the extra cost of

23

a customized contract usually not worth the benefit of dickering, but in many situations a standardized contract is a better one: there is more information available concerning a standardized form; important terms have been clarified by interpretation; and error costs and information costs are less than in individually negotiated deals.[87] It follows that the terms of corporate charters should be presumed to be the consequence of a meaningful bargaining process.[88]

Implicit and hypothetical contracts. Adherents of the regulatory theory argue that the corporation should not be regarded as fundamentally contractual, because many of the terms governing the corporate relationship are merely "implicit bargains" and not real contracts.[89] An implicit bargain is a term used in labor economics to refer to terms that, like real bargains, involve an economic quid pro quo. They are not "real" contracts because they are enforced by market, rather than legal, mechanisms.[90]

The fact that many of the parties to a corporation are governed largely by implicit terms supports rather than undermines the contractual theory of the corporation. The choice of implicit and explicit terms is one of many examples of how the parties, if unhindered by legal rules, choose the combination of legal and extralegal devices appropriate to their relationship. It is a clear non sequitur to say that because the parties to firms sometimes choose implicit instead of legally enforceable terms they should be forced to submit to mandatory legal rules.

The "lemons market" and the regulatory theory. Corporate regulators argue that the terms of the corporate contract are priced in a "lemons market,"[91] in which there are inadequate incentives to offer optimal protection against managerial misconduct.[92] These critics assert that there is a market failure in the ability of securities markets to evaluate accurately firm-specific corporate governance information, including the risk of managerial shirking or diversion inherent in certain contracts. The important implication of the market's failure to price contract terms accurately is that such terms are suboptimal, and resources are not allocated to their highest value uses. Because of the importance of this argument to the regulatory approach to managerial duties, it is crucial to consider whether it has any validity.

Unlike most areas of legal discourse, where it is unlikely that the correct answer can be proved, the incorrect application of economics can be demonstrated. The lemons-market failure argument, which is an economics argument, is seriously flawed. Most important, the argument is based on a misapprehension of the workings of efficient capital markets. As discussed previously, these markets ensure that a corporate shareholder gets what he is paying for both in the terms of the contract and in the substantive nature of the product, including the quality of management. This means that a lemons-market phenomenon will not occur in securities markets, and thus shareholders are protected. Accordingly, there is no a priori reason for subjecting corporate governance to more extensive government regulation than would be applied to other contracts.

The Case against Mandatory Rules. The above subsections provide strong evidence that government regulation of corporate contract terms is unnecessary. But even if the corporate regulators were correct and there were a strong case for government regulation because of market failure, this alone would not justify regulation without a further showing that regulation is likely to produce better corporate arrangements than private ordering. In this subsection, we show the dangers of the "nirvana fallacy"—the naive assumption that regulation will function perfectly if markets do not.

Institutional defects of mandatory rules. Even if anticontractarian law professors can think of better mandatory rules than those that currently exist, courts and legislatures are unlikely to adopt such rules or to change them in response to changing circumstances.

There are serious deficiencies in the courts' abilities to formulate governance rules.[93] First, in deciding particular cases, courts are virtually always confronted with bad results. Some commentators believe that this sample bias causes courts erroneously to assume that the bad result was a product of poor managerial performance.[94] Rules made on the basis of false assumptions can have perverse effects on corporations. Second, most courts, particularly those outside Delaware, decide corporate cases only sporadically and lack specific skill in corporate matters. Third, even if a case is correctly decided, it leads to a result on particular facts that has only uncertain application to other cases. Fourth, unlike managers, judges are not inspired to write optimal corporate rules by a proprietary interest or by shareholder monitoring. Fifth, even if the court attempts to formulate a general rule, it is limited in its ability to formulate policy by its own resources and by the nature of the adversarial process.[95]

There are also serious questions concerning legislators' ability to formulate efficient governance rules. Corporate agents' incentives to act contrary to shareholder welfare are no greater than legislators' incentives to serve narrow interest groups rather than a majority of the voters.[96] Moreover, throwing corporate governance issues into the legislative arena would only compound corporate agency problems, because managers surely possess a comparative advantage at getting legislation passed. The recent passage of takeover-specific antitake-over statutes illustrates the political problems that can arise when the managers are free to use corporate resources to rewrite corporate governance contracts through the political process.[97] Failures of private corporate contracts, if such failures exist at all, are surely less costly than attempting to solve these failures by resorting to political markets.

The motivations of political agents are, in fact, an important part of our story of the application of the Constitution to the corporation. Both the contract clause (see chapter 2) and the commerce clause (see chapter 4) can be explained as constraints on state legislators. For them, political power over the corporation under the regulatory approach to the corporation represents a lucrative source of political rents. At the same time, regulation of corporate political speech cannot be justified under the first amendment on the ground that, without such regulation, corporations would have excessive political power.

Both legislative and judicial rule making share the institutional problems of generality and stasis. Even a rule that is formulated by an all-wise and disinterested policy maker cannot suit every business equally well, any more than a well-made suit is right for every body. As discussed above, the literature on the theory of the firm reveals a wide range of organizational forms and governance rules, each adapted to different circumstances. Organizations that have to own substantial resources or that involve complex decision processes will look very different from smaller, simpler firms, and they will adopt very different governance structures. Within general types of organization there are many subvariations, such as whether the firm operates in a regulated industry.[98] Moreover, even a rule that is initially well suited to a particular firm may become unsuitable over time as a result of rapidly changing business conditions. Both legislative and judicial rules tend to remain past their welcome.

For the above reasons, even assuming a case can be made in this area for market failure, there is substantial reason to believe that a process of evolution of corporate rules through private ordering is preferable to a system of mandatory rules.[99]

The inevitability of contract. The discussion so far in this section has assumed that regulation of corporate contract terms is feasible. In fact, formidable practical difficulties attend this type of regulation, even if it was otherwise warranted on policy grounds. The reason is that any regulation that proscribed certain terms would inevitably leave room for substitution of other terms, or at least for a substitution of forms of organization.[100] Thus, for example, it is unclear how statutes mandating appraisal rights in the event of a merger should apply to such merger-like transactions as asset sales[101] or changes in control or structure.[102] With regard to substitution of forms, limitations of the voting structure of corporations (that is, by forbidding dual class common) can be circumvented by forming limited partnerships[103] or limited liability companies.[104] The partnership technique would also be available for circumvention of limits on opting out of fiduciary duties.[105] In general, the possibilities are endless because, as was discussed earlier, the corporation is part of a continuum of contractual forms that includes not only forms of business organization, but other types of relational contracts.

The normative assumption and the burden of proof. The approach throughout the law of contract is to presume in favor of private ordering until some type of market failure can be shown. The only reason for departing from this presumption in the corporate context would be if the corporation were not regarded as a contractual relationship. As discussed above, however, the dominant trend in corporate law over the past 200 years has been to free corporate law from its state concession origins and treat it as a contractual relationship. Therefore, if the general presumption from private ordering is departed from in this context, it must be because of adherence to the historical rather than the modern position. The time has come to reject the historical position in favor of the contractual theory and to shift the presumption to one favoring contract.

Conclusion

This book considers the implications of the contractual theory outlined above for the application of constitutional law to the governance of the corporation. The book is based on two general principles. First, in deciding how to apply constitutional principles, the corporation should be viewed as a set of private contractual relationships subject to complex market forces. Second, an important implication of this view is that corporations, like other contracts, must be protected from the acts of political agents and private parties who seek to circumvent contracts through the political process.

Economic analysis represents a major advance in our understanding of the nature of corporation law and the proper role of government in the corporation. The contractual theory that is supported by economic analysis offers a new perspective on the corporation and the role of corporation law. The corporation is in no sense a ward of the state, but rather is the product of contracts among the owners and others. This approach has forced legal commentators on corporation law and securities regulation to show a greater appreciation for the economic implications of alternative legal rules. Once this theory is finally recognized by judges, legislators, and commentators, the corporate form may finally be free of unnecessary and intrusive legal chains. It is our hope that this book is a significant step in that direction.

2
Constitutional Protection of the Corporate Contract

The contract clause, Article I, section 10 of the Constitution, states: "No state shall . . . pass any . . . Law impairing the obligations of contracts." This provision was a significant legal predicate for the economic success of this country because it prevented states from restricting the contractual rights of private citizens, and it can play an important role in ensuring the stability of internal corporate arrangements. If, as argued in this book, the corporation is treated as a set of private contracts, these contracts should be entitled to the same level of protection under the contract clause as other contracts.

Introduction

Efficient corporate contract terms will develop only if private ordering in corporations is enforced and state laws are allowed to compete in the market for corporate charter.[1] Where states refuse to enforce private arrangements according to their terms, the terms are, in effect, formulated by politicians and judges who lack incentives comparable to those of the contracting parties to make efficient contracts. Thus, application of the contract clause can be regarded as an integral aspect of the contractual theory of the corporation because it is a vitally important safeguard against government interference with corporate governance arrangements.

In this chapter we demonstrate why the contract clause is applicable to the corporate contract and how it can be applied to several different types of changes in state corporation law. In the next section, we discuss the origins, rationale, and interpretations of the contract clause and then set out the general considerations that affect its application. Next, we discuss the applicability of the clause to the corporation in light of the contractual theory of the corporation. We conclude that the considerations set forth in the second section support application of the contract clause to the corporate contract. Even state reserved power clauses, which are inserted into corporation laws to allow for future modification and thus appear to be part of the corporate contract, are unable to prevent the contract clause from being used as a barrier to state manipulation of private ordering. In the next section, we consider the ramifications of application of the clause to specific statutory changes. Finally, we offer some concluding comments about the importance of the contract clause to maintaining stability in the governance of the corporation.

The Contract Clause

This section introduces the history, rationale, and general application of the contract clause. The next section then demonstrates that they are consistent with the application of the clause to the corporate contract.

Origins of the Contract Clause. Perhaps the best modern summary of the background of the contract clause is in Justice Sutherland's dissenting opinion in *Home Bldg. & L. Assn. v. Blaisdell.*[2] In the wake of the destruction of commerce in the American Revolution, impoverished debtors successfully sought relief from state legislators. The result was that "bonds of men whose ability to pay their debts was unquestionable could not be negotiated except at discounts of thirty, forty, or fifty percent."[3] Although some legislators advocated permitting the states to relieve debtors' contractual burdens during emergencies, James Madison and others, who favored limiting this power, prevailed. As Madison stated in *Federalist* 44:

> The sober people of America are weary of the fluctuating policy which has directed the public councils. They have seen with regret, and with indignation, that sudden changes, and legislative interferences, in cases affecting personal rights, become jobs in the hands of enterprising and influential speculators; and snares to the more industrious and less informed part of the community. . . . [S]ome thorough reform is wanting, which will banish speculations on public measures, inspire a general prudence and industry, and give a regular course to the business of society.

This early background of the contract clause shows that the framers were aware of and sought to avoid the particular harm that results from government interference with private agreements.

The economic problem addressed by the contract clause is not simply the harm to the parties whose contract rights are impaired by the statute at issue, but the harm that the threat of such interference causes ex ante by deterring contractual arrangements and forcing the parties to discount heavily for uncertainty the value of all obligations. Without a "regular course to the business of society," allocation of resources through private ordering and markets is reduced, and the role of the state is accordingly increased. In short, the existence of the contract clause as an explicit limit on the power of states to impair private contracts is essential to the development of a market economy.

The Rationale of the Contract Clause. The constitutional history of the contract clause indicates that the clause was inserted to ensure the stability of contracts, thereby increasing their value and encouraging private ordering.

But although it is an important rationale for the clause, stability cannot be the whole story, because it applies to all property rights, and therefore does not explain why contracts have been singled out for protection. Any efficient acquisition or development of property can be deterred by the threat of government interference. This raises the question of why private contracts are singled out from other property rights for special attention in the Constitution. The question is important because the particular function of the contract clause should be relevant in determining the situations in which the clause should be applied.

An important reason for special constitutional protection of contracts is to discourage state government officials[4] from earning "rents," such as campaign contributions and other benefits, by engineering wealth redistributions to interest groups.[5] Because the wealth redistribution is a zero-sum game, the rent-seeking expenditures invested in the transfer are unlikely to be outweighed by any positive results of the expenditures.[6] Although this is a general problem with government,[7] it is a particular problem where the winners and losers from a potential wealth redistribution are clearly defined. This is the case where government action impairs contracts, thereby redistributing wealth from the parties who stand to gain, ex post, from further enforcement of the contract to those who stand to lose.[8]

Another reason why contract impairment is constitutionally protected separately from other state takings of property is that state government does not benefit from impairment of a contract unless it is a party to the contract.[9] This explains why the prohibition on contract impairment is not qualified by a duty to pay just compensation. If the state paid for an impairment from which it did not benefit, this would merely redistribute wealth from the taxpayers to a contracting party, rather than between contracting parties. The wasteful redistribution would remain.

The contract clause has been qualified in several ways that are arguably consistent with its central purpose of prohibiting a particular type of regulation that encourages wealth-redistributing rent seeking. The Supreme Court held quite early that the clause does not apply to laws that prospectively limit the power to contract but do not affect existing contracts.[10] Although this permits substantial interference with private ordering,[11] and much wasteful rent seeking, prospective limits on contracting do not present the same danger of redistribution as retrospective impairments. Winners and losers from prospectively applied laws cannot necessarily be identified at the time of enactment, because the parties to postregulation contracts can contractually allocate the burdens of the regulation.[12]

There is another reason for believing that contract-impairing legislation as a class is likely to be inefficient. A principal justification for legal regulation is that it substitutes for private ordering where private ordering is frustrated by transaction costs and other market imperfections. But instead of substituting for private ordering, contract-impairing legislation necessarily frustrates it.

It does not necessarily follow from the above discussion that all contract-impairing legislation is inefficient. The impairment may eliminate negative externalities, for example—nonnegotiated adverse effects on third parties—caused by the contract. But despite some possible overinclusiveness, much can be said for a categorical rule banning a particularly troublesome regulation in favor of costly, case-by-case judicial review of the efficiency of state legislation.[13]

These specific qualifications of the contract clause preserve policy-making latitude for state lawmakers while restraining one category of obvious abuse. Unfortunately, as demonstrated in the next subsection, the courts have rejected this precise pruning of the clause in favor of a broader and vaguer limitation.

Judicial Interpretation of the Corporate Contract. The historical background of the contract clause indicates that it was specifically intended to deal with state interference with debtor-creditor relations. Nevertheless, in the most important early contract clause case, the Supreme Court applied the clause to a case that was within its literal terms but was not envisioned by the framers. In *Trustees of Dartmouth College v. Woodward*,[14] in an opinion by Justice John Marshall, the Supreme Court invalidated under the contract clause a New Hampshire statute that altered the terms of a British crown charter granted to Dartmouth College. Justice Marshall described the charter as

a contract, on the faith of which, real and personal estate has been conveyed [by the donors] to the corporation. It is then a contract within the letter of the constitution. . . . It is more than possible that the preservation of rights of this description was not particularly in the view of the framers of the constitution, when the clause under consideration was introduced into that instrument. . . . But although a particular and a rare case may not, in itself, be of sufficient magnitude to induce a rule, yet it must be governed by the rule, when established, unless some plain and strong reason for excluding it can be given. It is not enough to say, that this particular case was not in the mind of the Convention, when the article was framed. . . . The case being within the words of the rule, must be within its operation likewise, unless there be something in the literal construction so obviously absurd, or mischievous, or repugnant to the general spirit of the instrument, as to justify those who expound the Constitution in making it an exception.[15]

The contract clause has had a checkered history in the courts. Broadly speaking, after *Dartmouth College* it initially flourished as a significant protection of property right. Its role was ultimately supplanted, however, by the Fourteenth Amendment as the primary constitutional restraint on state regulation of economic activity, although that provision itself was ultimately interpreted as having little role in this area.[16]

The period of broad application of the contract clause ended with the Supreme Court's opinion in *Home Bldg. & L. Assn. v. Blaisdell.*[17] The Court there upheld a Minnesota statute that reduced the rights of mortgagees by, among other things, extending mortgagors' period of redemption. The Court reasoned that, despite the constitutional limit on contract impairment,

The State . . . continues to possess authority to safeguard the vital interests of its people. . . . Reservation of essential attributes of sovereign power is . . . read into contracts as a postulate of the legal order. The policy of protecting contracts against impairment presupposes the maintenance of a government . . . which retains adequate authority to secure the peace and good order of society.[18]

But the Court hedged its rule:

The reserved power cannot be construed so as to destroy the limitation, nor is the limitation to be construed to destroy the reserved power in its essential aspects. They must be construed in harmony with each other.[19]

Thus, the Court carefully noted five circumstances that justified the impairment: there was an emergency; the legislation was not for a mere private advantage; the relief was appropriate to the emergency; the relief from contractual obligations was reasonable, since the mortgage obligation continued and the mortgagor was required to pay the rental value of the property toward the mortgagee's carrying charges; and the legislation was only temporary.[20] Nevertheless, Justice Sutherland registered a strong dissent, noting that the impairment of creditors' rights during economic emergencies was precisely the situation the contract clause was intended to deal with.[21] By the end of the 1930s, however, the Court proved unable to resist the onslaught of "emergency" claims.[22]

The Court's holding in *Blaisdell*[23] has been sharply criticized as unnecessary to protect the state's police power in the light of other limitations on operation of the clause, and as contrary to the purpose of the clause as a protection against destabilizing and wealth-redistributing impairments in the name of expediency.[24]

In the four decades beginning with the late 1930s, the contract clause was rarely applied to overturn a state statute.[25] Instead, the Court frequently relied on the state's need to "safeguard the vital interests of its people." Thus, for example, in *El Paso v. Simmons*,[26] the Court upheld under *Blaisdell* a Texas statute that changed the reinstatement period of purchasers who defaulted under contracts for purchase of public lands. Justice Hugo Black, in a strong dissent that adverted to Madison's defense of the contract clause, said "today's majority holds that people are not protected from the fluctuating policy of the legislature, so long as the legislature acts in accordance with the fluctuating policy of this Court."[27]

Two cases in the late 1970s marked a revival of the contract clause. In the first, *United States Trust Co. v. New Jersey*,[28] the Court struck down a New Jersey statute that impaired the rights of bondholders by repealing a covenant that prevented use of bond funds for deficit mass transit projects. The Court said that "neither [*Blaisdell* nor *El Paso*] indicated that the Contract Clause was without meaning in modern constitutional jurisprudence, or that its limitation on state power was illusory."[29] Although the state's goals of encouraging mass transportation to conserve energy and protect the environment were important, the statute was not saved by the state's reserved power under *Blaisdell* because the impairment was not "necessary." Less drastic impairments might have served the state's goals, including diverting only the additional revenues raised from tolls to mass transit, or modifying the formula for permitted deficits. The state also might have achieved its goals in ways other than by impairing the bondholders, as by discouraging automobile use. The Court indicated that it would more readily second-guess a state legislative judgment of the reasonableness and necessity of impairing its own financial obligations than it would an impairment of private obligations.[30]

A year after *United States Trust*, the Supreme Court in *Allied Structural Steel Co. v. Spannaus*[31] invalidated a state statutory impairment of a private agreement. The statute required an employer who terminated a plan or left the state to fund pensions for employees with at least ten years' service, even if their rights had not vested under the original terms of the plan. The statute was not within the state's reserved power under *Blaisdell* because, among other reasons, it did not deal with an economic emergency or a broad social problem; it permanently changed contractual relationships; it operated on a relatively narrow class; and it entered an area that had not formerly been regulated by the state.

The *Allied* opinion elucidates in several respects the modern application of the state's reserved power to impair contracts. First, the Court reiterated its intimation in *United States Trust* that it would subject impairment of the state's own contracts to stricter scrutiny than impairment of private agreements.[32] Second, the Court explicitly linked the scrutiny level to the severity of the impairment,[33] noting that the impairment in the present case was particularly severe because the employer had relied on vesting provisions in the earlier act and there was no provision for phasing in of statutory requirements or grace periods.[34] Third, the Court relied partly on the fact that the statute had a narrow focus, applying only to large private employers that have voluntary private pension plans and that leave the state. Moreover, the statute was to apply only during the nine-month period before the Employment Retirement Income Security Act of 1974 was to become effective. In fact, there was an indication that the statute was aimed at one company, White Motor Corporation, which had attempted to leave the state and terminate its pension plan for its operations there.[35]

The Supreme Court, although it has not announced a change in direction, apparently has backtracked to some extent in its application of the contract clause to three cases it has decided since *Allied* on this issue—*Energy Reserve Group v. Kansas Power & Light*,[36] *Exxon Corp. v. Eagerton*,[37] and *Keystone Bituminous Coal Ass'n. v. DeBenedictis*.[38] First, these cases involved supposed impairment of private contracts, and the Court has made increasingly clear that it will defer to the state's judgment of reasonableness and necessity unless the state has impaired its own contract.[39] Second, the Court has indicated that it would scrutinize less closely statutes of general application that incidentally operate to impair contracts than statutes that are specifically directed at contract impairment. In *Exxon Corp. v. Eagerton*, the

Court noted that, unlike the statutes in *United States Trust* and in *Allied*, whose sole effect was on existing contracts, the statutory prohibition on pass-through of a severance tax was a "generally applicable rule of conduct." Its effect on existing contracts "was incidental to its main effect of shielding consumers from the burden of the tax increase."[40]

Notwithstanding this wavering by the Court, the rationale underlying the contract clause remains at least as viable today as when the Constitution was adopted.[41] Wealth redistributions engineered by rent-seeking lawmakers are as much if not more of a problem today as ever before. Consequently, courts should again look to the contract clause as providing significant constitutional protection from impairment of economic rights.

Application of the Contract Clause in General. Before discussing specific application of the contract clause to the corporate contract, let us briefly review the criteria for its application that have emerged from the case law.

The first prerequisite for applying the contract clause is, of course, that the legal rule in question actually impair the contract. As discussed above, impairment occurs when the rule alters existing obligations, but not when it limits contracts to be formed in the future. Impairment occurs whether the rule imposes new conditions on the contracting parties or changes these parties' power to change the rules. But there is plainly no impairment under the contract clause if the contracting parties themselves, such as corporate shareholders, amend the contract within a preexisting amendment power.

The courts have qualified application of the contract clause by permitting impairments that are reasonable and necessary to further an important state interest. While this qualification is certainly questionable in light of the absolute language of the clause,[42] it is entrenched in the case law and it will be accepted here. As demonstrated in this subsection, even if state corporation laws are regarded as protecting shareholders or third parties rather than simply providing standard form contracts, this does not necessarily justify corporate laws that alter existing contracts.

The Supreme Court has indicated that the intensity with which the justification for the statute will be scrutinized depends on several factors:

- whether the statute impairs the state's own contract or a private contract
- the degree of impairment

- whether the statute impairs contracts incidentally to a broader purpose or is specifically directed toward contract impairment
- the extent of the statute's application—that is, whether it was aimed at a particular party

These factors are discussed separately below.

The state-private distinction. The Supreme Court in recent cases has indicated that a state must bear a higher burden in justifying impairment of its own statutes than impairment of private agreements. The dual burden has only been intimated, and the precise difference between the two burdens is unclear—particularly since the last case in which the Court struck down a state law under the contract clause, *Allied Structural Steel Co. v. Spannaus*,[43] involved impairment of a private agreement. Application of this dual burden would make it difficult to invalidate state antitakeover statutes because, under the contractual theory of the corporation, the corporate agreements impaired by these statutes are entirely among private parties. But some strong arguments against applying a dual burden may ultimately persuade the Court not to pursue the suggestions in its recent opinions, or at least to minimize any difference between impairment of state and private contracts.

First, the precedential and historical basis of the dual burden is suspect. The Court initially noted the dual burden in invalidating an impairment of the state's own contract in *United States Trust Co. v. New Jersey*.[44] The Court relied on a case involving the validity of federal legislation abrogating contractual clauses requiring payment in gold.[45] Justice William Brennan, dissenting, argued that the "gold clause" case's distinction between private and government contracts was inapplicable in the contract clause context because the case construed the government's power to "regulate the Value" of money under Article I, section 8 of the Constitution, which explicitly applies only to impairment of private contracts.[46]

Brennan also questioned whether the contract clause is even applicable to the state's own contracts.[47] As we discussed above, the contract clause was apparently intended specifically to limit the states' power to interfere with debtor-creditor relations, which had been a serious problem in the period between the American Revolution and the drafting of the Constitution. Although this historical background should not preclude application of the contract clause to contracts clearly within its literal terms, the background at least suggests that interference with private agreements should not be treated more lightly than interference with government contracts.

The *United States Trust Co.* Court's policy basis for differentiating between government and private contracts is also questionable. The Court said:

> Complete deference to a legislative assessment of reasonableness and necessity is not appropriate because the State's self-interest is at stake. A governmental entity can always find a use for extra money, especially when taxes do not have to be raised. If a State could reduce its financial obligations whenever it wanted to spend money for what it regarded as an important public purpose, the Contract Clause would provide no protection at all.[48]

It makes no sense to distinguish impairment of state and private agreements on the basis of "the state's self-interest." The self-interest that matters in questioning the reasonableness of the statute is that of those who actually enact the statute—the legislators. The legislators, like other economic actors, certainly are motivated by self-interest in wanting to capture rents in the form of increased power, campaign funding, and votes from competing lobbying groups.[49] Legislators' self-interest is obviously a potential factor in passage of all legislation, whether the legislation impairs contracts, whether it serves the public interest, and whether the impaired contracts are state or private in nature.

Moreover, even accepting the state-private distinction on its own terms—that is, assuming that a state's interests are relevant—the contract clause is necessary less to discipline impairment of the state's contracts than to discipline private impairments. Justice Brennan pointed out in his dissent in *United States Trust* that the state's conduct in impairing its own bond contracts is disciplined by the bond market, which "is apt to exact 'justice' that is quicker and surer than anything that this Court can hope to offer."[50] While ultimately the state bears the direct cost of impairing its own contracts in terms of reduction of its credit rating, the state does not bear the cost of impairing private agreements, except in the attenuated sense that this may erode its tax base by establishing a poor business climate within the state. States are also disciplined in impairing their own contracts by the constitutional obligation to compensate owners of property rights.[51] Thus, states may have significant incentives to abrogate private agreements, since they can reduce their financial obligations by either method. In *Spannaus*, for example, instead of the state's requiring private employers to bear the cost of vesting additional pensions, it could have borne the cost itself. Similarly, an obvious alternative to antitakeover statutes in preventing local companies from moving out of state would be for the state to offer tax and other financial incentives to induce the corporation to remain.

The severity of the impairment. The Court has sensibly concluded that the state's justification for severe contract impairments would be subject to greater scrutiny than for lesser impairments. This effectively balances the benefits of the impairment against its costs to contracting parties.

Direct versus indirect impairments. The Court has indicated that it would scrutinize less intensely the reasonableness and necessity of statutes that incidentally impair contracts as part of a broader scheme of regulation than statutes that are specifically directed at contract impairment. As with the severity of the impairment, this factor balances costs and benefits of impairment. A broad scheme of regulation is more likely to involve social benefits and less likely to constitute mere wealth redistribution than a statute aimed at abrogating existing contracts.

Specificity of application. In invalidating the state statute at issue in the *Spannaus* case, the Supreme Court emphasized that the statute was so narrowly focused as to appear to be directed at a single company. The Court hinted at why this is relevant in *Energy Reserves Group, Inc. v. Kansas Power & Light Co.*[52] when, distinguishing *Spannaus*, it rejected a contention that the legislation at issue was special interest legislation because it applied only to the defendant utility company. Unlike *Spannaus*, in which a few employers were "singled out from the larger group," in the *Energy Reserves* case, regulation of sales to public utilities necessitated application to a small number of companies.[53] There was, therefore, no "indication that the Kansas political process had broken down" to justify not leaving determinations of reasonableness and necessity to the discretion of the legislature.[54] Thus, the Court apparently believes that narrowly focused statutes like the one involved in *Spannaus* are more likely the product of rent-seeking behavior by politicians than of the legislators' concern for the public welfare.[55]

The Court's self-seeking-legislator scenario is unsatisfying because it erroneously assumes, first, that some legislation results from the legislators' genuine concern for the public interest, wholly detached from their self-interest; and second, that legislation motivated by the rent-seeking conduct of the legislators is more likely to be "bad" than to be public-interest legislation. In fact, because legislators do not cease to be economic actors when they enter the public arena, virtually all legislation results from rent-seeking of some sort, in which the legislators consciously seek to increase their power and secure reelection.[56]

As indicated above, the problem with specifically focused statutes is not that they are more likely the product of rent-seeking politicians, but rather that they are more likely to involve a particularly nonproductive form of rent seeking. A focused statute is almost certainly the result of lobbying by the benefited party to obtain a wealth transfer from the other contracting party. The lobbying party's decision to pursue the legislative route indicates that this was less costly than bargaining with the other party—that is, that the other party would have exacted a high price for parting with its contract rights. In other words, the legislation almost certainly involves wealth transfer rather than wealth creation.

In general, most of the factors discussed in this subsection make sense in light of the purpose of the contract clause to reduce wasteful legislative wealth redistributions. As discussed in the next section, these factors justify close judicial scrutiny of legislation that impairs corporate contracts.

Application to the Corporate Contract

The underlying rationale for the contract clause makes it particularly applicable to the corporation. Many of the contractual terms discussed in chapter 1 are intended to constrain the conduct of managers vis-à-vis common shareholders. Corporate managers can use their control over corporate resources to buy political power to effect ex post changes in these terms—precisely the type of problem the contract clause is intended to address.

The contract clause is not only one solution to the problem of ex post wealth redistributions in corporations—it is also the best solution. As discussed below in chapter 3, limitations on corporate political activity are purportedly designed to protect shareholders from this sort of conduct by managers. Given the costs and dubious benefits of these limitations discussed in chapter 3, however, the shareholders would be better protected by limiting contract impairment than by regulating corporate political activity. States' propensities to redistribute wealth also can be disciplined to some extent by the state competition for corporate charters. The states can compete for chartering business by bonding against future expropriations.[57] State legislators have perverse incentives, however, not to compete for chartering business.[58] Moreover, as discussed in chapter 5, the market for governance rules is limited by restrictive rules on enforcing contractual choice of law.

Despite the particular relevance of the contract clause to contracting in the corporation, its applicability has always been questionable because of the concept that the states can reserve the power to amend unilaterally the corporate contract by inserting the power to do so in the corporation statute. This section reviews the origins and basis of these provisions and concludes that they are a historical anomaly, and therefore irrelevant to modern corporation law.

The Concession Origin of Reserved Power Provisions. Reserved power provisions were spurred by the *Dartmouth College* case—the case that first applied the contract clause to corporations.[59] In the light of ensuing developments, the most important aspect of the *Dartmouth College* case proved to be a comment in Justice Joseph Story's concurring opinion that "rights legally vested in a corporation, cannot be controlled or destroyed by any subsequent statute unless power for that purpose be reserved to the legislature in the act of incorporation."[60] Following Justice Story's implicit suggestion, the states routinely came to insert in their corporation statutes just such a reservation of power.

A typical example is the provision in the Delaware statute:

This chapter may be amended or repealed, at the pleasure of the Legislature, but any amendment or repeal shall not take away or impair any remedy under this chapter against any corporation or its officers for any liability which shall have been previously incurred. This chapter and all amendments thereof shall be a part of the charter or certificate of incorporation of every corporation except so far as the same are inapplicable and inappropriate to the objects of the corporation.[61]

These statutes have been applied to permit new statutory provisions to change existing corporate contracts.[62]

In an analysis of the basis of reserved-power provisions, it is important to bear in mind that they have traditionally been applied only to corporations and not to other contracts. This stems from the outdated view that a corporation is a concession of the state rather than a private contract.

If corporations are, indeed, concessions of state power, it arguably follows that the state can make its grant conditional.[63] This approach makes some sense where the state grants a monopoly power, as was often the case at the time of Story's opinion. It makes less sense when applied to a corporation like Dartmouth College that derives no monopoly power from the state, but is at least understandable in light of the common early association between special charters and granting of monopoly privileges. And it makes no sense as to modern corporations formed under general incorporation laws, where the state merely provides a standard form and a filing mechanism.

Many cases adopted a more modern view of the corporation and held that reserved-power provisions do not apply to, and therefore do not permit retroactive alteration of, private contracts among shareholders.[64] Moreover, reserved-power provisions traditionally have not been included in partnership statutes, which were never used to convey monopoly or franchise privileges.[65]

Modern Bases for the Reserved Power. The reserved-power provisions originated in a view of the corporation that has long been outdated. But the same can be said of many legal rules that are still enforced. The question remains whether some modern basis has emerged to replace the concession basis of reserved-power provisions. Three possible modern bases for enforcement of the reserved-power provisions are discussed and rejected in this subsection.

The reserved power and the state's power to regulate. One potential modern basis of the reserved power is that it simply preserves the state's power to regulate corporations, just as the state reserves the power to regulate other matters. Parties to corporations accept the state's power to change internal corporate rules just as they accept the potential for tax changes and price controls.

The problem with this reasoning is that it ignores the rationale of the contract clause. The clause is not aimed at all state tampering with property rights, but rather at only a narrow category of regulation that is particularly likely to cause costly wealth redistributions. By permitting this type of regulation, the reserved power raises the precise problem that the contract clause was intended to prevent.

The reserved power as conditioning a government subsidy. Another possible justification for the reserved power is that it is a quid pro quo for the tort immunity conferred on incorporating shareholders. Unlike the limited liability to contract creditors, limited liability to tort victims does not seem to be the product of private ordering. Rather, it might be regarded as a government subsidy to encourage business activity. Just as the federal government can condition awards of highway funds on maintaining speed limits, the argument runs, so can the states condition the tort subsidy on acceptance of the reserved power. There are several problems with this reasoning.

First, as explained in chapter 1,[66] shareholders' limited liability to tort creditors is simply a legal consequence of contract and does not justify extraordinary regulation of the corporate form. Second, even if limited tort liability is appropriately characterized as a subsidy, this does not justify the reserved power. The reserved power, unlike the speed limit, has no connection with the tort immunity for which it is purportedly exchanged. The reserved power is not exchanged for contractual terms that are analogous to limited liability, such as the priority of secured creditors.

A third and more potent refutation of the subsidy argument on constitutional grounds is the principle of unconstitutional conditions—that is, that the government cannot condition granting of privileges on waiver of constitutional rights.[67] Richard Epstein has argued that the principle should apply where costly governmental abuse of discretion associated with the condition reduces the social value of the privilege to which the condition is attached.[68] The first example Epstein gives is the rent-seeking costs associated with giving government the power to sell special charters prior to the emergence of general incorporation laws.[69] An even stronger argument can be made for prohibiting the government from conditioning the tort "subsidy" on waiver of the contract clause, where rent-seeking costs are at the heart of the constitutional protection. These costs should not be tolerated merely because the government is able to attach them to a valuable privilege.

The reserved power as a contract term. A third modern argument for validity of reserved-power provisions is that the parties' expectations, and therefore their contract, should be determined in light of the reserved power provision. This would, in effect, let states opt out of the contract clause as long as they do not deprive contracting parties of substantive due process and equal protection. As Justice John Marshall recognized long ago, however, in his dissenting opinion in *Ogden v. Saunders*,[70] this reasoning potentially eliminates any constitutional limit on impairment of contracts by permitting the state to decide what contracts it will enforce. In arguing that the contract clause forbids prospective as well as retrospective impairments, Justice Marshall said:

If one law enters into all subsequent contracts, so does every other law which relates to the subject. A legislative act, then, declaring that all contracts should be subject to legislative control, and should be discharged as the legislature might prescribe, would become a component part of every contract, and be one of its conditions. Thus, one of the most important features in the constitution of the United States, one which the state of the times most urgently required, one on which the good and the wise reposed confidently for securing the prosperity and harmony of our citizens, would

43

lie prostrate, and be construed into an inanimate, inoperative, unmeaning clause.[71]

It is inadequate to respond to this argument by claiming that the contract clause protects what people are entitled to expect, rather than merely what they actually expect, and is therefore "essentially coextensive with the reach of substantive due process and equal protection."[72] This approach ignores the separate interest protected by the contract clause—the need for certainty of legal enforcement to facilitate private ordering. The ultimate question is whether to let people decide for themselves what they want through the interactions of a market economy, or to leave it to the courts in determining what interests are protected by the Fifth and Fourteenth Amendments.

The effectiveness of the contract clause limitation on state power arguably can be protected only by making it clear that, while the state generally reserves power under *Blaisdell* to impair contracts to protect important public interests, the Constitution precludes enforceability of blanket statutory reservations of power. This constitutional protection, and not statutory reservations, would then shape the parties' actual expectations. In other words, subject to the public interest limitation, there would be no difference between what contracting parties would be entitled to expect and what they actually expect.

In analyzing the reserved power as a contract term, it is important to keep in mind that the state's opt-out of the contract clause is not wholly unilateral. Because corporations voluntarily select the state of incorporation, the reserved-power provision can be regarded as having been voluntarily included in the corporate contract. In other words, the contracting parties themselves opt out of the contract clause. Because the parties to corporations cannot foresee future developments, and because shareholder amendment can be costly, they may wish to empower the state to make state-of-the-art modifications in the corporate contract. Perhaps corporations should be able to decide whether this benefit is worth the risk of potential wealth-redistributive legislation. After all, as discussed in chapter 1, corporate statutory terms are priced out in the financial markets, and states can compete for chartering business by offering "tight" statutes without reserved-power provisions.

Several factors suggest, however, that the ubiquity of reserved-power provisions is not attributable to corporations' finding them to be efficient. First, lawmakers' incentives are not perfectly aligned with the taxpayers' interests. Although the taxpayers of an incorporating jurisdiction would want to maximize net revenues from the franchise tax, they are not a coherent interest group capable of paying rents to legislators.[73] But legislators, as the producers and sellers of interest group legislation, do gain from engineering the wealth redistributions that are permitted by reserved-power provisions. Lawmakers therefore would lose more than they would gain by offering statutes without reserved-power provisions.

Second, even if legislators wanted to increase franchise tax revenues, it is not clear that they could do so substantially by deleting reserved-power provisions. In at least some corporations, reserved-power provisions serve managers' more than shareholders' interests,[74] and so are likely to be deleted only at the shareholders' insistence. But shareholders can force deletion only by overcoming free-rider problems, as through the market for control. The expected costs resulting from the use of the reserved power, while substantial in the aggregate, are unlikely to be great for any given corporation. Thus, one could not ordinarily gain by purchasing control in order to reincorporate under a statute that does not include a reserved-power provision. This minimizes the potential benefit to a state that seeks to compete for chartering business by offering a tight corporation law.[75]

Third, even if a tight statute offered substantial benefits to some corporations, these benefits might be offset by the costs of adopting the statute. Thus, Delaware competes for incorporation business by offering a bond in the form of an investment in reputation that cannot readily be duplicated by other states.[76] This bond provides a margin within which Delaware legislators' rent-seeking gains cannot be wrested by other states.

Fourth, efficiency-based explanations of reserved-power provisions do not explain why they are not waivable. Even if most parties to corporations found such provisions to be efficient, there is no basis to assume that all parties would. The more likely explanation for not permitting shareholders to waive reserved-power provisions is that these provisions do not serve shareholders' interests.

It is no answer to these arguments to say that shareholders are not injured by reserved-power provisions because the risk of prospective impairment is priced out ex ante. If efficiency and wealth maximization are the goals, the parties should not be able to opt out of constraints on contract impairment because the rent-seeking expenditures invested in statutory wealth redistribution are a social cost. By reducing the gains from contracting, contract impairment allocates resources from productive contracting to wasteful rent seeking. Indeed, as discussed above, just such a situation occurred in the chaotic period following the American Revolution, when debtor-relief statutes proliferated and commercial activity ground to a halt. This

45

era was fresh in the framers' minds at the time of drafting the Constitution. The contract clause represents the framers' preference for productive over political activity.

Judicial application of reserved-power provisions. Although, as discussed above, use of reserved-power provisions to evade the contract clause appears to be entrenched through application in numerous cases since *Dartmouth College,* the appearance of universal acceptance is deceptive. In fact, many of the cases enforcing such provisions involve special fact situations to which the contract clause may not even be applicable. At least four types of fact situations may be identified.

First, courts sometimes apply reserved-power provisions to let the state revoke a privilege that was at least arguably terminable at will.[77] Second, courts have applied reserved-power provisions to permit "changes" that were at least arguably within the contract, or at least anticipated by the shareholders. The reserved power, for example, was applied to sustain a statute clarifying that minority shareholders can be compelled in a short-form merger to surrender their shares for cash where the former statute permitted exchange of "other securities," including cashlike instruments.[78] Third, some cases apply reserved-power provisions where the affected shareholders receive appraisal rights,[79] and so arguably are compensated for their contract rights.[80] Finally, reserved-power provisions have been applied to corporations whose charters explicitly provide for change by the legislature.[81] As discussed above, some contracting parties may desire the flexibility afforded by these provisions. Also, incorporating such a provision in the charter may simply clarify the terminability at will of a state grant of monopoly power.[82]

The special circumstances of many of the cases in which reserved-power provisions have been applied, coupled with the cases cited above in which the courts have refused to use such provisions to sustain retroactive application of statutory amendments, provide strong evidence that the reserved power actually plays little role in sustaining amendments of corporate statutes.

Statutory Changes in the Corporate Contract

This section discusses specific issues concerning the application of the contract clause to state corporation statutes.[83] The first three subsections discuss, respectively, state antitakeover statutes, statutes permitting consideration of nonshareholder interests, and statutes that provide for direct alteration of the standard of conduct or liability. These statutory provisions clearly raise concerns under the contract clause, because they change the terms of the corporate contract without a shareholder vote. The fourth subsection discusses statutes expanding shareholders' amending power—a kind of statutory provision that raises different issues under the contract clause because it applies to a corporation only if adopted by shareholder vote.

State Antitakeover Statutes. Because the threat of takeover is an important means of disciplining managers, antitakeover defenses can improve life for managers while imposing costs on shareholders. Not surprisingly, managers would like to adopt these defenses, particularly if they can do so unilaterally without having to accept such offsetting contractual adjustments as pay reductions or alternative monitoring devices. To be sure, modern corporation laws have always had many provisions that could be characterized as antitakeover in the sense that they impeded corporate acquisition. State statutes, for example, commonly permit staggered boards of directors (that is, election of only a portion of the board each year) and supermajority approval requirements for certain corporate transactions or certificate amendments. But the problem with these provisions from the standpoint of incumbent corporate management is that they must be adopted as part of the corporate governance structure by shareholder vote. Managers' control of the proxy machinery, coupled with the usual passivity of the shareholders of public corporations, ensures adoption of most corporate changes proposed by management. But shareholders, particularly sophisticated institutional ones, can be expected sometimes to balk at provisions that would prevent them from selling their stock at the substantial premiums over market offered by hostile bidders. Thus, managers have reason to fear a "slave revolt" on this issue.[84]

Against this background, in the late 1970s and early 1980s, corporations with substantial economic clout, particularly in rust belt states, turned to their state legislatures for help. Faced with the specter that jobs would move elsewhere in the wake of takeovers, thirty-seven states passed statutes that substantially impeded tender offers made to shareholders in their states by, among other things, providing for lengthy notice periods and approval by state regulators. In 1982, the validity of all these statutes was cast in considerable doubt by the Supreme Court's decision in *Edgar v. MTE Corp.*[85] In that case the majority of the Court held that the Illinois statute unconstitutionally burdened interstate commerce, and a plurality held that the statute was unconstitutional under the supremacy

47

clause because it conflicted with federal tender offer legislation aimed solely at protecting shareholders from coercive takeovers rather than at protecting the jobs of incumbent managers.

After *Edgar*, incumbent managers and their advisers went back to their drawing boards. The result was a "second generation" of state antitakeover statutes that sought to avoid commerce clause and supremacy clause problems. These statutes eliminated notice periods and administrative approval, applied only to corporations incorporated in the enacting state, and regulated the second-stage transactions that followed the tender offer rather than the offer itself. This new strategy to impose costs on shareholders worked. In *CTS Corporation v. Dynamics Corp. of America*,[86] the Court upheld on commerce and supremacy clause grounds the Indiana statute, which provided that "control shares" obtained by hostile tender offers would be nonvoting unless a majority of disinterested shareholders voted to make them voting shares at the next regularly scheduled shareholder meeting, or at a special meeting called by the tender offeror within fifty days of the offer.

While *CTS* may have been appropriate on the grounds considered by the Court,[87] the discussion below makes clear that Indiana-type antitakeover statutes are unconstitutional under the contract clause.

Impairment. In general, managerial defensive tactics have been the subject of an intense debate in the legal and economic literature. While some commentators have argued that managerial defensive tactics should be prohibited because, as discussed above, they circumvent the vital protection against agency costs provided by the market for control,[88] other commentators have shown how some shareholders may find it efficient to permit corporate managers to defend against takeovers.[89] Under the latter view, the extent of managers' power to defend against takeovers is a term of the corporate contract, negotiated in advance of the takeover.[90] In some cases the shareholders may want their managers to defend against takeovers to encourage them to make firm-specific investments of human capital, while in others the costs of permitting entrenchment may outweigh the benefits, so the managers may trade job protection for higher compensation.

State antitakeover statutes of the type involved in *CTS* involve a potential violation of the contract clause because they impair the contracts both of shareholders generally, whose power to transfer control rights is changed, and of shareholders who bought stock expecting to be able to acquire control without the conditions later imposed by the act. The impairment is not ameliorated by the shareholders' ability to opt out by selling their shares or reincorporating. The new statute reduces the present value of expected future returns for any corporation for which the antitakeover statute is an inefficient term. This reduction in value is reflected in the market price of the stock. Because reincorporation requires costly mobilization of shareholder votes, any costs imposed by an antitakeover statute will be tolerated if they are less than the costs of reversing the standard by reincorporating. More important, the statute itself frustrates exit through reincorporation by inhibiting acquisition of control to effect this result.

Because antitakeover statutes clearly impair corporate contracts, it is important to determine whether the state can show a sufficient justification of the impairment to avoid invalidation of the statute under the contract clause. This is considered in the following two subsections.

Scrutiny level. The justification of the impairment should be scrutinized closely because of the severity of the impairment. Any change in the degree of management entrenchment is likely to be a significant change in the contract because of the importance of the market for corporate control to corporate governance.[91] The impairment is particularly likely to be severe where it results from lobbying by a specific corporation for relief from a particular bidder, because the winning party presumably pursued the legislative route precisely because it was less costly than dealing with the shareholders.

Although Indiana-type statutes do not eliminate control transfers, their impact is significant because additional risks attached to the takeover increase its cost, thereby reducing the bidders' gains from the takeover and deterring the bid.[92] Inhibiting the bidder's ability to effect a second-stage transaction, such as a sell-off of one or more divisions, may eliminate the very improvement the gains of which the bidder sought to capture by making the bid. This would remove the power of the market for control to discipline incumbent managers' refusal to do the transaction. Although the shareholders can vote to confer control share status, this involves the bidder in a proxy contest with incumbent managers, who have access to the corporation's proxy machinery—that is, who can wage the campaign at the company's expense. This, again, soaks up the bidder's potential gains, eliminating or substantially reducing the bidder's incentive to make the bid.

Indiana-type antitakeover statutes also require extra scrutiny

49

because they are a good example of specifically focused statutes. Substantial evidence indicates that in Indiana and elsewhere, state antitakeover statutes were passed to prevent the hostile takeover of specific corporations by publicly identified potential acquirers.[93] More generally, Roberta Romano has explained passage of this type of statute as the result of lobbying by specific firms that were dominant in their respective states rather than by a coalition of interests that might be affected by takeovers.[94] The Indiana act itself was apparently passed at the urging of Arvin Industries,[95] and many other "second generation" antitakeover statutes seem to conform to this explanation.[96] Romano shows that corporations that lobby for this type of statute usually have high concentration ratios of ownership, and she concludes that the shareholders of such corporations would be most likely to reject control-share–type provisions.[97] These facts are consistent with managers' exerting political influence to increase their job security, even if they traded job security for other benefits in their initial contract. This reworking of the contract redistributes wealth from shareholders to managers.

Reasonableness and necessity. The purported justifications of the impairment cannot stand up to the scrutiny level just described. The principal purported justification for state antitakeover provisions has been protection of shareholders of target corporations, and this was a basis on which the Supreme Court upheld the Indiana statute in *CTS.* The Court held that the statute was consistent with the Williams Act and therefore valid on supremacy clause grounds, because the statute protected shareholders from coercive tender offers. The Court also rejected a commerce clause challenge, concluding that the Indiana statute neither discriminated against interstate commerce nor subjected interstate activities to inconsistent regulations. It stressed the state's interest in protecting the shareholders of its corporations from coercive tender offers, adding:

> A State has an interest in promoting stable relationships among parties involved in the corporations it charters, as well as in ensuring that investors in such corporations have an effective voice in corporate affairs.[98]

It is not clear whether the Court would take the same approach in justifying the statute on contract clause grounds. The Court's opinion not only addresses a different constitutional provision, but also was endorsed by only four members of the current Court.[99]

The Court's reasoning clearly should not be adopted under the contract clause. The Court was led into error at the outset by its mistaken characterization of the corporation as a creature of state law rather than of private contract.[100] Almost sixty years ago, a writer characterized the argument under the contract clause that Delaware had a public interest in protecting its supposed creatures as follows:

It may be remarked that the picture of the paternal interest of the state in its corporate creatures is very affecting and that Delaware, with its ever-increasing progeny of "corporate creatures," is certainly entitled to give expression to its paternal instincts. But the thought of parental solicitude following some eighty thousand corporations created by this state, most of whom have wandered far abroad without even a sentimental attachment to the parental roof, surpasses a legal fiction in its demands upon faith.[101]

The state's role vis-à-vis antitakeover statutes is simply to minimize transaction costs by establishing standard forms shareholders can opt into. Problems relating to takeovers should be resolved by their contract,[102] perhaps utilizing the state's standard form, and not by the state acting as guardian for the shareholders.

Even assuming that the state has a role in protecting shareholders from tender offers, it is neither reasonable nor necessary for states to impair the shareholders' contract in order to do so. The impairment in the antitakeover statute is the automatic application of the statute to the shareholders by director action. The state's supposed interest in shareholder protection is not furthered by forcing this protection on the shareholders. Even in *United States Trust*,[103] in which the Court held that the bond contract could not be impaired on the basis of environmental and other concerns that could be served in other ways, at least the deletion of the bond covenant did, in fact, further the state's goals.

The states may defend their antitakeover statutes from a contract clause challenge by confessing to what is, perhaps, the real motivation for the statutes: protection of employees and others in the state from exit of important citizens as a result of takeovers. Unlike the shareholder-protection rationale, the protection-from-exit story at least has the virtue of presenting a real state interest that is furthered by the impairment.

But there are two major problems with the protection-from-exit justification. First, as in *United States Trust*, the state has many other nonimpairing options, including financial inducements to stay or requiring notice or lag periods before departure from the state. Also, the means—regulating transfers of stock—do not relate to the end, which is preventing movement of assets. In the light of the state's other options and the lack of a fit between means and ends, the state's justification should not stand up to the relatively high-level

51

scrutiny we have concluded the Court should apply to antitakeover statutes. Moreover, even if the state were justified in limiting control transfers to impede corporate exit from the state, this would clearly redistribute wealth from the shareholders to the state. This would entitle the shareholders to reasonable compensation.[104]

Thus, state antitakeover statutes not only impair corporate contracts, but also cannot be justified as reasonable and necessary. It follows that these statutes are unconstitutional under the contracts clause.

Nonshareholder Constituency Statutes. State corporation statutes have been amended in a majority of states explicitly to permit directors to consider the interests of nonshareholder constituencies in making decisions, including decisions connected with a change of corporate control.[105] The Minnesota statute, for example, provides that

> in discharging the duties of the position of director, a director may, in considering the best interests of the corporation, consider the interests of the corporation's employees, customers, suppliers, and creditors, the economy of the state and nation, community and societal considerations, and the long-term as well as short-term interests of the corporation and its shareholders including the possibility that these interests may be best served by the continued independence of the corporation.[106]

It is unclear whether these statutes change the corporate contract.[107] Managers clearly owe contractual duties to nonshareholder constituencies, including workers and consumers. Some cases have held that managers may act in the interests of nonshareholder constituencies.[108] In particular, the Delaware Supreme Court has allowed directors to act broadly within the business judgment rule to protect the corporation's interests, even if this means precluding shareholders from accepting a takeover offer at a price significantly in excess of current market value.[109]

Although the point is not clear, on balance several types of statutes permitting consideration of nonshareholder constituencies apparently do change the law and therefore impair the corporate contract.[110] In particular, some statutes provide that the directors are not required to give primacy to shareholder interests.[111] Since shareholders would not willingly accept these terms, they should be subjected to them only by clear prospective regulation. The mere intimation in some court decisions that the directors may consider nonshareholder interests does not meet this test.

52

Assuming nonshareholder-constituency statutes impair the corporate contract, they can be sustained only if they are "reasonable and necessary" to protect a public interest.[112] The scrutiny level would not be as intense as with antitakeover statutes, because the statutes do not specifically limit shareholders' power to transfer control[113] and do not appear to be aimed at specific corporations.

Despite the lower scrutiny level, nonshareholder constituency statutes cannot be justified as reasonable and necessary. One potential justification is that these statutes allegedly protect citizens of the state from precipitous exit of businesses that are important to the local economy. In one sense, the statutes fulfill this purpose better than state antitakeover statutes, which, as discussed above, impede any change in control, whether or not connected with a corporate exit that is potentially costly to third parties.[114]

There are, however, three problems with the protection-from-exit justification. First, the purpose itself is suspect because, by preventing the highest bidder from taking control, it inhibits efficient use of assets located in the state. Second, the statutes are not well designed to protect local state interests. They apply on the basis of incorporation rather than of presence in the state. Moreover, the state could accomplish its goal through means that less directly and less severely impair corporate contracts, such as by financially inducing local corporations to remain in the state. Third, even if these statutes were "reasonable and necessary" to fulfill an important state interest, the statutes effect a partial condemnation of the value of shareholders' investments for an allegedly public purpose, and the state should compensate for this.[115] Therefore, statutes that permit managers to consider nonshareholder interests in making corporate decisions are unconstitutional under the contract clause, because they impair the corporate contract and are difficult to justify as reasonable and necessary to protect an important state interest.

Direct Alteration of the Standard of Conduct or Liability. Several statutes alter the managers' standard of conduct and of liability. Some provide that directors (and sometimes officers) can be held liable only on the basis of, for example, "improper personal benefit" or "willful misconduct."[116] Others adjust the managers' liability for breach of the applicable standard of conduct or the method or grounds of indemnifying managers.[117]

Statutes that alter the standard of conduct or liability of managers without shareholder vote are troubling under the contract clause. Fiduciary duties of managers are properly regarded as part of the shareholder-manager contract rather than as imposed by law. As

53

discussed in chapter 1, these contracts reflect sensitive trade-offs between the costs and benefits of fiduciary duties. Reducing fiduciary duties or liability may be inconsistent with the trade-offs in the original contract. Loosening the duty of loyalty, for example, might enable managers to have the benefits of a higher explicit level of compensation without commensurate limitations on implicit compensation. Similarly, loosening the duty of care may reverse the parties' decision to rely on this duty instead of, for example, precisely calibrated incentive compensation or tight monitoring. The result of the change may be to leave managers with the benefits of flat compensation or greater job security without the commensurate constraints of fiduciary duties.

Thus, the statutes that alter fiduciary duties or liability without shareholder approval arguably impair corporate contracts. There would probably be no impairment if these provisions simply eliminated manager liability for negligence,[118] because there have been very few cases in which managers have been held liable on this ground.[119] Such provisions could be regarded as simply correcting the misinterpretation or impairment of the corporate contract by cases like *Smith v. Van Gorkom*.[120] To the extent that the statutes also eliminate the directors' duty to act nonrecklessly, however, they arguably go beyond even pre–*Van Gorkom* case law, thereby impairing the contract between shareholders and managers.

Precisely the same considerations are raised by statutes that adjust managers' liability for breach of the applicable standard of conduct rather than the standard itself. Thus, a Virginia statute limits director and officer liability to the greater of $100,000 or the manager's compensation in the year preceding the breach, unless the charter limits liability even further or unless the manager has engaged in willful misconduct or a knowing law violation.[121] To similar effect, a Wisconsin statute requires indemnification of managers against liability for merely reckless conduct.[122] While these statutes do not preclude injunctions against transactions effected in breach of the applicable standard of conduct, the extent of liability for breach of duty is just as important a part of the shareholder-manager contract as the standard of conduct under which such liability is imposed. It follows that any statutory alteration of this liability is subject to the contract clause.

The statute may constitute an impairment even if it changes only the extent to which the corporation may indemnify managers.[123] If the indemnification decision is made by shareholders—as where the statute permits charter provisions that vary from the statute—the situation is analogous to statutory provisions like those discussed in the next subsection, which enlarge the shareholders' amendment power. But enlargement of the power of directors or other corporate agents to make indemnification does constitute a direct change in the contract, and it is subject to the same considerations discussed above in this subsection.

A statute that changes the managers' duties or liabilities is not "saved" from impairing the corporate contract by permitting the shareholders to opt out of coverage, any more than by allowing the shareholders to reincorporate. Such a statute significantly changes the shareholders' rights because of the cost of obtaining a shareholder vote. It follows that the statute is also not saved by delaying the effective date from the time the statute is enacted, or the date enactment becomes certain, because the managers' duties will be changed on a certain date unless the shareholders have taken costly action to reincorporate before then. An inefficient contract term can be expected immediately to depress the price of the company's stock to reflect the net cost of the change discounted for the possibility that the shareholders will act to reverse it.

Since statutory alteration of fiduciary duties or liability for breach impairs the corporate contract, it is unconstitutional under the contract clause unless it is reasonable and necessary. The principal factor affecting the degree with which the courts will scrutinize the justification of this type of statute is the extent to which the statute departs from earlier law. Thus, a statute altering the duty of care or liability for breach may be subject to a low scrutiny level because, *Van Gorkom* notwithstanding, the cases appear to be generally opposed to such liability.[124]

If the statutes alter the contract, they are probably not reasonable and necessary. The statutes cannot be sustained merely on the ground that they represent a better contract term. This conclusion is supported by at least one case invalidating under the contract clause an attempt to impose cumulative voting.[125] Although cumulative voting arguably protects minority shareholders by ensuring them board representation, this is something that the shareholders themselves should determine. Altering the corporate contract to improve it can stand only if a corporation is regarded as a "creature," and therefore in a sense a ward, of the state. The alteration falls if the corporation is correctly viewed as a conventional contract.

Nor can the statutes be sustained on the theory that, by correctly anticipating a contract change some shareholders would approve, they save the transaction costs of such approval. There is little reason to believe that state legislatures can anticipate the preferences of corporate shareholders generally, particularly since different contract terms are appropriate for different companies. Moreover, the costs of a shareholder opt-in, as distinguished from those of opt-out discussed above, are minimal. As with respect to antitakeover statutes, this is the type of change likely to be initiated by management, thus avoiding the costs of shareholder coordination.

Expanding the Shareholders' Amendment Power by Opting out of Fiduciary Duties. The statutory provisions discussed above all change the corporate contract without a shareholder vote. This subsection discusses statutory provisions that permit the shareholders to vote for a change in the corporate charter. Some of these statutes may be unconstitutional under the contract clause.

At first blush this type of statute may not seem to present any contract clause problems because it permits change only by the shareholder. But the statute does alter the corporate contract to the extent that it enlarges the shareholders' power to amend the charter. Moreover, this kind of alteration raises the same kinds of problems as the others discussed in this section. The amendment power provided for in the original charter, like other contractual terms, reflects complex trade-offs. On the one hand, the shareholders may desire flexibility in light of the impossibility of drafting a fully contingent long-term corporate contract. On the other hand, as discussed in chapter 1,[126] as a condition of granting amendment power to the majority, minority shareholders may have insisted on protection from abuse of this voting power in the form of a limitation on the changes that could be wrought by majority vote. Enlargement of the amendment power may subvert this protection.

The problem of enlarging shareholder amendment power was recognized in some early cases that invalidated statutory amendments on the ground that they infringed shareholders' "vested rights."[127] While a leading case ultimately rejected the vested rights approach,[128] that case did not raise the contract clause problem because the corporation was formed after amendment of the statute. Thus, the contract clause problem raised by retroactive application of an expanded amendment power has not been settled.

A prominent example of possible impairment through alteration of the amendment power is recent statutory provisions that permit the shareholders to adopt charter provisions limiting director (and sometimes officer) liability for breach of fiduciary duties. These statutes were passed in the wake of *Smith v. Van Gorkom*,[129] which for the first time appeared to recognize director liability for merely negligent conduct. Delaware passed the first statute, which became the prototype for many of the others.[130] The Delaware statute permitted the following type of charter provision:

A provision eliminating or limiting the personal liability of a director to the corporation or its stockholders for monetary damages for breach of fiduciary duty as a director, provided that such provision shall not eliminate or limit the liability of a director (i) for any breach of the director's duty of loyalty to the corporation or its stockholders, (ii) for acts or omissions not in good faith or which involve intentional misconduct or a knowing violation of law, (iii) under section 174 of this title, or (iv) for any transaction from which the director derived an improper personal benefit. No such provision shall eliminate or limit the liability of a director for any act or omission occurring prior to the date when such provision becomes effective. All references in this subsection to a director shall also be deemed to refer to a member of the governing body of a corporation which is not authorized to issue capital stock.[131]

A provision like this probably does not violate the contract clause because it does not actually enlarge the amendment power. The Delaware statute permits amendment "in any and as many respects as may be desired; so long as its certificate of incorporation as amended would contain only such provisions as it would be lawful and proper to insert in an original certificate of incorporation filed at the time of the filing of the amendment."[132] The provision on the contents of the certificate permits the certificate to include, among other things, "any provision creating, defining, limiting and regulating the powers of the . . . directors."[133] The Delaware fiduciary duty opt-out is not inconsistent with any existing statutory provision, since the statute nowhere defines the directors' duty of care. Nor did the prior case law preclude changes of the sort made by the new Delaware provision. It prevented complete abrogation of director duties,[134] but it validated charter provisions that adjusted fiduciary duties in a way that was not inconsistent with existing law.[135]

A charter provision that, contrary to existing law, allowed complete abrogation of fiduciary duties would raise a more serious contract clause question. To be sure, the statutory amendment power must be broad to accommodate needed flexibility in a long-term corporate contract. Moreover, shareholders would normally have no reason to prohibit this type of amendment because they are protected by their common interest in optimizing agency cost. Where this common interest does not protect the shareholders, however, as where the managers themselves hold a controlling class of stock, perhaps the contract should be interpreted as prohibiting this type of amendment.

Statutory amendments that remove explicit limitations on the statutory amendment power are least likely to withstand contract clause analysis. An example would be an amendment that removed the requirement for class voting on amendments that affect the rights of a particular class.[136] Because such a limitation on the amendment power protects limited-vote shareholders from abrogation of their contracts by controlling shareholders, the limitation is an important part of the corporate contract and is accordingly protected from impairment by the contract clause.

The same principle would invalidate other statutory amendments that permit voting shareholders to remove rights of parties who are protected by mandatory provisions of the corporate statute. The Delaware fiduciary duty opt-out recognizes this problem by excepting limitation of director liability for improper dividends—a liability that is imposed to protect nonvoting creditors.

In general, this section demonstrates the important role that the contract clause can play in protecting contract rights of parties to corporations from unjustified state legislative interference. Such legislation often involves the protection of purely local interests, usually managers of local corporations, at the expense of dispersed shareholders and the national economy. These statutes accordingly involve the problem of dead-weight wealth-redistribution that is addressed by the contract clause.

Conclusion

Understanding the contractual theory of the corporation teaches us that legal regulation of the corporate form beyond the establishment of standard form contracts is neither necessary nor desirable. Legal regulation is not necessary because optimal arrangements will develop through private ordering, and it is not desirable to the extent that it impairs these arrangements. For this reason it is vital to understand how the Constitution, through the contract clause, guards the integrity of corporate contracts. Moreover, the importance of this constitutional protection is increasing as developments in corporate finance and acquisitions challenge courts and legislators to settle disputes among parties to the corporate contract. These disputes must be settled through interpretation of the contract rather than application of outmoded legal norms.

3
Corporate Campaign Activities

The First Amendment both protects the self-expression rights of individual speakers and serves society as a whole by fostering the production and dissemination of information.[1] As Justices Oliver Wendell Holmes and Louis Brandeis said in their famous *Abrams* dissent, "the best test of truth is the power of thought to get itself accepted in the competition of the market."[2]

Introduction

Speech is important in a democratic society in assisting not only political decisions,[3] but all decisions free people make for themselves.[4] Accordingly, the relevance of the First Amendment to corporate speech—such as corporate political campaign activities and corporate governance communications with shareholders—cannot be dismissed, even by those who care little about the rights of corporations and other for-profit entities.

Because of the importance of First Amendment rights, proponents of regulating speech should have to overcome a strong burden of justification. Even stringent government regulation of speech, however, may be constitutionally justified. First Amendment analysis necessarily entails pragmatic balancing of the importance of speech and the need to accommodate other social interests.[5] The government can, for example, restrict false advertising or forbid cries of "Fire!" in a public theater. As discussed in this and the following chapter, proponents of regulating corporate speech have cited several benefits from regulation to justify the laws under the First Amendment.

This chapter shows that whether restrictions on corporate speech can withstand scrutiny under the First Amendment depends on whether these restrictions are consistent with the contractual or with the regulatory theory of the corporation. Under the contractual theory, corporate campaign activities and other corporate speech would be restricted only by contracts intended to minimize agency costs in the firm. Managers' use of corporate assets to support political causes that they favor but that are inconsistent with shareholder interests, for example, does not differ significantly from any other type of managerial misbehavior. Similarly, managers' control over corporate disclosures to hide their misconduct and proxy speech by dissident shareholders intended to replace errant managers are both aspects of the control of agency costs. Firms may adopt default rules provided by state corporate codes that are intended to minimize agency costs by directly controlling managerial misuse of corporate assets, or by increasing the shareholders' voice in corporate affairs. Such rules should not raise significant constitutional concerns. Although the rules may amount to direct restrictions on speech, the contractual theory of the corporation holds that the benefits of these contracted-for default restrictions are likely to outweigh the costs, because the rules must compete in efficient capital markets.

Nevertheless, restrictions on corporate speech that are consistent with the regulatory theory of the corporation, such as mandatory federal and state election laws, raise significant First Amendment concerns. First, there is no reason to assume that mandatory rules, which need not compete in capital markets, will appropriately balance the costs and benefits of speech restrictions. Second, the purported justification for mandatory rules is government's supposed interest in exercising political control over the corporation. Thus, regulation of corporate speech is often intended to, and in fact does, affect the balance of political power in society. Not-for-profit activist corporations,[6] for example, and noncommercial speech[7] may be less regulated and more constitutionally protected than the activities of commercial enterprises. Because of this potential for recognition of a government-imposed orthodoxy, regulation of corporate speech requires the highest level of First Amendment scrutiny.

Corporate Political Activity and the Court

The Supreme Court decided in *Austin v. Michigan Chamber of Commerce*[8] that laws restricting corporate political activity are not unconstitutional under the First Amendment. As discussed briefly in this section, that decision brought full circle a series of cases, beginning with broad recognition of corporate First Amendment rights in Justice Lewis Powell's decision in *First National Bank of Boston v. Bellotti*.[9]

Bellotti invalidated under the First and Fourteenth Amendments a Massachusetts statute that prohibited certain business corporations from making contributions or expenditures "for the purpose of . . . influencing or affecting the vote on any question submitted to the voters, other than one materially affecting any of the property, business or assets of the corporation." The Court reasoned that speech that is otherwise protected does not lose its protection because the speaker is a corporation—that speech is protected not merely as a property right, but as a part of the guarantee of liberty to all natural and artificial persons.[10]

The Court also held that potential state interests, in preventing corporations from unduly influencing referendum votes, offsetting state-conferred advantages such as limited liability,[11] protecting shareholders from use of their investments in corporations to support views with which they disagreed, were insufficiently compelling to sustain the statute.[12]

Justice Powell's opinion in *Bellotti* stands as the high point of the Court's protection of corporate political speech. The *Bellotti* dissents foreshadowed the erosion that would occur in subsequent opinions. Justice Byron White, who wrote in dissent for Justices William Brennan and Thurgood Marshall, reasoned that corporate speech should be protected only when it furthers self-expression by the shareholders, as is the case with corporations formed solely to advance particular causes, or press corporations, or commercial speech, which "may be viewed as a means of furthering the desires of individual shareholders."[13] Justice White also defended the restrictions on the ground that shareholders should not be forced to support speech with which they disagree.[14] Justice William Rehnquist dissented in *Bellotti* on the basis of the Court's holding in *Dartmouth College v. Woodward*[15] that a corporation "possesses only those properties which the [state-conferred] charter of creation confers on it, either expressly, or as incidental to its very existence."[16] In the case of a nonpress commercial corporation, these "properties" do not include a right of political expression.[17] Thus, according to Rehnquist, the state need not even justify corporate speech restrictions under the First Amendment.[18]

The first case eroding the basic protection in *Bellotti* was *Federal Election Commission v. National Right to Work Committee (NRWC)*,[19] in which the Court held that Congress constitutionally could prohibit a nonprofit corporation from mass soliciting from "nonmembers" political contributions to a segregated fund. The statute's limitation on associational freedom was justified by the interests in protecting against use of "substantial aggregations of wealth amassed by the special advantages which go with the corporate form of organization" and in protecting individuals from having their money used for candidates they oppose.[20] The Court distinguished *Bellotti* as applying to state referendums rather than to candidate elections.[21]

In *Federal Election Commission v. Massachusetts Citizens for Life, Inc. (MCFL)*,[22] the Court, by Justice Brennan, held that a federal prohibition of use of corporate treasury funds for expenditures in a federal

61

election, as distinguished from the less-protected activity of campaign contributions involved in *NRWC*, would unconstitutionally burden the exercise of First Amendment rights. Although the Court struck down the law, it narrowly focused the application of the First Amendment in this area by emphasizing that the newsletter was published by a nonprofit corporation organized to oppose abortion. The Court held that the state's interest in preventing political use of corporate wealth amassed in the economic marketplace did not apply to MCFL-type companies whose resources reflected the political views of its contributors.

The Court made this narrow focus even clearer in *Austin v. Michigan Chamber of Commerce*,[23] which held that a Michigan statute's prohibition on the use of corporate treasury funds for expenditures for or against candidates for state office was not unconstitutional under the First and Fourteenth Amendments, as applied to a newspaper advertisement placed by the Michigan Chamber of Commerce. The Court reasoned that the statute was constitutionally justified by the state's interest in protecting against "corruption" in the form of "the corrosive and distorting effects of immense aggregations of wealth that are accumulated with the help of the corporate form and that have little or no correlation to the public's support for the corporation's political ideas."[24]

The Court distinguished the chamber from the MCFL on the grounds that the former, although nonprofit, was not formed for the express purpose of promoting political ideas, that members received nonpolitical benefits from the chamber and so would be reluctant to disassociate, and that the chamber could be used to funnel money from business corporations. The Court emphasized the chamber's adoption of the corporate form—"the unique state-conferred corporate structure that facilitates the amassing of large treasuries."[25]

Thus, the post-*Bellotti* cases culminating in *Austin* whittled Justice Powell's broad recognition of First Amendment protection of corporate political speech down to protection of corporate political activities in referendum contests, and of the speech of narrowly defined MCFL-type nonprofit corporations. Members of the Court have reasoned that regulation of corporate political activity can be justified on three types of grounds: (1) for protection of shareholders from use of their investments to support speech with which they disagree; (2) because corporations are peculiarly subject to regulation, as a creature of state law; and (3) in order to constrain corporate political power. The following three sections show that these arguments, which appear to reflect the Court's continued acceptance of the outmoded regulatory theory of the corporation, should not sustain restrictions of corporate political activity under the First Amendment.

Shareholder Protection and Agency Costs

Several members of the Court have argued that government restrictions on corporate political speech are justified under the First Amendment by the need to protect shareholders from managers.[26] This section shows that while contract-based restrictions are justified, mandatory regulation of corporate political activities under election laws should not survive First Amendment scrutiny.

Whose Speech Is It? Before discussing whether government restrictions on corporate political speech can be justified as shareholder protection, we should consider whether managers of publicly held corporations who speak as agents have any constitutionally protected right to speak. Some commentators[27] and members of the Court[28] question whether individuals' rights of self-expression are at stake in the speech of corporate managers. This line of reasoning reflects the suspicion of corporate agents that is at the heart of the contractual theory. Nevertheless, the argument is deficient because it mischaracterizes and derives erroneous constitutional implications from the contracts between managers and shareholders.

Managers' speech cannot be attributed to the shareholders in publicly held corporations. Managers obviously have a constitutionally protected interest in speech they make on their own behalf and support with their own compensation or with corporate funds authorized for managers' "personal" speech.[29] Managers' personal speech also should be protected even if they spend shareholders' money without authority, as where the speech is purportedly made on behalf of the corporation but actually serves managers' interests.[30] A speaker should not have to trace the source of the funds supporting the speech in order to be entitled to First Amendment protection.

Moreover, whether the managers technically have authority to speak should not determine whether the speech is attributed to the shareholders for First Amendment purposes. Shareholders do not "approve" managers' corporate speech, except in the attenuated sense that they can sue errant managers for breach of fiduciary duty or vote them out of office for conduct that is significantly contrary to their interests.[31] Passive shareholders in public corporations cannot be regarded in any meaningful sense as controlling or monitoring corporate activity, including corporate speech.[32]

Because political speech by managers of publicly held firms can generally be considered the expression of the individual managers from whom the speech originates, regulation of this speech presents a potential First Amendment concern. If the agency relationship between managers and shareholders matters at all under the First Amendment, it is only because speech restrictions are purportedly justified by the need to protect shareholders' property. As discussed in the following sections, however, regulation of corporate political speech also cannot appropriately be justified on that ground.

Agency Costs and Agency Contracts. Commentators[33] and some members of the Court[34] have sought to invoke a contract or agency theory to justify government restrictions on corporate campaign activities, on the ground that such rules protect shareholders from having to support views with which they disagree. To the extent that this argument assumes that shareholders are like employees in a closed shop who are compelled to contribute money to support a union's political activities with which the employees disagree,[35] the argument is patently misguided. As the *Bellotti* majority noted,[36] corporate shareholders are free to decide where to invest their money.[37] The shareholder-protection argument, however, may be based on the more subtle economic argument that managers' use of corporate funds to invest in speech contrary to investors' interests or beliefs can be regarded as a type of agency cost. In fact, despite shareholders' freedom to sell their stock, managers' and shareholders' interests are likely to diverge regarding speech. Managers may, for example, advocate pet causes that do not relate to the corporation. Even managers' political activity that is clearly in the firm's best interest may not be in the shareholders' best interests. Managers may want to advocate wealth transfers to their own firms from others, while shareholders would regard such transfers as shifting wealth within their portfolios while imposing dead-weight transfer costs.[38]

The parties to the corporation can invest in corporate governance devices that minimize this divergence of interest. They will do so up to the point that the cost of the devices exceeds the costs saved by instituting the controls. This contractual view was pointed out by Justice Antonin Scalia in his *Austin* dissent, when he said that a shareholder

> knows that management may take any action that is ultimately in accord with what the majority (or a specified supermajority) of the shareholders wishes, so long as that action is designed to make a profit. That is the deal.[39]

The cost of the devices could include direct enforcement costs or, less directly, the reduction of benefits from turning control of corporate political speech over to managers. Firms would adopt such contractual restrictions only up to the point that the benefits of restrictions exceed costs.

Contracts restricting managers' speech do not raise significant First Amendment concerns. The First Amendment would permit, if not even protect, contracts that restrict the managers' right to use corporate funds to engage in political speech. By the same token, the First Amendment would permit default provisions in the state's corporation statute limiting corporate speech that corporations could adopt by shareholder vote. In other words, it is appropriate to rely on the traditional state role of defining shareholder rights to defend speech restrictions of this sort.[40] As discussed in the next subsection, however, this theory does not justify the regulation that actually exists under campaign statutes.

Minimal Benefits to Shareholders from Regulation. Although contractual rules and default statutory provisions restricting corporate political activity should pass First Amendment scrutiny, mandatory corporate campaign finance laws are an entirely different matter. Such regulation is not entitled to the same presumption in favor of validity that is appropriate in evaluating private contractual provisions. In order to pass First Amendment scrutiny, such regulation must be shown to be a cost-justified means of minimizing agency cost inherent in the shareholder-manager contract. As shown in this and the following subsections, however, these rules only minimally benefit shareholders and impose high regulatory costs.

The cost to shareholders of corporate political activity is likely to be very low since, as discussed above, most public corporation shareholders are indifferent to the speech of "their" corporations, and in any event can protect themselves from unwanted speech simply by selling when they disagree, as Justice Scalia pointed out in his *Austin* dissent.[41] Although Justice Brennan asserted in *Austin* that sale would cause "financial sacrifice,"[42] that is plainly not the case. Because the public corporations to which the shareholder-protection rationale supposedly applies are traded in efficient securities markets, the stock and its current market price are fungible.[43] To be sure, if corporate managers engage in speech that reduces the market price of the corporation's stock because it indicates a lack of management probity, sale by individual shareholders at the reduced price is not a complete remedy. But shareholders can mount a proxy contest or tender offer to remove the managers or sue for breach of fiduciary duty.[44] In other words, shareholders have the familiar alternatives of "exit" and "voice" as means of obtaining redress.[45] That neither is fully effective, particularly in public corporations, does not necessarily justify statutes forbidding corporate political speech. Because managers' political speech rarely costs the shareholders much, the costs of prohibiting it discussed in the next subsection probably outweigh the benefits.

High Costs to Shareholders. Even if shareholders need protection from managers' use of corporate funds for political activity, prohibiting corporate political contributions and expenditures may be an excessively costly way of providing this protection. Like insider trading,[46] speech that benefits the managers personally may be an efficient form of managerial compensation in the sense that the managers value the power over corporate political activity more highly than the cost to the shareholders of granting this power. The forgone benefit from this efficient compensation may exceed the benefit from guarding against the extremely unlikely event of managers' engaging in highly offensive speech.

Moreover, corporate speech restrictions may exacerbate residual agency loss because campaign laws channel corporate political activity into political action committees (PACs) that corporations may organize and operate. Corporate PACs solicit funds primarily from managerial employees.[47] This is not surprising, since shareholders have no more reason to spend their personal funds than to have corporate assets spent on political activity.

Channeling corporate activity into PACs may cause corporate political speech to reflect managers' interests even more than it would if it were channeled through the corporation.[48] Managers may choose to use their PACs to advocate laws, such as antitakeover statutes, that shift corporate power and resources from shareholders to managers. If the managers sought to use corporate treasury funds that way, they would be at least potentially subject to shareholder discipline. And if corporations could use treasury funds for political purposes, shareholders might be able to force managers to act politically through the corporation rather than funding PACs. Thus, by permitting corporations to organize PACs but prohibiting them to act directly, current law reduces shareholder power over corporate political activity.[49]

In sum, the regulation of corporate political activity saves shareholders from the probably small agency cost of having their invested funds used in ways they would oppose at the potentially larger agency cost of weakening incentive devices and increasing the political power of managers vis-à-vis shareholders through PACs.

Corporate Finance Laws Are an Inappropriate Means of Protecting Shareholders. It is important to distinguish regulation of corporate political speech like the one upheld in *Austin* from contractual restrictions on corporate speech. Even seemingly "mandatory" provisions in state corporation laws could be characterized as contractual, because shareholders who opposed the provision could choose to invest in firms incorporated elsewhere.[50] Such provisions might protect shareholders who are unable to organize effectively against the charter amendments. But federal campaign contribution limitations and state campaign laws that apply to campaign activity by all corporations in the regulating state cannot be defended on similar grounds, because shareholders cannot choose whether to invest in corporations that are bound by the restrictions.

Austin-type regulation can be justified on agency cost grounds only if (1) shareholders are incapable of choosing protection against the supposed agency costs inherent in corporate political speech; or (2) shareholders need protection against managers' pushing through a move to reincorporate from a regulating to a nonregulating state.[51] The first ground ignores the powerful market forces discussed in chapter 1, which discipline the terms of state corporation laws. The second ground has no particular application to corporate political activities.

Moreover, these conditions justify mandatory laws only if the benefits of such laws outweigh the inflexibility and other significant costs of mandatory rules discussed in chapter 1. And even if mandatory statutes are theoretically justified on these grounds, the justifications would be suspect. The fact that government has acted through election statutes rather than through corporation statutes indicates that these are intended as direct speech restrictions rather than as shareholder protection that only indirectly affects speech. As discussed above, such restrictions raise serious doubts about the sincerity of a nonspeech-related justification.[52]

In short, the shareholder-protection rationale for the current scheme of restrictions on corporate political activity assumes not only that shareholders incur agency costs from permitting corporate political activity, but also that such costs are best constrained by mandatory rules. Such reasoning is wholly inconsistent with the contractual theory of the corporation, and should be rejected for the reasons discussed in chapter 1.[53]

The State-Creation Argument

A second reason articulated for allowing state restrictions on corporate political speech is the argument that because states created corporations, they may restrict their speech. The *Austin* Court relied on this reasoning, as evidenced by its emphasis on the "unique state-conferred corporate structure."[54] Justice Rehnquist also reasoned in his *Bellotti* dissent that corporate political speech is merely a privilege that states can choose not to confer on their legal creations.[55] Although the *Bellotti* majority firmly rejected this position,[56] the broad view of the state's power to regulate corporate speech adopted in such recent cases as *NRWC* (an opinion written by Justice Rehnquist) and *Austin* indicates that the theory may at least be operating in the background.[57] The Court also has cited the "state-privilege" theory in other contexts: as a basis for the corporate tax,[58] and to justify state antitakeover legislation against a commerce clause challenge.[59]

The state-creation theory is deeply flawed. As discussed in chapter 1, it is wholly inconsistent with the economic reality of the modern corporation. Under the contractual theory of the corporation, the parties to a corporation derive their rights from private contracting rather than from the state. Moreover, even if individuals doing business in the corporate form did derive their powers from the state rather than from private contract, the states may not unconstitutionally condition exercise of these privileges.[60] Thus, it makes no sense to say that government regulation of corporate political speech should pass First Amendment muster because corporations are created by the state.[61]

Controlling Corporate Political Power

The third reason articulated in *Austin* for why government restrictions on corporate political speech are justified is that corporate political power must be constrained for the benefit of society. Indeed, all of the Court's cases on corporate political speech embrace to some degree the notion that government may legitimately constrain the political power of corporations to avoid "corruption" of the political system. This argument has profound implications for public policy toward corporations in general, because it supports making corporate governance fundamentally a matter of state control rather than of private ordering.

One version of the corruption argument is that corporate contributions facilitate "capture" of politicians by interest groups rather than ideology.[62] This argument, however, does not distinguish corporate from noncorporate speech. Capture results from the ability of interest groups of all kinds to supply the financial support politicians need.[63] Indeed, the Court reasoned in *Buckley v. Valeo* that the Federal Election Campaign Act's (FECA's) limits on all sorts of political contributions were justified, because "large contributions are given to secure a political quid pro quo from current and potential office holders."[64] Removing corporations from the field would merely reallocate strength to other interest groups, rather than eliminate the financial quid pro quo.[65]

Another version of the corruption argument is that regulation is necessary to prevent corporations from having access to political influence that is disproportionate to voter support. Under this "equality" theory, the First Amendment lets government serve as a sort of traffic cop in allocating communication channels so that all ideas get a fair hearing.[66]

The equality idea was an important basis of the earliest restrictions on corporate political activity,[67] and it was later urged by some influential commentators.[68] The Court first rejected the idea in *Buckley v. Valeo*[69] and in *Bellotti*.[70] It emerged in Justice White's *Bellotti* dissent,[71] in *NRWC*,[72] and in *MCFL*, where, as just noted, it provided a basis for distinguishing ideological and business corporations. In *Austin*, this version of the corruption argument became the central basis for limiting corporate speech.[73] *Austin* characterized disproportionate influence as a "different type of corruption" from the danger of "financial quid pro quo" corruption relied on in *Buckley*.[74]

This section demonstrates that the Supreme Court had it right in *Buckley* and *Bellotti*. Inequalities of resources and opportunities for communication are pervasive, complete equality is unachievable, and implementation of an equality principle would necessitate pervasive government interference and inevitably difficult choices about what sorts of inequalities should be tolerated.[75] Moreover, restraining corporate political power is not constitutionally justified in the light of modern interest-group theory, because it amounts simply to an improper weighting of some groups' participation in the political process over others'.

Interest-Group Theory and the Cost of Regulation. Restrictions on corporate political speech are the product of the state legislative process. Although these restrictions are almost always cloaked in public interest rhetoric—for example, the regulation is justified to protect shareholders or control corporate power—the true purpose of the restrictions can be inferred from the consequences. Interest-group theory, because it describes the forces that actually produce government action, is obviously relevant to analyzing these consequences. indeed, interest-group theory is important for any analysis of the application of the First Amendment to political speech.

Interest-group theory shows how politicians broker wealth

transfers (such as subsidies, tax reductions, and trade barriers) to interest groups that function as demanders of legislation.[76] These groups pay politicians (in the form of votes, contributions, expenditures, junkets, employment for politicians' associates, and so forth) to effect these transfers. A group will pay no more than $1 to receive $1 of transfers and, by a parity of reasoning, will suffer a $1 transfer if it would have to pay more than $1 to avoid the transfer. Interest-group theory shows how wealth transfers occur because of differing organizational costs among interest groups.[77] In particular, many interest groups, including both for-profit and nonprofit corporations, have important nonpolitical features, such as mutual assistance of the members or profit-making activities. These groups can support political activities out of profits from their nonpolitical activities. Such organizations have low marginal costs of political organization because they obtain political benefits as a "byproduct" of their organization for nonpolitical reasons.[78]

Some members of the Court have asserted that individuals are only trivially affected by corporate campaign rules, because regulating corporate speech leaves individuals connected with the corporation free to support political action directly.[79] Individual managers or shareholders may act politically both independently and through political action committees.[80] Election laws currently let corporations use treasury funds to administer PACs,[81] and there are many wealthy and active business-oriented political action committees.[82] Moreover, corporations can engage directly in such political activities as lobbying and sponsoring political advertisements,[83] and they can achieve similar goals through nonpolitical activity, such as litigation. Thus, in the Court's view, restrictions on corporate political speech are almost inconsequential.

This reasoning is on its face suspect because it raises the question of why anyone bothered to pass the laws. The Court's view also ignores the economics of interest groups discussed above. Limiting corporate speech forces corporate participants to incur additional organizational costs in order to act collectively,[84] and it therefore reduces political representation of some corporate interests in favor of others. Moreover, corporate activities other than direct contributions and expenditures in support of particular candidates may have limited effect. Firms may want to influence individual candidates on a range of regulatory issues, for example, rather than on a single issue. Moreover, since contributions buy access to candidates, lobbying without such contributions is likely to be less effective.[85] Campaign activities through the corporate form are, therefore, a nontrivial means of expression, and restrictions on use of the mechanism raise significant First Amendment concerns.

The rechanneling of corporate political activity is nontrivial not only because it redistributes political power, but because this redistribution of power may have significant social costs. First, as elaborated below,[86] restricting corporate political activity could cause laws to be inefficient by permitting noncorporate groups or issue-oriented corporations to dominate the political process. Indeed, all the arguments used to justify restrictions on corporate political speech can also be used to argue why corporations should have countervailing power to deal with anticorporate interests, such as unions.

Second, restrictions on corporate political activity may increase the agency costs imposed by politicians. Interest groups can constrain politicians to act in their constituents' interests.[87] Because challengers need access to funds from interest groups to fund the costly campaigns necessary to unseat incumbents, campaign spending by challengers is particularly influential in determining election outcomes.[88] Accordingly, laws that restrict interest-group activity tend to favor incumbents.[89] This, in turn, makes incumbents more secure in office and more able to indulge their personal ideologies or other preferences instead of constituents' preferences. This insight supports Justice Scalia's view in his *Austin* dissent that corporations are an important private check against abuse of official power.[90]

A third way restrictions on corporate political activity may impose social costs is by reducing the quantity and balance of information available to voters. This consideration is particularly relevant to restrictions on corporate political speech like those on campaign expenditures that were upheld in *Austin*. Because of the free-rider problem, voters often have little incentive to acquire information about political choices.[91] This is one of the factors that lets relatively small interest groups obtain wealth transfers from much larger groups with higher organizational (including free-rider) costs. Permitting expenditures by all competing groups can result in a more informed electoral choice and thus benefit voters generally even more than it benefits the competing interest group.[92] Thus, the Court was wrong in assuming that sterilizing corporate political activity is innocuous or improves the political process.

Reducing Influence of For-Profit Firms. The substantial potential costs of regulating corporate political speech raise the question of whether this regulation can be justified by a sufficient state interest in limiting the supposed corruption resulting from corporate political power. The corruption argument is based largely on the supposed

71

ability of for-profit firms to seek collective goods as a "byproduct" of support for their profit-making activities. In other words, shareholders invest and consumers buy the firm's products not because of the firm's political goals, but because they are offered consumers' surplus or a financial return on their investment. It follows that for-profit firms can support political views that are not necessarily supported by the investors who fund this power. By contrast, according to *MCFL*, shareholders in "ideological" corporations could withdraw if displeased with the firm's political goals without suffering an economic penalty.[93]

The history of corporate speech restrictions like the one involved in *Austin* shows that the restrictions did not originate from a realistic evaluation of the dangers of corporate political speech. The first such restrictions were passed in the early part of the twentieth century,[94] during a time of general distrust of large institutions that fueled the Populist and Progressive movements.[95] It was also a time of distrust of large corporations that had recently broken loose from state control as a result of the development of a national market in corporate charters. Just as the antitrust laws sought to reduce the scale of enterprise,[96] the first restrictions on corporate political activity sought to reduce corporations' political power. These sentiments were never based on legitimate policy considerations, and they are irrelevant today, now that direct and indirect ownership of corporate stock has become ubiquitous and large corporations have become widely accepted.

From the standpoint of interest-group theory, equalizing corporate power is clearly not justified in order to prevent large wealth-transfers to corporations. The byproduct theory of collective action, in which firms use surplus from noncollective activity to support political action, applies to both for-profit and ideological firms. Many ideological firms grow large and powerful by combining selective incentives and political goals,[97] such as the outdoor activities offered by the Sierra Club.[98] Labor unions and farm groups in particular have amassed considerable membership by offering economic benefits, such as insurance, that are separate from the organizations' political goals.[99] In fact, it is often difficult to determine whether membership in such groups is motivated primarily by selective incentives, ideology, or other considerations.[100]

Even if for-profit firms have more surplus potentially available for political activity than have nonprofits, the former's political advantage cannot be determined without comparing the firms' opportunity costs for their surplus. Corporate managers who are acting in their principals' interests will invest the firm's surplus in nonpolitical activities if its risk-adjusted return from doing so exceeds that from investing in political activities. For-profit firms extensively engaged in productive activities probably face significantly higher opportunity costs for their surplus than do nonprofit firms engaged primarily in political activities.[101]

Even if for-profits have some advantage under the byproduct theory in generating surplus for collective action, ideological groups may be able to overcome this advantage by organizing at lower cost, because of forceful leaders who serve out of initial commitment to a cause as "political entrepreneurs";[102] or because many members have sufficient moral or political commitment to the cause or group that they are willing to incur the costs of membership without being offered selective incentives;[103] or because geographical proximity of members makes the group relatively easy to organize;[104] or because interest groups offer social or relational incentives to join[105] or provide prominent rallying points for people with shared ideologies.[106]

Moreover, interest groups' ability to compete in political markets does not depend solely on financial resources. Some organizations, such as civil rights groups, have had a significant impact primarily because their members contribute time to such activities as marches and vote drives.[107] Groups also may be strong simply because politicians realize that a comparatively small membership may, precisely because of the difficulty of collective action, represent a much larger supply of votes.[108] And groups' influence depends partly on their ability to coordinate their activities. Labor PACs may be able to compete effectively with corporate PACs because, like cartels, they are better able to concentrate their resources on, and therefore control, particular politicians.[109]

In light of the significant power of noncorporate interest groups, restricting corporate speech may upset or prevent a desirable equilibrium among competing interest groups. James Madison recognized the inevitability of "factions" and that, in a large republic, no single faction could dominate.[110] Gary Becker has shown that interest-group competition may cause laws to be Kaldor-Hicks efficient because some interest groups offset the influence of others.[111] As government subsidies rise, so do transferrers' benefits from resisting, while transferees' benefits decline because they share the increasing deadweight costs from the subsidies.[112] Thus, unless a particular group is very effective at seeking influence, the competition among groups tends to produce laws whose benefits outweigh their costs.[113] Indeed, there may be significant efficiency benefits from allowing corporations to act as a counterforce against other interest groups and political agents.[114] Finally, it is important to emphasize that, even if corporations' political strength is disproportionate to their popular support, by itself this merely reduces to the argument that corporate power should be distributed to other groups. Obviously the winners will prefer this outcome, but that alone does not make the laws constitutional.[115]

Equalizing the Influence of Corporate Managers. Another form of the corruption argument is that unrestricted corporate political speech gives "undue" power to corporate managers. This form of the argument asserts that managers can use resources contributed by shareholders and others to finance managers' views that are not supported by other corporate participants. This argument underlies the *MCFL* Court's distinction between members of for-profit and members of ideological corporations, regarding their support for the organization's political goals. But it merely restates the agency-cost justification for regulating corporate political speech rejected earlier in this chapter. Just as there is no basis for concluding that regulation is necessary to protect shareholders of for-profit corporations from corporate speech with which they disagree, so there is no basis for distinguishing for-profit and ideological groups in this regard.

Indeed, an ideological group's political goals may differ even more from those of the members than do the goals of corporations, particularly with respect to members who have joined for nonpolitical reasons.[116] This membership support can become, in turn, the basis of political action.[117] Exit is often less an option for members of ideological groups who disagree with the group's positions than it is for corporate shareholders. Members who joined for selective idiosyncratic incentives may lose the benefits entirely rather than obtain cash that is fungible with their investments. Moreover, a given group may be the only one representing a certain ideological position, so that a dissatisfied member would have to incur the significant costs of organizing another group.[118] Even if there are available substitutes, they may involve significantly higher costs of joining.[119] Finally, members who have difficulty exiting usually do not have as effective a voting mechanism as have shareholders in for-profit firms.

Corporate power may, in fact, better represent voter support than the groups that would gain from a reallocation of power. Managers who expend corporate funds for speech risk offending not only shareholders but also, among others, workers, consumers, and members of local communities who can exercise displeasure through voice (as with shareholders) or through exit (as with customers) by refraining from dealing with the firm.[120] This forces most corporate speech to conform at least generally with the views of a cross section of the community. Conversely, in the most purely ideological associations, wealthier voters may dominate because a member's financial "vote" for a particular organization represents not merely the strength of his commitment to the cause, but also the number of dollars the member has made available to commit.[121]

Reducing Rent-seeking Costs

The preceding two sections demonstrate that the purported justifications for regulating corporate political speech asserted by the Court do not pass First Amendment muster. This section analyzes an additional justification for regulating corporate speech regulation that was not articulated by the Court—reducing the dead-weight costs of rent seeking. This justification is worth evaluating because it makes some superficial sense and because, as discussed in chapter 2, it is an important rationale for invalidating state regulation under the contract clause. This section shows, however, that the rent-seeking cost justification cannot justify regulation of corporate political speech under the First Amendment, once again because of the alternative of private contracting within the firm.

As discussed in chapter 2, government officials can earn "rents," such as campaign contributions and other benefits, by engineering wealth-redistributions to interest groups.[122] Because the wealth-redistribution is a zero-sum game, the amounts invested in effecting the transfers, including amounts spent in seeking government action, in seeking political office, and in shifting in and out of activities for purposes of obtaining transfers, are unlikely to be outweighed by any positive results of the expenditures. Rent seeking is inefficient not because of who wins and loses, but because there are costs in creating winners and losers.[123]

Minimizing rent-seeking costs has been shown to be an important policy underlying several aspects of the Constitution in addition to the contract clause. The Constitution establishes procedures that reduce rent seeking by raising its cost, for example, including separation of powers, election of different parts of government by different sets of voters, and limiting delegations of legislative authority to bureaucratic agencies.[124] Even groups who may expect occasionally to gain from political wealth-redistributions would favor such provisions, because they do not know whether they will be winners or losers from rent seeking, but they do know they will bear part of the dead-weight costs of rent seeking.

Corporate political speakers might particularly favor statutory restrictions on their political speech because such limitations help overcome collective action problems. All corporations might come out ahead if none participated in political activity. Yet individual firms cannot afford to refuse to participate in the game, because they may lose more by wealth transfers to participating firms than they would save in rent-seeking costs. Indeed, corporations may contribute not so much to support particular legislators or legislation, but as a kind of "protection money" to avoid being hurt for not contributing.[125] Prohibiting corporate political activity is a way out of this classic prisoners' dilemma. If winners and losers from corporate speech cannot be identified in advance, all firms would favor the prohibition.[126] The rent-seeking cost theory may even explain why corporations do not use their supposed clout to lobby or litigate against restrictions on corporate political speech. The theory is also supported by the fact that major legislation restricting corporate political activity has tended to follow episodes of flagrant "shake-downs" of corporations by political fund-raisers.[127]

There are serious problems, however, with the rent-seeking cost theory as a First Amendment justification for regulating corporate political speech. Most important, as with the other justifications discussed above, a legislative solution does not offer clear benefits over private contracting. The problem of dead-weight costs from rent seeking is simply another version of the agency cost problem discussed in the section on corporate political activity—diversified shareholders do not gain as much as managers do from expenditures to obtain intraportfolio wealth transfers. While firms may not be willing to refrain from seeking wealth transfers if they fear that others will not also refrain, legislation is unnecessary to solve this problem, since shareholders can contract for bonding devices that ensure that managers do not incur dead-weight rent-seeking costs.[128]

Moreover, even if the rent-seeking cost justification made theoretical sense, it could not practicably be applied without imposing significant regulatory burdens on speech. Because all political activity involves rent seeking, giving legislatures a broad power to restrict rent seeking involves a high risk of error in sorting out "legitimate" from "rent-seeking" legislation.

There are several respects in which a rent-seeking cost theory of the First Amendment would be difficult to limit. First, there is no reason to distinguish among types of corporate political activity. At the limit, lobbying expenditures, PAC spending, and all corporate political activity could be curbed. Second, there is no basis for distinguishing on rent-seeking grounds between for-profit and ideological firms. Under a rent-seeking theory, it is necessary to show that political activity by for-profit firms is more likely than other political activity to divert resources from privately creating rents to merely seeking government-engineered transfers. But political activities of nonprofit organizations and unorganized individuals also may divert resources from wealth-creating activity or savings. If political speech by ideological groups were restricted, these groups might either substitute other forms of rent seeking, such as litigation,[129] or reduce their total expenditure of resources. The latter course of action might both return resources to productive use and reduce the need for responsive rent seeking by for-profit groups.

Third, as discussed in more detail in the next chapter, there is no reason to distinguish between commercial and political speech. Much commercial speech involving competition between firms in the same industry is aimed at wealth-transferring market share increases rather than at wealth creation. At the same time, as discussed above, there are real benefits from some political speech. Of course, the rent-seeking cost analysis does not support a distinction between expenditures by media corporations and by nonmedia firms, apart from any support for such a distinction by the "press clause" of the First Amendment.[130] Just as with commercial speech, expenditures by media firms can be characterized as productive, rent-creating activity rather than as dead-weight rent seeking. While media communications increase voters' information costs and, accordingly, their ability to constrain wealth transfers to interest groups, the same can be said of some corporate political speech. Moreover, media expenditures can enhance their political influence, just as corporate political speech does generally.

Fourth, the rent-seeking justification does not support a distinction between for-profit corporations and partnerships and other types of for-profit firms. Perhaps the distinction could be based on a rough split between large and small firms. But it is far from clear that large firms are disproportionately responsible for wasteful political rent seeking. Indeed, if anything, the opposite may be the case: large firms, at least in concentrated industries, do not need to act politically, because they can achieve the same benefits through privately coordinated activity.[131] In all events, many small corporations are not exempted from the regulation. This indicates that the corporate-noncorporate distinction is really based on the outmoded state-privilege argument, or is simply a holdover from the distrust of the corporate form that motivated the first corporate campaign statutes.

Conclusion

This chapter shows that most of the rules restricting corporate political speech do not pass constitutional muster. The rules can be constitutionally justified only under the contractual theory of the corporation—that is, only as contract or statutory default rules that are intended to minimize agency costs. But the regulation of corporate campaign activity that has been subjected to First Amendment review is not, in fact, consistent with that theory. Instead, it is based on one or more versions of the regulatory theory of the corporation: that shareholders must be protected by means of mandatory rules; that corporations are creatures of state law; or that corporate political power must be limited. None of these regulatory approaches can pass muster under the First Amendment. Mandatory rules protecting shareholders are neither necessary nor appropriate; the state-creation view of corporations is outmoded; and regulation of corporate campaign activity imposes costly restrictions on speech that improperly limit without providing corresponding benefits.[132]

4
Corporate Governance Speech and the First Amendment

The federal government regulates what corporations and their agents can say about many aspects of corporate governance, particularly including communicating with existing shareholders in proxy statements during director elections, communicating to securities markets in filed documents and press releases, and buying and selling their securities and those of other companies. Because this is a broad category of speech that affects economically significant activities, it is important to consider whether and to what extent the First Amendment could be used to strike down regulation of corporate governance speech.

To answer this question, we must consider the appropriate scope of the commercial speech doctrine, which holds that "commercial" speech is entitled to a lower level of protection than "political" speech.[1] The commercial-political distinction is difficult to draw under the best circumstances, because much conventional commercial advertising, such as "corporate image" advertisements, has political implications. The distinction is particularly troubling as applied to corporate governance speech. Communications by corporate managers to shareholders often sound like the speeches of politicians to their constituents.

In light of the theoretical foundations of the commercial speech doctrine, at least one category of corporate governance speech—proxy-related speech—should be characterized as political speech and therefore subject to the highest level of First Amendment protection. Like the most clearly "political" speech, regulation of proxy-related speech can serve the interests of legislators and bureaucrats by slanting the public debate on regulation. Moreover, because participants in corporate elections receive only a small portion of the benefits of their speech and each speaker must bear a disproportionate share of regulatory costs, the costs imposed by proxy regulation can have a significant negative impact on the amount of such speech.

Finally, it is unlikely that government regulators can improve on the highly efficient markets in which proxy speech occurs.

A lower level of First Amendment protection is appropriate for nonproxy corporate governance speech. Nevertheless, federal regulation of this speech may be unconstitutional. First, because such speech resembles political speech in important respects, it should be placed in a hybrid category rather than being treated as ordinary advertising. Second, even under the lowest commercial speech standard, particularly under recent Supreme Court decisions that have clarified that standard, federal regulation of corporate governance speech goes much further than is reasonably necessary to protect the regulatory interest at stake.

It is important to recognize, with respect to all corporate governance speech, that the federal disclosure standards do not raise the only problems under the First Amendment; these obligations are also imposed as mandatory rules that cannot be avoided without significantly changing the structure of the transaction. In this respect, federal regulation of corporate governance speech goes against the grain of most corporate law, which recognizes that corporations are fundamentally contractual relationships.[2] Consistent with this contractual theory of the corporation, most corporate law is enabling either in the literal sense of default rules or in the substantive sense that it can be avoided by choosing the incorporating jurisdiction.[3] Such default rules raise no First Amendment problem because the restrictions are basically voluntary and in any event are presumptively reasonable, because they are disciplined by market forces. Mandatory federal regulation of corporate governance speech is not entitled to a similar presumption.[4] Moreover, federal regulation that turns corporate elections into political contests should be subject to the stronger First Amendment protection accorded speech in political campaigns, and not to the lower level of protection accorded speech in essentially commercial transactions.[5]

The speech and corporate governance analysis below is a brief discussion of the commercial-political speech distinction that the Supreme Court has developed to provide different levels of government-regulation scrutiny for different types of speech. This section shows that corporate governance speech is difficult to characterize under the commercial-political distinction, and that the few court decisions on the issue are inconclusive. The succeeding section discusses the theoretical bases of the commercial-political distinction. This discussion is helpful in determining how to treat proxy and other corporate-governance speech. The next section shows that proxy speech almost certainly should be characterized as political speech and, accordingly, that regulation of such speech should be scrutinized strictly under the First Amendment.

The final section discusses other federal securities regulation of corporate governance speech, including regulation of sale of securities, continuous disclosure, insider trading, and takeovers. It shows that, although much of this speech probably should be characterized as commercial speech, the constitutionality of federal regulation is questionable under recent Supreme Court commercial speech cases. This conclusion follows from the success of enabling state law to regulate most areas of the corporation, and from the questionable economic basis of regulation of the securities markets. In short, voiding of the securities laws would be both good economic policy and good constitutional law.[6]

Speech and Corporate Governance

The commercial speech doctrine emerged from an era in which there was little, if any, First Amendment protection of corporate or commercial communications. The Supreme Court initially indicated in *Valentine v. Christensen*[7] that advertising and other speech connected with commercial transactions was not constitutionally protected. The Court created the modern commercial speech doctrine in the 1976 case of *Virginia State Board of Pharmacy v. Virginia Citizens Consumer Council, Inc.*,[8] in which it struck down regulation of prescription drug price advertising, holding that such commercial speech is not wholly outside First Amendment protection. The majority opinion in *Virginia Pharmacy* repudiated paternalistic consumer-protection legislation, saying that it was better to "open the channels of communication."[9] Nevertheless, the Court made clear that commercial speech is entitled to something less than full First Amendment protection. This section discusses the commercial speech doctrine and its application to corporate governance speech.

Identifying "Commercial" Speech. Although the distinction between commercial and noncommercial speech may seem clear at first, in fact it presents troubling questions. Some prominent commentators maintain that there should be no distinction between commercial and other forms of speech.[10] Even the most blatantly commercial advertising is a form of expression of ideas regarding choices that are just as important to most people as the selection among political candidates. Indeed, some protected types of speech, such as pornography, seem far less important to most people than advertising about the characteristics of essential goods and services. Moreover, there is

81

no clear distinction between advertising that sells a specific product, more political advertising that is intended to influence public opinion concerning regulation of the company's products,[11] and genuine political advertising concerning a candidate's philosophy about regulatory policy.

In light of these inherent problems of distinguishing between commercial and noncommercial speech, it is not surprising that the Court has struggled with a definition. Although the Court has said that commercial speech may include the broad category of speech "related solely to the economic interests of the speaker and its audience,"[12] more recently the Court has apparently narrowed the category to speech that proposes a commercial transaction.[13] Moreover, at least one member of the Court supports full First Amendment protection of all commercial speech, other than time-place-manner regulation or regulation of speech that is deceptive or proposes unlawful transactions.[14] The Court's failure clearly to define commercial speech has led it to make some questionable distinctions. The Court has restricted regulation of lawyer advertising,[15] for example, and in-person solicitation by ACLU lawyers[16] and CPAs,[17] but it has permitted regulation of in-person solicitations and other types of promotional activities by lawyers.[18]

The Standard for Commercial Speech. If the regulated speech is characterized as commercial, the regulation is subject to the following test set forth in the leading case of *Central Hudson Gas & Elec. Corp. v. Public Serv. Comm'n of New York:*[19]

> For commercial speech to come within [First Amendment protection], it at least must concern lawful activity and not be misleading. Next, we ask whether the asserted governmental interest is substantial. If both inquiries yield positive answers, we must determine whether the regulation directly advances the governmental interest asserted, and whether it is not more extensive than is necessary to serve that interest.

Thus, the commercial speech doctrine has a four-part test for determining whether the regulations violate the constitution: (1) only lawful and nonmisleading speech is protected; (2) the government interest must be "substantial"; (3) the regulation must be one that "directly advances" the government interest; and (4) the regulation must be "not more extensive" than is necessary to serve that interest.[20]

The Court has held that the "not more extensive than is necessary" language in the *Central Hudson* test does not necessarily compel the government to adopt the least restrictive means of achieving the governmental interest. In particular, in *Board of Trustees of State University v. Fox*,[21] the Court said:

> What our decisions require is a fit "between the legislature's ends and the means chosen to accomplish those ends," . . . a fit that is not necessarily perfect, but reasonable; that represents not necessarily the single best disposition but one whose scope is in proportion to the interest served . . . ; that employs not necessarily the least restrictive means, but . . . a means narrowly tailored to achieve the desired objective.

At the same time, however, the Court has made it clear in its most recent commercial speech cases that "reasonable fit" requires a careful cost-benefit analysis. In other words, it is not enough for the government to show that a substantial purpose is furthered in some way by the restriction. In *City of Cincinnati v. Discovery Network*,[22] the Court struck down a city's removal of sixty-two newsracks that distributed magazines consisting primarily of advertising. The Court reasoned that the city's purpose of improving the appearance of its streets was not sufficiently furthered by singling out sixty-two "commercial" newsracks from a total of 1,500 to 2,000 newsracks on public property. In other words, the city could not single out petitioner's newsracks for its beautification campaign merely because these newsracks were commercial. In *Edenfield v. Fane*,[23] the Court struck down a ban on solicitations by CPAs, reasoning that the state had not shown a sufficient likelihood that permitting such solicitation would compromise the independence of CPAs or result in fraud or overreaching.[24]

In short, the Court has indicated that the category of commercial speech may be a relatively narrow one, and that even speech clearly belonging in this category is protected from regulation that goes further than is reasonably necessary to protect government interests. As discussed below,[25] in light of the scant theoretical and empirical support for mandatory federal regulation of securities disclosures, even regulation of corporate governance speech that is commercial in nature probably does not meet this tightened standard of justification.

Application to Corporate Governance Speech. It is far from clear how corporate governance speech should be characterized under the commercial speech doctrine. Such speech arguably concerns the economic interests of the speaker and listener and therefore is commercial under the broadest version of the Court's definition.[26] Apart from prospectus disclosures, however, much of the speech cannot be characterized as proposing a commercial transaction. Speech in investment newsletters similar to newspaper copy, and portions of proxy statements dealing with important issues of corporate policy appear just as political as speech by candidates for political office. Accordingly, it is more appropriate to recognize the hybrid nature of corporate governance speech than to attempt to force it into either of the artificial categories the Court has created.

Recent cases illustrate the hybrid nature of corporate governance speech. The most important case dealing specifically with it involved proxy disclosures. In *Long Island Lighting Co. v. Barbash*,[27] an issuer sought to apply proxy disclosure rules to an advertisement concerning the question of municipal ownership of a utility. The court avoided the First Amendment issue by holding that the issuer was entitled to discovery on the question of whether the advertisement was a covered solicitation. Yet it is hard to see how the court could characterize statements made in a contest for control of a public utility raising the issue of municipal ownership as anything other than political.[28]

Two other leading cases involve statements about corporate securities in investment newsletters. In both cases, investment publications with obvious similarities to newspapers were not given the same sort of First Amendment protection that clearly would have been applied to newspapers. In *Lowe v. SEC*,[29] which involved the question of whether the SEC could prohibit unlicensed publication of an investment newsletter, a majority of the Court avoided the First Amendment question by holding that the Investment Advisers Act regulated only face-to-face professional advice. Three concurring justices said that the First Amendment prohibited application of the act to broad restraint of a publication without regard to its quality whether or not the speech was characterized as commercial. In *SEC v. Wall Street Publishing Institute, Inc.*,[30] the Court held that the First Amendment did not prevent the SEC from enjoining publication of monthly magazines by an investment adviser under 17(b) of the Securities Act of 1933,[31] because it failed to disclose that the publisher received consideration in the form of free text from the subject firms. The Court emphasized that, unlike *Lowe*, the case did not involve prior restraint without review of the contents, there were misleading statements, and the SEC was requiring only additional disclosure rather than censoring contents. Surprisingly, the Court said that regulation in an area of extensive federal regulation should be sustained even without weighing its merits. Although the Court upheld the regulation, however, it characterized the speech as not clearly commercial, but more like a news story. The foregoing discussion shows that the courts have not settled on a clear definition of commercial speech, and that they have had particular problems characterizing speech relating to corporate governance and corporate securities. Moreover, the Court's most recent commercial speech cases demonstrate that even the most clearly commercial speech is entitled to substantial First Amendment protection. Accordingly, even if the definition of commercial speech were settled, it may be unclear on a case-by-case basis whether particular regulation will survive First Amendment scrutiny. Yet before the Court can provide more meaningful guidance on these questions, a more coherent theoretical understanding of the distinction between political and commercial speech is necessary.

A Theoretical Analysis of the Commercial Speech Doctrine

This section attempts to clarify the appropriate definition and treatment of corporate speech by developing a theory for distinguishing commercial and political speech. It begins by questioning the appropriateness of any a priori distinction between speech that is and speech that is not related to democratic processes. It then identifies pragmatic grounds for the distinction.[32]

Relation of Speech to Democratic Processes. Several commentators advocate denying First Amendment protection to commercial speech on the ground that the framers intended the First Amendment to protect only speech relevant to our representative form of government.[33] There are several problems, however, with this type of analysis.

First, even if the First Amendment does no more than protect democratic processes, political speech cannot be clearly distinguished from commercial speech because even pure advertising has political ramifications. Advertising develops and expresses public opinion relating to the decisions that are made both in grocery stores and in Congress. Indeed, much clearly political debate concerns purely economic decisions,[34] including decisions as to the amount of political control of the capital markets.[35] Alcohol or cigarette advertising that stresses the sophisticated pleasures of these products, for example, arguably has an effect similar to that of a "political" advertisement against a "sin" tax on these products.

Second, neither courts nor commentators generally accept the principle that the First Amendment is intended solely to protect the political process. The case law under the First Amendment has extended its protection far beyond "political" speech.[36] Influential theorists have argued that the First Amendment generally protects self-realization or self-expression, and it would therefore clearly include at least some commercial as well as political speech.[37] Indeed, broad protection of free expression may be at the heart of the First Amendment's protection of democratic processes. As Justice Powell said in *Virginia Pharmacy*:

> So long as we preserve a predominantly free enterprise economy, the allocation of our resources in large measure will be made through numerous private economic decisions. It is a matter of public interest that those decisions, in the aggregate, be intelligent and well-informed. To this end, the free flow of commercial information is indispensable. And if it is indispensable to the proper allocation of resources in a free enterprise system, it is also indispensable to the formation of intelligent opinions as to how that system ought to be regulated or altered. Therefore, even if the First Amendment were thought to be primarily an instrument to enlighten public decision making in a democracy, we could not say that the free flow of information does not serve that goal.[38]

Thus, the commercial-political distinction cannot properly rest on the ground that the First Amendment is prima facie limited to a particular category of political speech. This suggests that it is appropriate to look to pragmatic considerations—that is, to costs and benefits of constraining government restrictions on speech.[39] These considerations are discussed in the ensuing subsections.

Regulators' Self-Interest. A second possible reason for distinguishing commercial from political speech concerns the different motivations of incumbent politicians and regulators with regard to the two types of speech. Other things being equal, regulators who are motivated to act in their constituents' interests can be expected to produce more efficient rules than self-interested regulators. Thus, it is important to consider the relative agency costs of regulators connected with various types of regulation.

Regulators' agency costs should be distinguished from whether the regulators act "fairly" or "evenhandedly." In a democratic society, legislation and regulation are inevitably shaped by interest-group pressures. Under standard interest-group theory, interest groups obtain wealth transfers through subsidies, tax reductions, and the like by "buying" laws from politicians with votes, contributions, and so forth, and wealth transfers occur because of differing organizational costs among interest groups.[40] It follows from interest-group theory that legislation cannot be expected to maximize social welfare. Indeed, because much legislation involves wealth transfers rather than wealth creation, the majority might conclude at the time of forming the constitution, before winners and losers can be identified, that expected rent-seeking costs from much government activity exceed their expected gains from legislation.

It does not follow, however, that the majority would favor constitutional restrictions on this basis. First, because interest-group pressures are pervasive, it would be impossible to isolate a particular category of interest-group legislation. Second, in the long run, the competition among interest groups is likely to drive regulation toward generally efficient results,[41] thereby minimizing the harm from such regulation and the need for drastic alterations in the political process. Third, even interest-group-motivated regulation may hurt the majority only weakly while strongly aiding a minority-interest group. Because at the time of agreeing to constitutional restrictions the majority will not expect to be systematically hurt and may expect occasionally to be members of beneficiary interest groups, they would not favor constitutionally restricting such legislation.

The same cannot be said for speech regulation that favors the politically empowered minority of legislators and bureaucrats. Such regulation may increase the agency costs of government by loosening effective constituent controls on regulators. At the extreme, politicians could perpetuate themselves in office by prohibiting speech against government and its agents. Moreover, politicians may have ideological preferences for proregulatory, anticapitalist views[42] that would lead them to favor particular types of speech. Indeed, economists have shown that these preferences combine with economic incentives to explain politicians' voting decisions.[43]

It follows that, at the time of forming constitutional rules, a majority of the population would view themselves as more likely to be harmed by regulation of certain types of political speech than by regulation of certain types of commercial speech.[44] This is similar to the argument by some commentators that government regulation of commercial speech involves a lower potential for error than regulation of political speech, because the government is generally less biased in regulating commercial speech than in regulating political speech.[45] Although neither the government nor the voters systematically care about commercial winners or losers, incumbent politicians are systematically interested in defeating challenges to their authority.

It is important to recognize, however, that incumbents' ideological preferences might cause them to discriminate as much against some commercial speech as speech by competing candidates. Moreover, incumbents entrench themselves not only by muzzling their opponents, but also by slanting the debate on issues so that it favors regulation over private ordering, and by establishing ground rules for debate favoring proregulatory points of view. Speech regulation, for example, can reduce advertising by affected interest groups, such as by an energy industry group opposed to an energy tax or by drug companies opposed to price controls, that would have informed voters who otherwise could not easily internalize information-search costs.[46] More broadly, any product advertising potentially conveys information that is relevant to the debate on the appropriate extent of regulation. Thus, a public that has been well informed about the benefits of new drugs may be more receptive to arguments about the dangers of price regulation that can limit research and development, or less resistant to high drug prices. These considerations underlie the arguments of economists and others who have questioned the viability of a commercial-political distinction on the ground that economic decisions have political implications.[47]

So even if the agency-cost argument supports a rough distinction between commercial and political speech, the argument should be applied with caution. Incumbents arguably have at least as much incentive to squelch debate on economic issues as on political issues. Indeed, the above discussion indicates that politicians might have more incentive to regulate speech relating to business or economic issues, because this category of speech has more rent-seeking potential than has cultural or political speech, and because of their own ideological preferences. At the least, there may be specific categories of speech—including speech in corporate elections—that are particularly susceptible to regulation tainted by incumbent self-interest.

Chilling Effect on Speech. A third reason for distinguishing commercial speech, and the reason the Court stressed in *Virginia Pharmacy*, is that profit-motivated speech is less likely to be chilled by regulation.[48] Like the argument based on regulators' self-interest, this reason is based on pragmatic cost-benefit considerations.[49] It assumes that regulating political speech would be more likely to deter socially valuable speech, and would therefore have a higher social cost, than regulating commercial speech.

This argument does justify a rough distinction between commercial and political speech. Commercial speakers generally reap a large portion of the total social benefit from their advertising through increased profits. While regulation increases the costs and therefore reduces the quantity of this speech, regulation is relatively unlikely to deter a large amount of socially beneficial advertising. But many individual participants in political debate realize little economic benefit, and only a small portion of the total social benefit, from their speech. Accordingly, even a small regulatory tax could significantly reduce socially beneficial political speech.

But, once again, this argument does not allow a sharp distinction between commercial and political speech. First, some commercial speakers may be on the margin in the sense that even a small increase in the cost of speech will cause them to decide not to speak or to say something else. Both political speakers and commercial speakers respond to incentives, and regulation of either type of speech affects their incentives—that is, chills their speech.

Second, the "chilling effect" argument erroneously assumes that politically oriented speakers are inherently less able than commercial speakers to internalize all the benefits of their speech-related activities—that is, that larger positive externalities are associated with political than with commercial speech. Wholly political interest groups of all types, however, can effectively overcome free-rider problems and internalize the benefits of their activity.[50] Indeed, even individuals, including politicians, may reap significant benefits, including enhanced reputation and satisfaction, from purely political speech.[51] Conversely, much commercial speech is made by firms whose managers act as agents and do not internalize all the gain from commercial or governance-related speech. Thus, regulation that penalizes those managers for such speech may have a greater chilling effect than analogous penalties on politically committed individuals or agents of not-for-profit organizations.

Likelihood and Cost of Regulatory Error. Even perfectly motivated politicians, bureaucrats, and courts can err. The commercial speech doctrine may be justified if there is a greater likelihood of costly error in regulating political than commercial speech. The following discussion concerns various aspects of the regulatory error point.

Expected harm from commercial speech. Costs from excessive regulation would be lower for commercial than for noncommercial speech if commercial speech were more likely to cause harm than political speech. In fact, the opposite is likely to be the case. Because the recipients of commercial speech are generally in contractual privity with the speakers, commercial speakers have extralegal market incentives to speak truthfully, which limit the potential harm from misleading statements.

Business firms that lie to their customers risk incurring a reputa-

89

tional penalty. Nevertheless, market constraints on speech by political candidates may be less effective.[52] Although politicians may also incur penalties, the heavy advantages of incumbency can protect them to a large extent.[53] Also, speech that is obviously profit oriented, and therefore clearly self-interested, may have less impact on listeners and is therefore less likely to mislead than speech that appears disinterested.[54] Thus there may be a greater regulatory benefit in suppressing, for example, apparently disinterested, erroneous statements by public interest organizations funded by trial lawyers than statements on the same issue by insurance companies.

There are several reasons, however, to question a sharp distinction between regulation of falsity and other speech regulation with regard to the expected harm from the speech. First, even deceptive speech can increase net social welfare. Forcing firms to respond truthfully to requests for information concerning merger offers, for example, could increase market efficiency but impose higher costs in terms of lost positive-net-present-value deals.[55] Second, the potential harm from deceitful speech varies according to the characteristics of the relevant market. Markets characterized by active trading, particularly securities markets, may allow false information to be rapidly reflected in market price; but they also facilitate rapid correction by new information, as long as the flow of information is not impeded by regulation.[56] Third, even regulation intended to limit only false speech necessarily deters valuable, truthful speech, because speakers cannot always determine ex ante whether they will be deemed ex post to have violated the law. The amount of truthful speech deterred depends both on how precisely the standard of liability is articulated and on the measure of damages.

Government's ability to assess harm. Some proponents of the commercial speech doctrine argue that government is better able to determine the truth of commercial speech than of other forms of speech.[57] It would follow from this argument that, even if commercial speech is not more likely than political speech to cause harm, at least commercial speech regulators will do a better job determining which speech to regulate.

This is a weak basis for distinguishing commercial from political speech. Even if some facts about commercially advertised products and services may be more readily verifiable than those concerning political or artistic issues, it does not necessarily follow that government is better able than markets to discern these facts.[58] In fact, the verification argument is inconsistent with the "chilling effect" argument discussed above. If speech is truly robust, then the market itself should be relatively able to correct errors.[59] Ford can be expected to rebut errors about Fords that Chevrolet makes in its ads. Indeed, regulating speech may even inhibit the market's capacity for self-correction.[60]

Moreover, even if lawmakers or regulators are expert in a general category of cases, they nevertheless may make inefficient decisions to maximize their support from well-organized interest groups. Indeed, this may be particularly likely to happen in highly technical areas regulated by experts far from public view.

In any event, even if the government is well suited to dealing with certain types of market failure, this only demonstrates that particular government interventions are justified, and not that government should be held to a lower burden of justifying regulation of a whole category of speech. In other words, the verification argument makes sense only if it is sufficiently likely to be the case that government can better regulate speech in commercial than in political markets. Then a presumption in favor of regulating commercial speech would be justified under the First Amendment.[61]

The commercial speech doctrine might be justified on this ground to the extent that it singles out false or deceptive commercial speech. Falsity is identified as one of the *Central Hudson* factors, and Justice Blackmun would make falsity the main characteristic of commercial speech that is not entitled to full First Amendment protection.[62] Deceptive speech generally involves net social harm, the argument would run, so regulation aimed at deceptive speech could generally be expected to increase social welfare.

Mandatory versus default rules. An important factor in evaluating the likelihood and cost of regulatory error is whether the regulation imposes mandatory rules on a class of transactions or only default rules that are subject to the parties' contrary agreement. Although both types of rules can significantly constrain speech, there is little reason to be concerned about potential regulatory error as long as the affected parties can easily contract around speech restraints.

Although mandatory and default speech restrictions should be distinguished under the First Amendment, the distinction may be unexpectedly hard to make. Parties must incur some contracting costs to avoid any default rule. Conversely, the parties can virtually always avoid a mandatory rule by contractually selecting the forum, legal regime, or category of transactions. Even the federal securities laws, for example, which would seem to be paradigmatic mandatory rules, might be avoided by choosing a form of transaction that does not involve the sale of a "security"[63] or that is not subject to U.S. law.[64] Thus, mandatory and default rules merge at the edges.

Fear of *Lochner*—Substantive Due Process and Commercial Speech.
A final argument for distinguishing commercial and noncommercial speech is based on jurisprudential rather than policy concerns: the Court will seek to avoid the impression that it is resurrecting *Lochner*-type substantive due process review of economic regulation.[65] Although some prominent commentators believe that resurrecting *Lochner* would be a good thing,[66] the Court will not lightly reverse, nor give the appearance it is reversing, a rule that is almost a century old. The Court seemingly endorsed this argument in *Posadas de Puerto Rico Associates v. Tourism Co.*,[67] in holding that the state's power to regulate an activity includes a power to regulate speech about the activity.

The courts can, however, strike down commercial speech regulation under the First Amendment without necessarily returning to *Lochner*. The First Amendment protects commercial speech because such speech, as Justice Powell has said, can "enlighten public decisionmaking in a democracy."[68] So even if the Court is unwilling to second-guess legislative decisions, it should ensure that the political process leading to those decisions is robust and well informed. As Justice Blackmun has said, regulating commercial speech can mean that "the state's policy choices are insulated from the visibility and scrutiny that direct regulation would entail and the conduct of citizens is molded by the information that government chooses to give them."[69] Moreover, legislators' motive to squelch criticism should be as suspect when they restrict speech about regulated commercial activities as when they regulate political speech.[70]

Summary. The foregoing discussion shows that there is at least some theoretical support for a rough distinction between political and commercial speech. In particular, because politicians are more likely to help themselves at the majority's expense in regulating campaign speech than in regulating commercial speech, regulating political speech is particularly likely to deter socially beneficial speech. These arguments also apply, however, to much economically motivated speech. Moreover, regulators are particularly likely to commit costly errors regarding commercial speech as compared with private market arrangements. Accordingly, any rule that applies only a low level of First Amendment protection to a broad category of commercial speech is likely to give a significant amount of such speech less protection than is socially desirable under a pragmatic approach to the First Amendment. This suggests that it is appropriate, if the commercial speech doctrine is to continue to have any vitality at all, to be careful in designating the speech categories that are entitled to lesser First Amendment protection. The following two sections make this careful delineation in the context of corporate governance speech.

Proxy Statements as Political Speech

This section analyzes the application of the First Amendment to regulation under the Securities Exchange Act of 1934 of disclosures to shareholders in connection with proxy solicitations and annual meetings.[71] The section shows that in light of the analysis in the preceding section, proxy-related speech is entitled to the highest level of First Amendment protection.

Proxy Speech and Democratic Processes. To the extent that the commercial speech doctrine is based on the framers' intent to protect only speech relating to democratic processes, much proxy speech looks like the most obviously political speech. Accordingly, even those who credit this questionable basis of the commercial speech doctrine should support giving proxy speech the highest level of First Amendment protection.

An important illustration of this point is the application of the shareholder proposal rule, SEC Rule 14a-8,[72] which ensures public access to corporate proxy statements.[73] The rule has often been used for blatantly political purposes. In *New York City Employees' Retirement System v. Dole Food Co., Inc.*,[74] for example, the court, under the shareholder proposal rule, enjoined Dole Food Company from excluding the following proposal made on behalf of its shareholder, the New York City Employees' Retirement System:

> WHEREAS: The Dole Food Company is concerned with remaining competitive in the domestic and world marketplace, acknowledging the positive relationship between the health and well-being of its employees and productivity, and the resulting effect on corporate growth and financial stability; and
>
> WHEREAS: Sustained double-digit increases in health care costs have put severe financial pressure on a company attempting to continue to provide adequate health care for its employees and their dependents; and
>
> WHEREAS: The company has a societal obligation to conduct its affairs in a way which promotes the health and well-being of all;
>
> BE IT THEREFORE RESOLVED: That the shareholders request the Board of Directors to establish a committee of the Board consisting of outside and independent directors for the purpose of evaluating the impact of a representative

93

cross section of the various health care reform proposals being considered by national policy makers on the company and their [sic] competitive standing in domestic and international markets. These various proposals can be grouped in three generic categories; the single payor model (as in the Canadian plan), the limited payor (as in the Pepper Commission Report) and the employer mandated (as in the Kennedy-Waxman legislation). Further, the aforementioned committee should be directed to prepare a report of its findings. The report should be prepared in a reasonable time, at a reasonable cost and should be made available to any shareholder upon written request.

Although the proposal was couched partly in terms of the company's costs, the political nature of the proposal is underscored by the fact that it was made by New York City Comptroller Elizabeth Holtzman, a 1992 candidate for the U.S. Senate, in her capacity as the custodian of the assets of NYCERS.

There are many other examples of the political nature of the shareholder proposal rule. One recent case required the company to include a shareholder proposal requiring the company to report on equal employment and affirmative action policies.[75] Another held that a company had misstated its record on the environment in response to a shareholder proposal urging adoption of the "Valdez principles," rejecting arguments that the information had been included in the company's 10-K SEC filings and annual report and in press reports.[76]

The political nature of proxy speech and proxy regulation is also evident from the main rationale for the regulation. Advocates of regulating large corporations have argued that on the one hand, because corporations have a government-like power to affect the economy, they should be regulated like quasi-political entities.[77] Such regulation would include giving all those affected by corporate activities direct access to corporate governance, including requiring managers to make disclosures in proxy statements and other disclosure materials as to matters of social policy.[78] In other words, corporate elections are regulated because they are regarded as functionally similar to political campaigns.

On the other hand, under the contractual theory of the corporation,[79] participation in corporate elections is governed by the long-term contracts between the parties in much the same way as any process of modification or adjustment in long-term contractual relationships.[80] The First Amendment should have no role to play regarding these contractual restrictions, even if some contract terms are supplied by statutory default rules.

In short, the political rationale for regulating corporate elections can be turned on its head to justify greater scrutiny of the regulation under the First Amendment. If speech connected with the governance of private corporations is an extension of the political process, it should be protected to the same extent as political speech under the First Amendment.[81]

Regulators' Self-Interest. The argument for constitutional constraints on political speech based on regulators' self-interest, although it cannot draw a sharp line between political and commercial speech, clearly supports constitutional protection for proxy speech. Because this type of speech directly affects participation of the largest economic actors in the debate on the appropriate degree of regulation, politicians have extraordinary incentives to manipulate this type of speech.

Mark Roe has furnished important background evidence for the incumbent self-interest basis of constraining corporate speech. Roe has shown how a wide variety of tax and financial regulation has combined to limit the role played by large financial institutions in corporate governance.[82] He argues that these political developments result partly from the political elite's desire to protect their power by fragmenting economic power and preventing a coalition between financial and industrial firms.[83] As long as these institutions hold both economic power, such as the ability to affect the availability of credit, and the resources to participate effectively in the public debate, the power of public officials is diminished.[84]

Thus, Roe cites Ferdinand Pecora, counsel to the Senate Banking Committee for the hearings that ultimately led to the federal securities laws (and for whom these hearings are popularly named), as saying that it was necessary to prevent the rise of the sort of powerful financial institutions that drove governments in Britain and France from power.[85]

Regulators' self-interest in crippling business institutions is particularly evident with respect to proxy regulation. Politicians have "democratized" corporate governance by giving a voice to widely dispersed and relatively small shareholders that is disproportionate to their financial holdings. Subsidizing speech by employees and consumers with low capital investments in the firm, who would favor more regulation of large corporations, slants the debate over the appropriate activities of these institutions.

Empowering nonshareholder interests helps legislators and regulators in several ways. First, the inclusion of proregulatory views in proxy statements can help persuade shareholders to accept regulation that could diminish the value of their investments in the firm. In this way, politicians could extract rents from increasing regulation[86] while at the same time minimizing the risk of being punished at the polls for this regulation. Second, the subsidizing of proxy speech by small shareholders could help persuade shareholders to favor, or at least not actively to oppose, their firms' willing compliance with hard-to-police regulation such as worker safety, pollution, and employment discrimination. This in turn increases the impact of the regulation and, again, the rents politicians and bureaucrats can earn or extract through the regulation.

Along similar lines, the shareholders could be persuaded not to support actively, or even to oppose, efforts to minimize the effect of regulation by exploiting jurisdictional competition. Plant closings and relocations, for example, take advantage of differences between states and countries regarding taxes and regulation. To the extent that firms can be persuaded through the proxy process to remain in high-tax, proregulatory jurisdictions even though this is inconsistent with shareholder welfare, state and federal politicians are freer to continue earning and extracting rents.

The effect of regulation that democratizes corporate governance may be even more important than regulation's effect in preventing concentrations of capital. Even if institutional holders, such as public pension funds, could wield greater power, it is far from clear that they would use any governance power they had to maximize shareholder wealth. Roberta Romano has shown how politicians have exerted pressure on public pension funds to favor such positions that serve the interests of politicians rather than of corporate shareholders.[87] Politicians might favor social investing, for example, to "camouflage the true cost of local projects from the public or transfer wealth from future to current taxpayers."[88] This suggests that it may be more important to manipulate how shareholders exercise their voice than to control which shareholders exercise power.

Regulation of proxy speech in general, and the shareholder proposal rule in particular, reflects these objectives of regulators. The shareholder proposal rule requires managers to include in proxy statements any proposal that a shareholder intends to make at a shareholder meeting, subject to certain exceptions. One of the most frequently litigated exceptions concerns the "ordinary business" of the company. This exception has been interpreted by the SEC and the courts to permit exclusion of matters relating to the company's economic well-being, unless they involve matters of general "policy." Thus, as already noted,[89] matters such as employment discrimination, health care, and the like must be brought before the shareholders. Nevertheless, matters that would seem to be of significant interest to the shareholders, including limits on capital expenditures,[90] are excluded as being entirely in the province of directors. This indicates that the regulation is intended to empower those with a political agenda rather than an economic stake in the enterprise.

The Court has indicated its concern with political interference with corporate communications. In *Pacific Gas & Electric Co. v. Public Utilities Commission*,[91] it held as unconstitutional under the First Amendment a state utility commission requirement that a utility company provide space in its billing envelope for opposing political viewpoints. The Court, however, questionably distinguished the shareholder proposal rule. The Court reasoned that corporations were free to express opinions "externally," citing the *Bellotti* case on corporate political speech,[92] but that managers have no interest in corporate property that would justify constitutionally protecting their internal governance speech.[93] But there is no difference in this respect between "external" and "internal" speech.[94] This subsection makes clear that even purely internal speech relating to corporate governance has important political ramifications, particularly including the issue of what political positions managers should take.[95]

Once again, the theoretical considerations underlying the commercial-political distinction support characterizing proxy speech as political and entitled to the highest level of First Amendment protection.

Chilling Effect. Commercial speech is arguably distinguishable from political speech on the ground that regulation of political speech is likely to have a greater impact on the quantity of speech because political speakers often do not reap much of the economic benefit from their speech. Although, like the other arguments for the commercial-political distinction, this rationale does not justify a sharp line between the categories, it does justify characterizing proxy speech as political.

Proxy regulation potentially has a serious impact on speech in corporate elections. The proxy rules broadly prohibit communications among shareholders,[96] require SEC preclearance of proxy materials,[97] and pose a risk of large civil fraud liability. Shareholders who oppose incumbent managers in proxy contests or tender offers may be unable cheaply to internalize gains from changes in management policy without owning a significant percentage of the corporation. These shareholders therefore are in a position very similar to that of voters and activists in political elections. Proxy regulation can significantly deter speech that would have high social value because it might bring about the replacement of inefficient managers.

Moreover, potentially large antifraud awards can significantly chill even managers' speech. Although managers may be fully compensated for their contributions to their firms,[98] they do not necessarily internalize all the benefit from all of their disclosure activities. Thus, exposure to liability from speaking as compared with remaining silent may outweigh any reputational or other benefit managers that would receive for making full disclosure. In this situation, proxy liability could chill speech.

Even rules that mandate only additional disclosure present a First Amendment problem.[99] Mandatory disclosure rules that burden disclosures that otherwise would be made voluntarily, such as rules requiring additional statements to present existing statements from being misleading,[100] can reduce the quantity of speech. Also, even if additional disclosures are otherwise costless for the speaker, they can affect the total meaning and impact of the speech, as by requiring the speaker to hedge particular statements, such as projections and appraisals.[101] Consistent with this analysis, the Supreme Court has struck down regulation requiring a utility company to include an insert in its bills.[102] The same reasoning should apply, for example, to mandatory rules requiring inclusion of shareholder proposals in managers' proxy statements[103] or requiring complete information in managers' rebuttals to shareholder proposals.[104]

Thus, the "chilling effect" theory underlying the commercial-political distinction clearly supports putting proxy speech in the political category.

Likelihood and Cost of Regulatory Error. Even assuming it is appropriate generally to distinguish commercial and political speech on the basis that regulatory error regarding the former is likely to be less costly, this does not justify applying a lower standard of protection for proxy speech. First, with regard to the likelihood of harm from the regulation, information about corporate activities and corporate performance is essential to making financial markets operate efficiently and in serving important management monitoring and re-source-allocation functions. Moreover, whle all political and commercial markets can be adversely affected by regulation that causes less information to reach the market, capital markets uniquely suffer from regulation that merely delays disclosure because of the effect of such delay on the pricing of securities and the importance of securities pricing in efficiently allocating resources.[105]

Second, government agencies have no advantage over markets

in regulating the complex financial and management disclosures that characterize corporate governance speech.[106] It is unlikely that regulators evaluating the shares of publicly held firms can do a better job than the sophisticated analysts who "follow" these firms and are compensated based on the quality and accuracy of their evaluations. Moreover, firms actively compete for capital, and therefore have ample extralegal incentives to disclose and to signal the quality of their disclosure in various ways, such as by hiring investment banking and accounting firms and by listing on stock exchanges.[107]

Third, regulatory error is particularly likely because of the mandatory nature of this regulation. In a world of free contracting, firms' contracts would require disclosure only up to the point that the benefits of disclosure outweigh the costs to the particular firm.[108] Investors could choose whether and at what price to invest in firms, and capital market competition would constrain firms to offer contracts that efficiently balance costs and benefits. Under such a regime, as with respect to much of corporate and commercial law, disclosure laws could offer standard form terms to minimize the costs of contracting, and corporations could decide not to be covered by a law that they believed was too restrictive. Because default rules would reduce the level of speech only to the extent justified for particular firms, there would be no First Amendment concern with erroneously prohibiting valuable speech.[109] By contrast, the federal securities laws impose constraints on any transaction that involves the purchase or sale of a "security" and cannot be avoided by contract, either directly by waiver or indirectly by choosing the applicable law. Because these legal rules do not compete in efficient capital markets, they pose a significant risk of regulatory error. Accordingly, First Amendment scrutiny is as important in this area as it is for political speech in reducing such error.

The First Amendment and Substantive Due Process. Restricting regulation of corporate governance speech under the First Amendment is not tantamount to *Lochner*-type review of substantive regulation. Regulating corporate governance speech is constitutionally suspect under the First Amendment not because it is economically unwise, but because it skews the public debate over whether regulation of corporate governance is appropriate. Restricting speech by dissident shareholders under the proxy rules, for example, can insulate from public scrutiny managers' arguments that they need government protection from takeovers; restricting defensive speech by managers, conversely, strengthens the arguments of those who favor regulation of takeover defenses. It does not matter under the First

99

Amendment which side of the debate is correct from an economic standpoint—only that the government should be required to remain neutral.

Application of Commercial Speech Standard. Proxy regulation may be unconstitutional even if proxy speech should be characterized as commercial rather than political. Although providing information to shareholders voting in corporate elections may be a substantial government goal under *Central Hudson*, mandating disclosure rules for all firms may not be a reasonable means of meeting that goal. Because firms' contracts for disclosure are disciplined by efficient capital markets,[110] penalizing even truthful speech unless it is accompanied by a regulation proxy statement is suspect under the First Amendment. Even worse, these requirements potentially interfere with a vast amount of legitimate activities, since they are triggered by any "solicitation," which includes any "communication" with a shareholder that is "reasonably calculated to result in the procurement, withholding or revocation of a proxy."[111] It follows that recent SEC rules mitigating these requirements[112] may have been not only good policy,[113] but also constitutionally compelled.[114]

Summary. The foregoing analysis strongly supports characterizing proxy regulation as political speech. Under this characterization, proxy regulation would have to survive the same level of scrutiny under the First Amendment as regulation of speech by candidates for political office. Indeed, *Pacific Gas & Electric* specifically holds that even a commercial corporation cannot constitutionally be subjected to regulation similar to SEC Rule 14a-8, implying that other aspects of proxy regulation would also be unconstitutional to the extent that political characterization is accepted. Moreover, even if proxy speech is characterized as commercial, proxy regulation may be unconstitutional on the ground that it goes much further than is reasonably necessary to serve the government's disclosure objective.

Constitutionality of Other Regulation of Corporate Governance Speech

This section extends the First Amendment analysis to regulation of corporate governance speech other than proxy regulation. With respect to each type of speech, the section discusses two important questions. First, should the speech be characterized as political or commercial speech? Second, is regulation of the speech constitutional under the applicable First Amendment standard? This section concludes that although much corporate governance speech is arguably characterized as commercial speech, regulation of this speech may not meet the standard the Court has recently applied to commercial speech.

Prospectus Regulation. The Securities Act of 1933[115] requires the delivery of a prospectus containing certain disclosures to purchasers of securities distributed by issuers; forbids most written communications unless accompanied or preceded by a statutory prospectus;[116] and forbids any speech, truthful or not, about the securities for a significant period of time while the offering is in preparation, until at least a preliminary version of the statutory prospectus is available.[117] The act also imposes liability for misstatements about these securities.[118] State securities laws similarly require registration and review by securities administrators.[119] Because firms cannot contract for application of a particular state's securities laws as they can with respect to corporate law,[120] state securities laws should be treated like federal securities regulation for First Amendment purposes.

Communications concerning new securities issues closely resemble advertising, and therefore conventional commercial speech.[121] First, because promoters and others internalize the benefits of stock sales, regulating speech relating to public offerings probably has a less chilling effect on speech than regulating corporate governance speech has. Second, this regulation ordinarily does not directly affect who controls large corporations, and therefore does not have political implications or involve potential bias of incumbent regulators who compete for power with large firms. Third, because the 1933 act most heavily affects new issues of securities, which ordinarily are not traded in robustly efficient markets, the advantages of market over regulatory evaluation is not as clear as for other regulation of corporate governance speech.[122]

Nevertheless, there are several important differences between prospectus regulation and regulation of ordinary product advertising in light of the policies underlying the commercial-political distinction:

• Regulating which new products or ideas can be touted in the financial markets, and what can be said about them, inhibits the expression of and the competition between entrepreneurial ideas that are an important part of democratic society.

• The 1933 act may have a significantly chilling effect on socially valuable speech, because it imposes substantial penalties on directors and other individuals in the firm who do not necessarily internalize benefits from the distribution.[123]

• Government regulators are no more able to evaluate complex financial disclosures in prospectuses than in other types of securities disclosures. As with respect to proxy disclosures,[124] the regulatory knowledge argument is particularly inapplicable to disclosures by the most widely held firms, whose shares are evaluated by sophisticated analysts in efficient securities markets. Although the SEC has taken the degree of market efficiency into account in determining the level of disclosure required under the 1933 act,[125] this affects only the ultimate determination of whether the regulation is constitutional,[126] and not the level of First Amendment protection that applies to the regulation.

• The 1933 act impedes disclosure of valuable financial information not only for new issues,[127] but also by reducing the flow of information from established issuers while they are in registration.[128]

These differences between prospectus regulation and other regulation of advertising suggest that speech about securities issues should be classified at least as a hybrid of political and commercial speech and entitled to a higher level of First Amendment protection than advertising.

Even if the speech regulated by the 1933 act should be given no more protection than ordinary commercial speech, at least three aspects of mandatory prospectus regulation under federal and state law raise serious concerns under the First Amendment.

First, under *Central Hudson,* the constitutionality of the 1933 act is doubtful to the extent that the act prohibits statements that are neither unlawful nor misleading—any statements made before the statutory prospectus is available, and written statements not accompanied or preceded by a statutory prospectus. The act might pass the first *Central Hudson* hurdle in that, although it regulates truthful statements, its rationale is the "substantial" government goal of ensuring that investors receive full disclosure, rather than one-sided sellers' hype, before making up their minds.[129] Even if these are substantial government goals, however, the act is too broad to be considered a "reasonable fit" with these goals. The act's requirement that a statutory prospectus accompany most written statements effectively outlaws general advertising of securities and forces most issuers to rely on elaborate securities syndications. The excessiveness of this regulation is indicated by the fact that it goes much further than regulation that applies to any other type of advertising, including such investment products as franchises and land sales.[130] That securities are traded in highly liquid capital markets informed by analysts, newspapers, and others suggests that there is even less need to regulate securities than these other investments.

A justification of the 1933 act's prohibition on general advertising would require showing that investors are much more likely to be misled as to securities than as to other products, including other investment products, and that the prospectus delivery requirement would protect them. Yet it is unlikely that the investors who are most likely to be misled by overbearing salesmen are likely either to read or to learn much from the prospectus.[131] Investors are much more likely to trust investment advisers or the market price than to invest time and resources in reading a complex prospectus. Moreover, any slight possibility that requiring delivery of prospectuses will prevent some people from making bad investments is clearly outweighed by the enormous costs imposed on issuers and on the market. Indeed, in many respects prospectus regulation resembles the blanket prohibition on solicitation that the Court struck down in *Edenfield*, despite the state's claim that the ban was necessary to prevent fraud.[132]

Second, even if it is constitutional to define the form of truthful disclosures broadly, the 1933 act may be unconstitutional in compelling even publicly held firms to deliver these disclosures (that is, the prospectuses) directly to investors. Since securities markets efficiently discount all publicly disclosed information, it is questionable whether there is a reasonable fit between the regulation and the federal goal of informing investors under the *Central Hudson* test. At the very least, the SEC's coordinated disclosure system, which effectively excuses the prospectus delivery requirement for securities traded by large public companies in highly efficient markets, may be constitutionally compelled.

Third, state "merit" regulation[133] of securities is highly suspect under the First Amendment. Merit regulation forbids firms from truthfully advertising securities in regulating states even if they make the full disclosure the law otherwise would require. This is precisely the sort of paternalistic prohibition of speech that the Court prohibited in *Virginia Pharmacy*.[134] Moreover, the regulation cannot be sustained on the ground that the state has the power to ban the sale of the security altogether, because prohibiting firms even to advertise in the state effectively blocks public debate on whether sales of the securities ought to be allowed.[135]

In short, the 1933 act should not only be subject to more intense First Amendment scrutiny than ordinary advertising regulation, but is probably unconstitutional even under the standard applied to advertising.

Periodic Disclosure. The commercial-political factors lead to similar conclusions regarding mandatory continuous reporting under the

Securities Exchange Act of 1934.[136] In several respects, this reporting does not resemble political speech. As with respect to the 1933 act, there is no special risk of regulatory bias. The law merely requires disclosures in filings to the SEC, which are unlikely to slant corporate governance debate. Indeed, a court recently assumed that the public generally ignored these filings insofar as they dealt with the firm's environmental activities.[137] Moreover, there is arguably less likelihood of regulatory error since, unlike prospectus disclosure, the regulation helps ensure pricing accuracy in efficient markets.

In one important respect, however, regulation of continuous disclosure raises a problem of regulatory error that is similar to that concerning proxy speech. As with proxy speech,[138] the optimal continuous disclosure regime will vary from firm to firm, and firms' contracts regarding disclosure are well disciplined by capital markets. Accordingly, investors should be able to choose among different contractual regimes regarding disclosure rather than having only the single choice prescribed by mandatory federal rules.

Assuming mandatory continuous disclosure should be characterized as commercial speech, the questions remain under *Central Hudson* whether the regulation is justified by a substantial regulatory interest and whether there is a reasonable fit between the regulation and the regulatory interest.[139] There is arguably a legitimate regulatory interest in maintaining fully informed markets. Moreover, unlike the 1933 act, the continuous disclosure regime under the 1934 act does not broadly forbid speech. The regulation is constitutionally suspect, however, in that it penalizes companies even if they do not speak falsely,[140] and in that it restricts speech by regulating the form and content of disclosure.

Accordingly, the First Amendment requires an examination of these restrictions to determine whether they reasonably fit the regulatory interest. Mandating disclosure on social issues that do not necessarily have an impact on investors,[141] for example, or requiring disclosures of breaches of fiduciary duty that impede state regulation of corporations by mandating a federal fiduciary standard[142] may raise First Amendment concerns.

Takeovers and the Williams Act. The Williams Act requires disclosures in connection with takeover bids and transfers of control.[143] This regulation raises issues similar to those concerning proxy regulation. Indeed, proxy contests and tender offers are alternative, and sometimes also complementary, mechanisms for the same objective of control of large corporations. In both contexts, the speech concerns acquisition of corporate control and potential problems of shareholder coordination that may make it difficult for shareholders to internalize the benefits of the speech. Accordingly, the application of the commercial-political factors to the two areas is virtually identical. Both types of regulation involve similar potential for government bias concerning control of large corporations, the same problems of regulatory expertise and high-value speech, and similar potential for chilling socially valuable speech.

The implications of imposing a high First Amendment scrutiny level on tender offer regulation are also similar to those regarding proxy regulation. While the government may be able to establish a regulatory interest in ensuring full disclosure that satisfies *Central Hudson*, rules going beyond disciplining fraud to regulating the timing or format of nonmisleading statements[144] may not reasonably fit this governmental interest.

Antifraud Liability. Section 10(b) of the Securities Exchange Act of 1934[145] and SEC Rule 10b-5[146] promulgated under that section generally discipline fraudulent and misleading conduct. This regulation can be applied to all the categories of speech discussed above in this section, and accordingly raises the same issues as those discussed above. Indeed, plaintiffs often allege 10b-5 causes of action for precisely the same speech that is covered by other parts of the securities laws.

To the extent that the antifraud rules impose federal liability for fraudulent statements, they may withstand constitutional scrutiny under *Central Hudson*. To the extent that these rules compel or regulate the timing of nonmisleading speech, such as disclosures concerning impending mergers, they raise considerations similar to those regarding continuous disclosure and proxy and tender offer regulation. Although the Court has held that merger negotiations may be material, it has not explicitly ruled that such disclosure is required under 10b-5.[147] This suggests that the duty, if any, may come from state law.[148] State duties are generally contractual in nature because, even if they are mandatory in form, they can be avoided through choice of business form or choice of the state of incorporation.[149] Thus, such duties do not raise a problem under the First Amendment. By the same token, federal liability triggered by these duties also may not raise a First Amendment problem if it is clear that the parties can effectively opt out of federal duties by opting out of the underlying state duties.

Insider Trading Liability. Section 10(b) and Rule 10b-5, as well as §16(b) of the 1934 act,[150] impose liability for insider trading. The

105

First Amendment probably does not apply at all to insider trading regulation. The nexus with speech regulation—that the regulation reaches only trading without regulation—is too thin to raise First Amendment concerns because the regulation neither prohibits nor limits speech.[151]

One aspect of insider trading regulation—liability for tipping true information to the market—arguably does raise a First Amendment concern under *Central Hudson* even if it is commercial speech. One way to deal with this problem is to characterize the liability as being based on breach of the tipper's contract with the owner of the information. To the extent that the liability is not contractual, however, because there is no fiduciary or other relationship that gives rise to an implied contract term, or because the parties have waived any fiduciary duty that might otherwise apply, tipper liability raises grave concern under the First Amendment.

Conclusion

Even if the dubious distinction between commercial and political speech continues to be accepted, regulation of corporate governance speech should be subject to a high level of scrutiny under the First Amendment. Governance speech shares enough of the underlying characteristics that supposedly distinguish political from commercial speech that such speech should be treated either as political speech or as a hybrid between commercial and political.

An understanding of the contractual nature of the corporation assists both in characterizing corporate governance speech and in determining whether regulation of the speech is constitutional. Although default rules and state corporation law that firms select when they choose the state of incorporation raise no First Amendment concerns, federal mandatory regulation of corporate governance speech cannot be adequately justified under the First Amendment. This is because of the dubious premises of the regulatory theory of the corporation on which such regulation is based. Moreover, the political underpinning of these mandatory rules supports the argument that such speech should be subject to the highest level of First Amendment protection.

Forcing investors in all firms to accept the same mandatory rules regarding corporate governance speech is both bad policy and, at least in some respects, unconstitutional. Constitutional constraints on this regulation would free the capital markets of unnecessary regulation and improve the resource-allocation function of these markets.

5
Choosing Law by Contract

A fundamental principle of corporate law is that the law of the state of incorporation governs the relationship among shareholders and managers, regardless of the location of the shareholders or of the corporate headquarters. The so-called internal-affairs rule lets the parties to the corporation "shop" for the corporate law most compatible with their needs, thereby facilitating a state competition for incorporation business and preventing states from imposing mandatory rules on corporations. This rule is consistent from a normative standpoint with the contractual theory of the corporation, and it is an important reason why the contractual theory accurately describes current corporate law.

Introduction

This chapter argues that the contractual choice of law implicit in the internal-affairs rule should be applied to all contracts, and that state enforcement of contractual choice of law is constitutionally compelled under the commerce clause.

The second section of this chapter demonstrates that, ironically, the existence of the internal-affairs rule is actually explained by the regulatory theory of the corporation. The courts often do not enforce choice-of-law clauses in noncorporate contracts. Thus, the internal-affairs rule is applied to corporations precisely because they are not viewed as ordinary contracts, but rather as special "creatures" of state law. The state-creation view, in turn, is an important basis of the regulatory theory, as discussed above in chapter 1.

The internal-affairs rule's basis in regulatory theory is important because it means, as discussed throughout this book, that corporations must pay a price, in the form of lost constitutional protection, to have their contractual choice of law enforced. The regulatory theory and the state-creation concept are important bases for denying corporations the full protection of the contract clause, as discussed in chapter 2, and of denying full protection of corporate political speech under the First Amendment, as discussed in chapter 3.

The third section of this chapter considers the efficiency of enforcing contractual choice-of-law clauses. The fourth section presents a political theory of why state legislators as well as state courts are hostile to allowing parties to select the applicable law. This political theory is the basis of the argument in the fifth section, that the commerce clause should be interpreted to protect contractual choice-of-law clauses. The final section offers some concluding comments and suggests that recognizing these principles not only would extend the scope of the internal-affairs rule itself, but also would provide a firm foundation for application of the contractual theory of the corporation under other constitutional provisions.

Conflict of Laws and the Corporation

This section contrasts the internal-affairs rule with the rules regarding enforcement of analogous choice-of-law clauses in other contracts. It shows that if corporations were treated like other contracts, as they should be under the contractual theory of the corporation, then the law chosen by the parties to the firm—usually the law of the state of incorporation—would not necessarily be enforced. It also shows that the basis for the internal-affairs rule is actually the regulatory theory of the corporation.

The Internal-Affairs Rule. The Restatement of Conflicts provides that rights among parties regarding the internal governance of a corporation are usually determined by the law selected by the parties—that is, the law of the state of incorporation.[1] The courts only rarely apply the law of a nonincorporating state.[2] In determining whether to apply the law of a nonincorporating state, the Restatement emphasizes the needs of parties to multistate transactions to have certainty, predictability, and, in particular, a single, uniform rule that determines the rights of all the parties to a single, multistate firm.[3] Consistent with this rationale, the courts have departed from the internal-affairs rule only for firms so closely connected with a single state that there was little danger more than one rule would apply,[4] or where the courts deemed the issue insufficiently related to the firm's internal affairs to make it necessary to have a single rule necessary.[5]

Application to the Contractual Theory—Choice-of-Law Clauses in Noncorporate Contracts. If corporations were treated as ordinary contracts, as they should be under the contractual theory of the corporation, enforcement of the law agreed to by the parties to the firm would be subject to an intricate and unpredictable patchwork of exceptions.

Early commentary generally opposed enforcing choice-of-law clauses because they are private legislation,[6] and there was no provision for contractual choice of law in the Restatement of Conflicts. The "private legislation" argument has been criticized on the ground that the contract does leave the ultimate decision with the court, based on the parties' choice of law and other factors.[7] Moreover, the courts did enforce choice-of-law clauses, particularly where the parties' contract clarified the choice among several potentially applicable jurisdictions.[8]

The Restatement (second) of Conflicts clearly supports enforceability of contractual choice of law by making enforcement of such contracts the basic conflicts rule for contracts,[9] except in the "absence of effective choice by the parties."[10] That rule, however, is seriously weakened by exceptions. Although the Restatement provides for enforcement of the parties' contractual choice of law as to interpretation issues the parties could have resolved by contract,[11] §187(2) provides that the contract is not enforced as to issues such as validity, when the choice of law matters most, if

> either (a) the chosen state has no substantial relationship to the parties or the transaction and there is no other reasonable basis for the parties' choice; or (b) application of the law of the chosen state would be contrary to a fundamental policy of a state that has a materially greater interest than the chosen state in the determination of the particular issue, and which, under the rule of §188, would be the state of the applicable law in the absence of an effective choice of law by the parties.[12]

With respect to the "substantial relationship" test in §187(2)(a), it is not clear whether "substantial" refers to the number of relevant contracts[13] or, like the rules for selecting the applicable law in the absence of a choice-of-law clause,[14] to how the parties' contacts with a jurisdiction relate to the general Restatement factors guiding choice of law.[15] It is also not clear why any contact with the chosen jurisdiction is necessary. There is no problem of "surprise" if the contract clearly discloses the selection, nor any proof problems as long as the parties choose the law of a U.S. jurisdiction. Nor is there any reason why the selected state should have an "interest" in the case, as long as the contracting parties have made the judgment to choose the state's law.[16] Thus, any contractual choice of law should be regarded as "reasonable."

The rule in Restatement §187(2)(b) that the court should defer to "a state which has a materially greater interest than the chosen state" and would be selected under the general rules determining the applicable law is a potentially more limiting constraint on enforcement of the parties' contractual choice of law.[17] The Restatement comments unhelpfully define a "fundamental" policy as "substantial,"[18] yet not necessarily "strong public policy."[19] The forum applies "its own legal principles" rather than those of the avoided state.[20] The varied case law applying this rule illustrates the indeterminacy of the fundamental-policy exception. The cases have split, for example, as to whether to apply an avoided state's law protecting franchisees and distributors from termination and other conduct by franchisers and manufacturers,[21] and as to whether to permit avoidance of restrictions on noncompetition agreements[22] and usury.[23]

The fundamental-policy rule mainly serves to prevent evasion of mandatory statutory rules that supposedly protect the state's residents. As examples of situations in which the nonselected state's policy applies, the Restatement gives "illegal" contracts or rules "designed to protect a person against the oppressive use of superior bargaining power."[24] The Restatement qualifies the court's discretion only in situations in which there is no need to protect a mandatory state rule: where the parties themselves could avoid the rule by providing for the appropriate formalities; where rules "tend to become obsolete," like those addressing the capacity of married women, and so do not represent current state policy; or in cases of "general rules of contract law, such as those concerned with the need for consideration."[25]

In summary, the legal constraints on contractual choice of law are vague and ill conceived. As discussed below, they are better explained by interest-group than by efficiency considerations.

The Internal-Affairs Rule and the Regulatory Theory. The conflicts rules that apply to corporations therefore differ substantially from those that apply to noncorporate contracts. For corporations, the parties' selection is nearly always honored, while in other contracts cases, courts have significant discretion to override the parties' choice.

To illustrate the contrast between corporate and noncorporate contracts, compare the following two situations: (1) a franchise contract between a corporation based in state X and a franchisee based in state Y that provides that it is governed by the law of X and for termination at will by the franchiser; and (2) a corporation incorporated in state X with shareholders and business operations centered in Y, whose charter provides for a limitation on the directors' duty of care. Assume that Y law provides that franchisees can be terminated only for cause and that the duty of care cannot be limited by contract, while X law permits freedom of contract on both issues. Applying the rules discussed above, a court could refuse to enforce the termination-at-will clause in the franchise contract under Y law, but it almost certainly could not refuse to enforce the corporate duty-of-care limitation. In other words, the parties' selection of X law would apply to the corporation that is connected with X mainly by the contract designation, but not to the franchise contract that has independent contacts with X as the franchiser's home state. These results follow solely because one contract is a corporation and the other is not. As is shown in the next subsection, there is no substantive basis for this distinction.

Indeed, corporations differ not only from other contracts generally, but also from other types of firms. The Restatement provides that the general contract choice-of-law rules apply to partnerships.[26] Similarly, formation-state law does not automatically govern other business associations, even if the parties explicitly have agreed to the application of particular law.[27] The Restatement provides, for example, that formation-state law governs the limited liability of corporate shareholders,[28] but that a limited partner's liability, like that of all partners, is determined by application of the general conflict-of-law criteria.[29] A noncorporate firm operating outside its formation state therefore cannot be assured of being governed by its formation-state rules, particularly the shareholders' limited liability, unless the state in which it transacts business has recognized foreign firms of that type through a limited partnership, limited liability company, or similar statute.[30]

Any sharp legal distinction between corporations and other types of contracts is, of course, inconsistent with the contractual theory of the corporation. Also, as discussed in the next section, the policy arguments favoring enforcement of contractual choice of law apply equally to both corporations and noncorporations. Even if corporations differed from other contracts, that surely does not justify distinguishing them from other types of firms, such as partnerships, limited liability companies, and business trusts. While the Restatement attempts to justify the distinction on the grounds that the parties to a partnership may have no real expectation concerning the applicable law,[31] that is plainly not true for some noncorporate firms where the law selection is clear, such as limited partnerships that organize by filing a certificate in a particular state, or even for general partnerships that clearly designate the law of a particular state.[32]

Indeed, the arguments for the regulatory theory of the corporation discussed in chapter 1 might support greater restrictions on contractual choice of law in corporations than in other contracts. Advocates of the regulatory theory have urged that the internal-affairs rule encourages a "race to the bottom," in which states offer rules favorable to managers and adverse to powerless shareholders. Moreover, they claim that even if initial corporate contracts are efficient, managers can effect reincorporations that injure shareholders by exploiting their rational ignorance and high coordination costs.[33] This suggests that the state-chartering competition may yield inefficient rules to the extent that it is a competition for reincorporations.[34] By contrast, in noncorporate contracts such as franchise agreements, changing the applicable law would require unanimous consent, and all affected parties would have ample incentives to resist any attempt by one of the parties to renegotiate the choice of law.

The internal-affairs rule's inconsistency with the normative arguments for the regulatory theory of the corporation is ironic in light of its basis in the same state-concession philosophy that underlies the regulatory theory. The corporation has long been viewed not as an ordinary contract but as a legal "person," created and endowed with certain attributes by the chartering state.[35] This characterization gives greater weight to the parties' selection of jurisdiction than would characterizing the corporation as a mere contract.[36] In other words, under the internal-affairs rule, the contract among parties to a corporate firm is legally protected only because the corporation is not viewed as an ordinary contract, but rather sui generis as a legal person.

The different treatment of corporate and noncorporate contracts regarding enforcement of contractual choice of law also relates to the regulatory theory in the sense that the distinction reinforces state mandatory corporate rules. State legislatures provide only a limited supply of corporate contracts, and not all legislatures participate in the chartering competition. If all governance terms were enforceable in every state regardless of the form of entity, the supply of corporate terms would be determined solely by private contracting rather than by whether legislators chose to approve particular terms. In effect, cross-elasticities of demand for business forms would widen the state-chartering competition by adding new competitors.[37] If legislators refused to permit contracting out of fiduciary duties in statutory limited liability firms, for example, contracting parties could form a nonstatutory, corporate-like firm that did not provide for fiduciary duties, and they could expect to have that contract fully enforced in all states. Interstate enforcement of noncorporate contracts would, in turn, pressure the states to adapt their corporation statutes so as not to lose incorporation business to these new business forms.

Thus, generally enforcing contractual choice of law would have important implications for the contractual and regulatory theories of the corporation.

Efficiency of Enforcing Choice-of-Law Terms

This section shows that there is no efficiency-based justification for broadly refusing to enforce choice-of-law clauses in any type of contract. It follows that courts should apply the law of the incorporation state because corporations are contracts and not because, as the regulatory theory would have it, corporations are creatures of state law.

Benefits of Enforcement. Enforcing choice-of-law clauses helps contracting parties in several ways. In general, these benefits arise from increasing the supply of law products parties can choose from to govern their contracts.[38] If choice-of-law clauses were not enforced, contracting parties would be limited to the products provided them by states connected with the contract under applicable choice-of-law principles. The following discussion analyzes the specific benefits to contracting parties from being able to choose among several different law products. The first and fourth headed subsections below focus on mandatory rules; the other two discuss benefits of contracting for choice of law that apply to both mandatory and nonmandatory rules.

Reducing error from mandatory rules. An important function of contractual choice of law is that it helps parties avoid inefficient mandatory rules. These rules may be inefficient because they are enacted to benefit a particular concentrated group,[39] because legislators simply made mistakes, or because a single rule cannot fit all firms.

To understand the risk of error from mandatory rules, consider state regulation of franchise contracts. Some states have passed mandatory laws restricting termination other than for "good cause" and regulating other aspects of franchise contracts.[40] On the one hand, termination at will can be an important right for franchisers, since it may be the only way they can effectively monitor their franchisees to prevent franchisees from free-riding on and decreasing the value of the franchiser's brand name.[41] Moreover, litigating over whether termination is wrongful can be costly.

On the other hand, relation-specific investments by franchisees let franchisers terminate or threaten to terminate opportunistically, and to appropriate some of the value of franchisees' business. This

113

increases franchisees' risk and, therefore, franchisers' cost of raising capital through the sale of franchised outlets, while decreasing the franchisees' incentives as owners to invest in developing goodwill.[42] Accordingly, restrictions on termination at will might be an efficient standard-form term for at least some franchise contracts.

The important question in all this is whether it is appropriate for a state to include particular terms in all franchise contracts.[43] There is strong reason to believe that no single group of legislators, no matter how well motivated, can determine the best single term for all the contracts subject to the laws they write.[44] Yet unless the parties can choose the applicable law, all contracts subject to the law of a particular jurisdiction must adhere to mandatory rules in that jurisdiction. This suggests that enforcing contractual choice of law will improve the law for many firms—that is, it will lead at least to a race to the corner if not to the top.

The effect of jurisdictional competition. Letting contracting parties choose their governing law gives states an incentive to compete for law business by providing efficient legal rules.[45] Competition works by encouraging states both to develop new terms to attract new legal business and to revise their laws to retain legal business. This advantage helps to produce not only efficient mandatory terms but also, as discussed below, efficient standard-form terms. Daniel Fischel's point that it is difficult for a state to impose costs on nonresident corporate shareholders through its corporate law[46] applies equally to any noncorporate contract in which the parties have selected the applicable law. If the selected state inefficiently changes its law or fails to make needed revisions, it will quickly lose the patronage of contracting parties. Legislators may be concerned about the effects of this loss of patronage on taxpayers or, more likely, on influential interest groups, such as lawyers.

An example of the potentially salutary effect of jurisdictional competition is the rapid development of the law of limited liability companies (UCs). The earlier statutes allowed little flexibility in agreements that related to continuing the firm after member dissociation and transferability of interests, because of concern about jeopardizing the partnership tax treatment of firms formed under flexible statutes.[47] Some more recent statutes, however, now permit greater flexibility,[48] because their drafters concluded that the costs of rigidity exceeded the tax risk for many firms. The evolution has resulted in a larger menu of choices and adaptation over time to new circumstances and more information. This process might have occurred even without contractual choice of law, particularly since most LLCs formed to date are local firms organized under the law of the state in which the firm's business is located. Nevertheless, the rapid spread of LLC statutes indicates that legislatures and bar groups have at least to some extent responded to potential competition from other states.[49]

Efficient standard-form terms. Contractual choice of law may reduce costs by supplying standard-form contract terms, even if the parties otherwise could avoid these terms by customized contracting, because such contracting may be costly.

In identifying the benefits of contractual choice of law regarding standard-form terms, we distinguish between two situations in which the parties may want standard-form terms. In one-shot deals involving relatively small amounts of money—the typical situation dealt with in the Uniform Commercial Code—standard-form rules are particularly useful for filling in many of the operational terms of the contract, such as standards of performance and allocation of risk of loss. In this situation, the parties' costs of negotiating the terms in each case may outweigh the benefits. Moreover, there are often strong similarities among categories of cases and trade usages that reduce the parties' need to negotiate customized terms.

In long-term contracts such as franchises, distributorships, and business associations, though, the need for standard-form terms probably does not cause many firms to select the law of a particular jurisdiction.[50] The amounts of money and time involved either in individual deals or similar deals entered into by a franchiser or other contracting party justify substantial investments in customized terms. Morever, parties to long-term contracts often have to negotiate idiosyncratic terms, because contract terms such as those constraining shirking and opportunism must deal with factors that are specific to the parties and the deal.

The main contracting function that the parties to long-term contracts cannot readily accomplish without the help of legal rules is providing for remote contingencies. Because remote contingencies are specific to relationships and transactions, most legal rules dealing with them are likely to be standards, such as good faith or fiduciary duties, that courts apply to particular situations.[51] The parties could formulate standards without the help of a legislature. Among other things, the parties could adopt codes developed by industry groups or private firms and have controversies adjudicated by private arbitrators. But for several reasons, the parties may prefer state laws to privately formulated standard-form terms.

First, embodying standards in state statutory or decisional law

115

facilitates developing a consistent body of case law applying the standards to particular facts, which is an important function of choice-of-law selection in long-term contracts.[52] Applying private codes or rules may not make publicly available as large a body of experience and precedent for interpreting the rules as may exist under state law. The parties to particular disputes would bear the costs of their arbitrators' preparing opinions, while benefits would accrue to the parties to future disputes. Probably for this reason, arbitrators do not commonly prepare opinions.[53]

Second, private rules could be trumped by state courts or legislatures. The courts or legislators could decide to enforce or to apply to particular disputes only general legal rules rather than privately enacted codes. Even if the parties attempted to escape these results by resorting to arbitrators, state lawmakers could decide not to enforce arbitrators' decisions or to review them *de novo*.[54] The parties could increase the chances that private rules or adjudication would be enforced by choosing the courts and law of a jurisdiction that recognized such enforcement.[55]

Third, selection of a body of state rules reduces the parties' costs of obtaining information about the applicable rules. There are scale and scope economies in publishing and distributing the law relating to private contracting, together with tax-supported publication of other state laws.

Multiple-state regulation. The parties may contract for choice of law in order to eliminate problems that arise when different state rules may apply to different aspects of or parties to the contract. Unless the same shareholder voting rules apply to all corporate shareholders with the same economic rights, for example, the corporation incurs transaction costs of dealing with, in effect, multiple classes of stock and of coordinating the differing voting rights.[56] The firm may even be unable to conduct a director election in which some shareholders can cumulate their votes for directors while others can cast only one vote for each director. More generally, multiple-state regulation poses problems whenever different contracts have a common nexus. Because there is considerable variation among the states in key areas of franchise law,[57] for example, a national franchiser who must deal with different sets of franchisee rights may forgo expanding into new states.[58]

The role of contractual choice of law in reducing problems of multiple-state regulation is closely related to its role in facilitating avoidance of mandatory rules discussed above. Enforcing contractual choice of law is, indeed, usually unnecessary to eliminate multiple-state regulation. Inconsistency is a problem only in the relatively rare situation in which the contracting parties must obey inconsistent mandatory rules—as where an interstate trucking firm must use different types of mudguards in the different states in which it operates.[59] If a state law requires a firm to do something that is not required elsewhere, enforcing choice-of-law clauses matters only in preventing the mandatory state from imposing regulatory burdens on nonresident interstate firms. In other words, contractual choice of law is important not so much in eliminating inconsistent regulation, but in ensuring that jurisdictional competition determines what rule applies.

The above considerations apply equally to corporations and to other types of contracts. Although it may be costly to apply multiple-state rules to some aspects of corporate governance, particularly in a publicly held firm to which many different state statutes could apply, the need for certainty and uniformity does not justify the courts' almost complete deference to the law of the chartering state in corporation cases.[60] Even for issues relating to internal corporate governance, such as shareholder voting, application of nonchartering state law need not cause either uncertainty or application of multiple rules. Like other contracting parties,[61] corporations can resolve a choice between a mandatory rule, such as cumulative voting or shareholder inspection rights, and other nonmandatory default rules simply by complying with the mandatory rule.[62] Even conflicts between mandatory rules can be resolved by litigation and application of *stare decisis* and collateral estoppel principles.[63] Although questions may arise concerning the binding effect of the litigation,[64] the resulting problems are not qualitatively different from those affecting noncorporate contracts.

Certainty and information costs. Contracting for choice of law enables the parties to determine easily what law governs the transaction. Under the "interest" analysis pioneered by Brainard Currie, the forum, which is often not determinable at the time of contracting, must apply multifactor standards to determine whether to apply its own law or that of another state that has an interest in applying its rules to a given issue.[65] These rules require the parties to investigate the facts and law relating to their transaction in order to try to predict what law will be applied, and they often make it difficult to predict the result even with such an investigation.

Uncertainty affects the parties' conduct both at the time of contracting and at the time of litigation. Uncertainty at the time of contracting means that the parties cannot easily determine the standard of conduct to which they should conform or how to price contract rights and duties.[66] If the parties to a franchise contract agree to terminability-at-will, for example, and know in advance that the courts will enforce the term, the franchiser can rely on the term as a monitoring device, the franchisee can determine the appropriate level of its firm-specific investment, and both parties can negotiate a price based on their costs and benefits under the contract. But if the franchisee might be able to circumvent terminability at will by litigating in a forum that does not enforce it, the franchiser cannot rely on terminability and will attempt to negotiate a price that reflects this uncertainty. The uncertainty about choice of law may even reduce the parties' joint gains from relying on the term to the point that it produces the same result as invalidating the term in all jurisdictions.

Uncertainty about choice of law at the time of litigation can increase both the costs and the frequency of litigation. In particular, the uncertainty may increase the parties' gains from litigating rather than settling.[67] Not only is this privately more costly for the parties, but it also imposes costs on the judicial system that are borne by taxpayers generally.

Enforcing contractual choice of law is only one way of reducing the costs of determining the applicable law. An alternative might be a relatively simple mandatory rule, such as applying the law where the contract is made.[68] This would save contracting parties the costs of determining if there is a hidden choice-of-law clause.[69] In comparing these alternatives, we need to take into account the significant benefits from enforcing choice-of-law clauses discussed here, and the fact that information costs can be reduced by mandating disclosure rather than by taking the more drastic step of invalidating the contracts.

Protecting against retroactive changes. Contracting parties may choose a particular legal regime in order to ensure that new statutory or judicial rules will not change their contract. To give an extreme example, creditors of foreign sovereign borrowers may want to designate the law of some other country to ensure that the sovereign does not try to escape liability simply by changing its law.[70] Although, as discussed in chapter 2, this result should be guaranteed by the contract clause, that provision does not fully protect contracting parties from retroactive law changes.[71] Because state legislators can gain by brokering wealth transfers between contracting parties, not all states will be able to easily to assure contracting parties that their legislators will be able to resist this temptation. Some states can offer such assurances, however, through procedural safeguards and reputational bonds.[72] Here, too, jurisdictional competition is important, since states can compete in part on the basis of their ability to offer safeguards and bonds.

Arguments against Enforcing Contractual Choice of Law. This subsection evaluates some arguments against enforcing contractual choice of law. In general, it shows that the arguments against enforcement are weaker than courts and commentators generally suppose. Only in a small category of cases are the arguments against enforcement credible, and even in these categories the significant benefits of enforcement discussed in the subsection above probably outweigh the costs.

Contractual evasion of mandatory rules. Enforcing contractual choice of law obviously raises the most serious questions where the parties are attempting to escape prohibitions on contract terms such as fiduciary duty waivers, usurious interest rates, and termination-at-will or noncompetition provisions.[73] The argument against enforcing the contractual choice of law in these situations may seem to be precisely the same as that supporting the mandatory rule itself. In other words, there is an important threshold question whether enforcement of contractual choice of law is ever consistent with the policies underlying mandatory rules that are evaded by such contracts. In fact, for several reasons the courts do[74] and should enforce choice-of-law clauses, even in situations in which they would refuse to enforce direct evasion of the mandatory rule.

First, using choice-of-law clauses requires applying a state law rather than solely the voluntary act of contracting parties. In other words, the parties cannot enter into a contract that is condemned by all jurisdictions. While a state might attempt to benefit its residents by allowing them to victimize nonresidents in oppressive deals, the fact that the state's law applies to its own residents reduces states' incentives to engage in this sort of conduct. States will not let firms enforce contracts signed by children, for example. Accordingly, this danger of enforcing contractual choice of law is limited to the situation in which most victims live outside the state.

Second, because choice of law necessarily entails a choice between mandatory and permissive legal rules, nonenforcement of mandatory rules inherently results from a federal system and not from choice-of-law clauses. The parties' choice of law is not obviously less appropriate than any other basis of selecting among potentially applicable state rules. Indeed, even without law-selection clauses, the courts often apply a conflicts rule that favors validation in usury

119

cases, on the theory that the parties intended to have a binding contract.[75] Although the parties may have chosen a law the courts would not otherwise have applied, a residence state does not clearly have a greater interest or other basis for regulating than a contractual state, particularly since the latter may have a strong policy of encouraging selection of its law.

Information costs. Choice-of-law terms arguably raise an issue of surprise, since their effect is apparent only to one who has studied the law and not from the face of the contract. If the contract is a form drafted by one party and presented as a completed document to the other, the party who drafted the law-selection clause and selected the applicable law may have an advantage. Indeed, choice-of-law terms often are found in contracts in which one party, such as a cruise line, insurer, or franchiser, enters into similar deals with a number of other parties. The party responsible for the term is probably better informed concerning the chosen law. Moreover, customers may be caught off guard because they assume that local protective rules apply. If law selection can be dictated by one contracting party, the states may tailor their rules to suit that party.

There are several problems, however, with this line of argument. First, the effect of the law-selection clause often is to choose a legal regime that literally enforces the contract.[76] This would surprise only the disingenuous party who purported to agree to a term while knowing or strongly believing that he could resist enforcement under the law of a jurisdiction other than the agreed one.

Second, in long-term contracts such as franchises and distributorships, the price is set in each case by negotiations among sophisticated and knowledgeable parties who have the ability and incentive to read the contract carefully or hire an attorney to do so. If such parties do not understand the effect of the clause, the price will reflect their uncertainty. Indeed, suspicious negotiators may assume the worst from the designation of a particular state's law, and consequently can overdiscount for the clause. In this setting, the party who chooses the law must reassure the other party or bear at least some of the cost of the other party's ignorance.

Third, even in relatively short-term deals in which one party may be relatively unsophisticated, the adversely affected party's ignorance of what law applies is not necessarily a problem, because firms that offer choice-of-law clauses are subject to market incentives to disclose and to constraints on cheating. These include the effects of reputation,[77] third-party monitors such as consumer magazines, and the presence of enough knowledgeable consumers in the marketplace that the general price reflects knowledgeable consumers' awareness of the effect of the choice-of-law provision.[78]

Even if the information costs associated with contractual choice of law are substantial and standard-form drafters lack sufficient private incentives to minimize them, it does not necessarily follow that the courts should invalidate choice-of-law clauses. Regulators could minimize information costs by mandating disclosure of unusual and significant law-selection terms in some circumstances. Consider, for example, a general partnership agreement that designates the law of a state that makes it relatively difficult for the creditors to collect from individual partners by requiring the creditors to exhaust remedies against the partnership before reaching partner assets.[79] Creditors dealing with the partnership in a different state may have no reason to know that the law of any state other than their own will apply.[80] Once the practice becomes widespread, however, creditors may discount their need for extra information, or they may insist on disclosures in their dealings with all partnerships. Under these circumstances, partnerships would favor a rule requiring filings or disclosures as to the law being applied. This may help explain the filing requirement for corporations and other limited liability firms.[81]

Even if information costs justified refusing to enforce some choice-of-law clauses, this problem could not explain generally distinguishing corporations under the internal affairs rule, since corporations involve the same potential costs as other contracts. Although corporations must make state filings that clearly identify which law applies, this difference suggests no more than that a filing or other disclosure should be required as to other types of contracts.[82] Nor is it significant that some corporate shares are traded on efficient securities markets that discount significant contract terms, while noncorporate contracts such as franchise and insurance agreements are not. Many corporate contracts are not traded in efficient markets, including close corporations and initial public offerings.[83] Moreover, critics of private ordering in corporations argue that even efficient securities markets do not accurately discount differences between state laws.[84] Most important, the presence or absence of efficient markets should not be a sine qua non of permitting private ordering, since contracting parties can be protected from bad deals by many alternative market and contracting devices.[85]

"Adhesion" contracts. Another argument against enforcing contractual choice of law is that choice-of-law clauses are adhesion contracts, imposed by one party on another.[86] There is no justification, however, for broadly attacking contracts as adhesive merely

121

because they were entered into without bargaining. First, the parties sensibly may have refrained from bargaining because they knew they could not gain enough from dickering over details to justify bargaining costs. That, of course, is why the law provides standard-form contracts. Second, the deal is not necessarily one-sided, even if one party drafted the contract. The accepting party may have decided to choose the contract bundle of rights and obligations from among competing bundles.

Some deals may be adhesive in the sense that they involve the information problems discussed in the previous section, or because of the offerer's unusual leverage or market power. A sophisticated seller, for example, might insert a new, surprise default term that prejudices an ordinary consumer who expected the "fair" rule of his own jurisdiction to apply. Until the market catches on, consumers may be hurt. Moreover, from an ex ante perspective, allowing manufacturers to do this forces consumers in all transactions to be more wary. But the courts can deal with these problems by condemning contracts as unconscionable based on specific facts.[87] Because there is no reason to believe that all choice-of-law clauses involve bargaining defects, there is no justification for a general rule invalidating choice-of-law clauses as per se unconscionable.[88]

Although courts should not invalidate contract terms merely because they are choice-of-law clauses, the parties arguably should not be able to evade state law that protects certain types of contracting parties from specific types of deals. But legislators cannot easily identify such suspect categories. Consider, for example, state laws protecting franchisees from oppressive franchise contracts, usually by mandating disclosure and forbidding certain types of conduct, such as bad faith and surprise terminations.[89] Although a contract that subjects franchisees to the risk of financial ruin from termination at will might seem at first glance to be adhesive, such terms are important in facilitating monitoring by franchisers of franchisees. Moreover, franchisees, rather than being helpless, can effectively coordinate resistance to the opportunism of franchisers by forming franchisee associations.[90] They are also protected from the worst forms of opportunistic termination by the fact that franchisers will pay for such opportunism when they attempt to sell future franchises. Indeed, it is improbable that, despite years of supposedly opportunistic conduct by franchisers, franchisees would continue voluntarily not only to enter into these arrangements, but also to persistently to underprice and underprotect themselves against the risk of franchiser opportunism.

States' incentives to compete. If states cannot internalize the benefits from efficient contract rules, they may have inadequate incentives to devote legislative and judicial resources to developing and maintaining efficient contract rules. This argument appears to distinguish corporations and noncorporate contracts, since states can use franchise and filing fees to internalize benefits of corporate law. But as we show below, such mechanisms are unnecessary to give states incentives to compete, and in any event, the existence of such incentives should not matter to whether contractual choice of law is enforced.

The states clearly have some incentives to compete to supply legal rules. They can earn revenue if enforcing choice of law attracts firms' operations to the state or enables the state to collect a fee for contracts that adopt the state's law.[91] Either of these mechanisms would, in effect, give the state property rights in application of its law.

This reasoning assumes, however, that the state, in the sense of taxpayers generally, receives the payoff. Interest-group theory suggests that, in fact, taxpayers are too large a group to coordinate effectively to seek gains, because no individual members of the group can capture enough benefits from legislative action to justify expending resources on legislation.[92] As applied to corporate law, Jonathan Macey and Geoffrey Miller have argued that lawyers are a more effective group than taxpayers, as shown by their significant influence on Delaware law.[93] Lawyers not only wield the conventional power of a cohesive interest group, but in most states draft complex business statutes. Judges' and legislators' interests are often aligned with those of lawyers, among other reasons because many of them are lawyers who are currently in practice or will be after they leave public office.[94]

Lawyers gain from increased legal business in a state that becomes a major center for a particular type of litigation. As experts and members of a specialized community that stays well informed about the law,[95] they can expect to get most of the litigation and other legal business based on that law. While lawyers might prefer legal rules that foster litigation excessively from the standpoint of social welfare,[96] lawyers cannot solely maximize litigation cost, because they must compete with other jurisdictions to attract choice-of-law clauses that would generate this business.

Moreover, lawyers are not a monolithic group. Commercial lawyers engaged in planning rather than litigation might favor rules that fostered ex ante contracting rather than litigation.[97] Accordingly, lawyers have incentives to make the law efficient comparable to those of legislators seeking to maximize franchise tax revenues.[98] Indeed, state statutes explicitly sanctioning contractual choice of law[99] suggest that states do have incentives to compete even apart from franchise revenues like those generated by incorporation business.

In any event, it is not clear why it matters whether either the state or interest groups within it have incentives to compete for law business. Lack of incentives means that, at worst, there is no reason to conclude that the selected rule is more efficient than the regulatory rule. But several of the other reasons remain, as discussed above, indicating why the contract should be enforced, including the parties' need for certainty and to avoid inappropriate mandatory rules.

Protecting third parties. A final reason for not enforcing law-selection clauses is that they may circumvent state policy protecting noncontracting parties. Contractual choice of law may, indeed, be inefficient when it imposes costs on third parties who could not contract with regard to the applicable law. Thus, the choice of the law of state X in an automobile insurance contract should not bind the insured's victim, a noncontractual creditor, to accept application of X state's tort law. But so-called third parties are often themselves parties to the contract. While termination of franchises, for example, undoubtedly affects the franchisee's creditors, long-term creditors such as banks are aware of this potential instability at the time of the loan and can take it into account in negotiating terms and charges. Their situation does not differ from that of creditors whose loans are jeopardized by a corporate leveraged buyout. Although the creditors are not, technically, parties to the corporate chartering decision, they are able to take into account the takeover law of the state of incorporation in making their initial credit decisions.[100]

A Political Theory of Contractual Choice of Law

The two previous sections raise serious questions concerning the efficiency of the legal rules on enforcing contractual choice of law. This section analyzes these legal rules from the somewhat different perspective of lawmakers' incentives to restrict contractual choice of law. It shows that lawmakers have self-interested reasons for refusing to enforce these contracts. This analysis is relevant for a normative evaluation of the resulting legal rules and for prescribing constitutional rules that would constrain state law restrictions on contracting.

Legislators. Courts often limit enforceability of choice-of-law clauses to prevent contracting parties from evading mandatory legislation. A political theory of contractual choice of law accordingly must begin with the incentives of legislators.

Under standard interest-group theory, state legislation is determined by the relative strength of the various groups that the legislation helps and hurts.[101] Legislation that is inefficient in the Kaldor-Hicks sense—that is, total costs outweigh benefits—may result if groups that are hurt are diffuse and therefore have higher organizational costs than those who are helped.[102]

To begin with, it is important to ask how a state regulation can help or hurt interest groups. Consider the example of a statute that limits termination at will of franchisees and explicitly precludes avoiding the statute by means of a choice-of-law clause in the agreement.[103] Limitations on termination reduce the franchiser's ability to discipline shirking or free-riding franchisees. This may help some franchisees at the expense of their franchisers. It also may help some brand-name owners and outlet operators at the expense of others, because some types of businesses require less monitoring than others. Operators who rely on local repeat business are less able to free-ride off the franchiser's brand name, and therefore they require less monitoring than those who rely on transient business.[104] Better established, brand-name owners are likely to have more company-owned stores than less-established owners, because the more-established firms have better credit than potential franchisees and have had an opportunity to observe which locations are most profitable.[105] Thus, rules restricting termination at will may give the brand-name owners with more company-owned stores in their mixture a competitive advantage over the (mostly newer) firms that rely more heavily on franchising.

The parties could try to neutralize the effect of the mandatory rule in the contract by pricing the offending term. But affected parties may not be able to price accurately the effect of such a statute, because they cannot predict whether the choice-of-law term will be enforced. Indeed, certainty for ax ante pricing and conduct is an important reason for enforcing these clauses.[106] While some adversely affected firms could avoid regulating states, for others the costs of staying out of these states may exceed the costs of the mandatory rule. Most important, the statute's effect is enhanced if it alters contract terms ex post. A recent study of franchisee termination statutes[107] showed that some of these statutes changed the contracts of existing franchisees and that, even in the states that did not change existing contracts, existing franchisees could expect to be covered on renewal of their contracts,[108] or could gain from reduced competition because the statutes increased the cost to franchisers of additional franchises.

If franchisees who are helped by the law are more effective

interest groups than those who are hurt, they will be able to secure enactment of antitermination laws even if these laws are inefficient. Conversely, franchisers who are hurt by the rule may be able to coordinate lobbying activity effectively to defeat the statute or supporting statutory rules that enable contractual choice of law.

Interest-group opposition to mandatory rules may be least effective if the law benefits the states' residents while imposing costs mostly on industries outside the state. Most of the costs of a statute restricting franchisee or distributor termination, for example, are imposed on out-of-state franchisers. Franchisees outnumber franchisers both nationally and within each state. While franchisers can effectively coordinate on the national level because of lower organizing costs,[109] franchisees within a given state may be more influential than the national franchiser organization.

Even if state franchisee organizations are more powerful within each state than national franchiser organizations, they have only a limited ability to shape legislation. Legislators may recognize that, over the long term, contracting parties who lose from mandatory laws may migrate to contract-enforcing states and avoid contacts with nonenforcing states.[110] This is a specific instance of the general insight that the threat of exit gives legislators within states an incentive to adopt efficient laws.[111] The strength of that incentive, however, depends on whether legislators will lose political support as a result of exit from the state. Although exit may cause a loss of tax revenues and may inconvenience local consumers, that will take time, and taxpayers as a whole may be too diffuse to exert much pressure on legislators. Thus, legislators may choose to risk causing exit from the state if the legal rules causing the exit had strong enough interest-group support to offset any political costs from exit.

The interest-group story of limitations on contractual choice of law is supported by recent evidence concerning franchise termination statutes.[112] The recent study of franchisee termination statutes discussed above[113] provides evidence refuting an efficiency explanation for the statutes. The study shows that the number of franchises diminished in states with franchisee termination laws, and that the drop was greatest in industries characterized by nonrepeat business, in which monitoring of franchisees through the power to terminate is most important. This suggests that the laws raised franchisers' costs of franchising simply by making franchising less efficient. Moreover, the study showed that share returns of franchisers around adoption of the California law indicated large wealth losses for shareholders of those companies.

There is also direct evidence of lobbying by franchisees to secure passage of franchisee termination statutes generally,[114] and in particular of the Iowa franchisee protection statute, which is currently the most aggressive state franchise regulation.[115] This is similar to the evidence discussed in chapter 2 of lobbying efforts connected with state antitakeover statutes.[116] There is also specific evidence that the legislation reflected a strategy by local franchisees to pressure home state legislators.[117]

The interest-group theory of enforcing choice of law also helps explain why the same restrictions have not been applied to corporate contracts. There may have been no coordinated interest groups within particular states that would seek regulation of corporate governance. The weakness of interest groups that would press for regulation of corporate governance is particularly significant in light of the courts' early acceptance of the state-creation theory that led to judicial acceptance of the internal affairs rule.[118] The entity theory helped create a legal momentum toward enforcement of contractual choice of law in corporations. Once such a momentum existed, it was important only that there were no strong interest groups to resist it.

Theories of Interpretation. Statutes must, of course, be applied by courts. Most statutes do not explicitly address choice-of-law clauses, and even explicit statutory invalidation of choice-of-law clauses would technically leave the court free to take the clause into account in deciding which state's law applies.

This raises questions about how the courts should and will interpret these statutes regarding choice of law. The courts could try to reconstruct the legislators' intent by, for example, considering what would be reasonable in the light of efficiency considerations and the general structure of the law.[119] In light of interest-group theory and the impossibility of determining ex post what the legislators as a group wanted to do, it is highly questionable whether courts can actually determine intent in any meaningful way.[120] Even if the courts cannot determine intent precisely, however, they probably can assume that the legislature did not want contracting parties to be able to evade their laws easily. Legislators would be left with little to sell to interest groups if their deals could be avoided by the simple mechanism of choosing another state's law.

A third judicial approach, advocated by some public-choice theorists, would be to interpret statutes so as to reduce interest-group deals by raising their costs. The courts could do this by narrowly interpreting statutes that reflect interest-group deals,[121] or by interpreting statutes consistent with their "public regarding" purpose unless the interest-group deal is made explicit.[122] In the present context, the courts could force interest groups to buy explicit statutory provisions invalidating choice-of-law clauses by liberally enforcing the clauses in the absence of explicit provisions.[123]

The problem with this analysis is that it is simply a normative theory of what the courts should do. Courts will not adopt a particular interpretation approach merely because academics suggest that they should. Accordingly, the following sections focus on the incentives of judges and others in the litigation process to reach particular decisions regarding enforcement of choice-of-law clauses.

Judges' Incentives. Judges clearly have some incentive to respond to the interests of legislators, because the latter control judges' salaries and tenure and can act to reduce the discretion of errant courts by enacting more explicit statutes. Thus, just as judges have the incentive to increase the durability and value of legislators' interest-group deals by enforcing them within the state,[124] they would seek to maximize the value of these deals by protecting them from dilution by choice-of-law clauses.

Judges' personal preferences regarding enforcement of contractual choice of law apart from their interests in satisfying legislators are less clear. Judges may act to enhance their power, prestige, job satisfaction, and the value of their human capital both on and off the bench.[125] Prestige-maximizing judges may, for example, attempt to increase citations by deciding cases so as to provoke litigation.[126] To be sure, judges act within constraints. Even prestige-conscious courts would not want to be known for making poorly reasoned or rent-motivated decisions.[127] Moreover, judges recognize that their decisions may be reversed by legislatures,[128] that their decisions must carry the force of law in order to be effective, and that legislators can respond to errant judges by manipulating their jurisdiction.[129]

The complications regarding judicial motivation are apparent with respect to enforcing choice-of-law clauses. Enforcing such clauses deprives judges of the power not only to make the choice-of-law determination, but also possibly to make new law on the relevant issue. It is also important to keep in mind that judges' decisions on choice of law may affect the quality and quantity of litigation brought in their courts. Litigants who gain under the contractually selected law have an incentive to sue in jurisdictions that enforce these clauses, including federal court, or to contract for arbitration.[130] Litigation-maximizing courts could try to enforce the clauses in the types of cases where this favors plaintiffs.[131] The party who selects the forum (usually the plaintiff), however, may be as likely to lose as to win from enforcement of the clause. A choice-of-law clause may, for

example, hurt a franchisee plaintiff who otherwise would be protected by a franchisee-termination statute, but it may help a franchiser
seeking a declaratory judgment on the right to terminate.

The conflict-of-laws rules discussed earlier indicate that the
courts are, in fact, enforcing rather than deterring interest-group
deals. The rule invalidating choice-of-law clauses that would interfere
with a fundamental policy of the statute invites the courts to effectuate interest groups' underlying goal. Conversely, courts taking an
antiinterest-group approach to interpretation would enforce choice-
of-law clauses, unless the statute explicitly precludes this interpretation.

Litigation and Interest Groups. Even if courts have incentives to
disfavor choice-of-law clauses, litigation may drive common-law rules
toward enforcing these clauses, because at least some categories of
losers from nonenforcement of contractual choice have the incentive
to litigate until the rule is changed.[132] More specifically, Paul Rubin
argues that whether a rule is litigated depends on whether the group
can capture the benefits of legal change.[133] In other words, litigation,
like legislation, can be explained by interest-group theory.

With respect to choice-of-law clauses, groups who lost at the
legislative stage may be able to win at the litigation stage by being
able to invest significant resources in litigating to uphold contractual
choice of law. The extensive litigation on choice of law in franchise
disputes,[134] for example, indicates that franchisees or franchisers or
both have formed cohesive interest groups that can capture the
benefits of legal rules that support enforcing or not enforcing these
contracts. If both groups can coordinate equally effectively, this may
cause courts ultimately to adopt the efficient rule, since the loser
from an inefficient rule would gain more than the winner from
litigating the rule.[135]

An interest group that has been able to solve free-rider problems
successfully enough to win or to oppose revision of a favorable
statute might nevertheless lose the litigation battle to protect the
statute from erosion by choice-of-law clauses. In the franchise situation, for example, while franchisees have mobilized to obtain passage
of franchisee-protection statutes,[136] franchisers also have a powerful
organization[137] through which they can coordinate litigation. But
while franchisees may have enough local power with legislatures to
secure enactment of mandatory statutes,[138] franchisers may be in a
better position to litigate nationally to enforce choice-of-law clauses.

While litigation is a potentially powerful countervailing force
against interest-group legislation, it does not trivialize the effect of

129

such legislation. At best, litigation is costly and takes time. Moreover, while the courts may have considerable discretion to interpret the statutes, they can do little in the face of a statute that explicitly invalidates choice-of-law clauses.

Lawyers. Lawyers are an important interest group because they can influence both legislation and litigation. Paul Rubin and Martin J. Bailey have shown how the organized trial bar has been able to increase litigation by weakening contract rules in products liability cases.[139] Lawyers could try to do the same thing regarding contractual choice of law, or through bar associations could support or oppose statutes that invalidate choice-of-law clauses.

Lawyers' interests in this respect, however, are ambiguous. Litigators have an incentive to maximize fees through legal rules that ensure that cases are tried rather than settled out of court, or through increasing the complexity of legal rules.[140] Accordingly, lawyers may want to prevent the parties from simplifying choice of law by contracting in advance to be governed by a particular law.

At the same time, litigators also want to increase their state's share of the general litigation market. This is certainly true, for example, with respect to franchise litigation, which will probably grow as new franchise protection legislation is passed.[141] Invalidating choice-of-law clauses would prevent this litigation from going to other states. Alternatively, lawyers might want to validate these clauses and attract more litigation to their jurisdictions.[142] The former strategy may work best for a jurisdiction that is not already a major commercial or litigation center.

Lawyers' motivations are complicated by the fact that state courts' refusal to enforce choice-of-law clauses might send such disputes into local federal courts or arbitration rather than out of state. Local lawyers might either share in that business or lose it to national specialists in federal litigation and arbitration. Moreover, many commercial lawyers specializing in planning rather than in litigation would lose business if regulated firms went elsewhere, even if their colleagues could litigate concerning whatever business remained. In short, although lawyers may be an important piece of the interest-group puzzle in individual cases, it is difficult to generalize about their motivations, and therefore about the effect they are likely to have on statutes and litigation.

Choosing the Forum and the Role of Federal Courts. By selecting the forum in their contracts, the parties can try to have the case heard by a court that not only will apply the chosen law, but will do so in the way the parties anticipated. The parties can choose the court or the adjudicator by some combination of contract clauses that provides that any disputes will be tried in a designated court, or that the parties consent to the jurisdiction of a designated court, or that the parties agree to submit disputes to arbitration.[143]

The parties also may be able to escape the interest-group orientation of state courts by litigating in federal court. Federal courts generally apply state choice-of-law rules in diversity cases brought in or removed to federal court.[144] The Supreme Court has ensured that federal adjudication does not change the applicable rule by holding that the parties to a diversity case cannot change the law by transferring to a federal court in another state,[145] and even by giving a plaintiff who sued in an inconvenient forum the benefit of that court's conflicts rule after the case was removed to a convenient forum.[146]

Although the federal courts apply the same rules as state courts, they tend to reach different results. Some federal cases, for example, have enforced choice-of-law clauses that would avoid franchisee-protection statutes where the courts found no need to protect the particular franchisees involved from franchiser oppression.[147] This is a "public-regarding" construction[148] that increases the cost of interest-group deals by requiring them to be made explicit.

A review of cases citing §187(1) of the Restatement (Second) of Conflicts, which sanctions enforcement of choice-of-law clauses, since its final adoption in 1971 shows that federal courts wrote opinions in 151 such cases, compared with 65 state opinions. The federal courts refused to enforce the clauses in 22.5 percent of these cases, while state courts refused to do so in 44 percent of the cases. There was, therefore, a striking difference between federal and state courts, both with respect to the total number of cases on this issue and the percentage in which the clause was enforced.[149]

This federal tendency to enforce contractual choice of law is reinforced by a strong federal rule favoring choice of forum and adjudicator. The Federal Arbitration Act[150] mandates enforceability of arbitration agreements involving transactions in interstate commerce[151] in state as well as federal court.[152] The Court has upheld arbitration clauses even against plaintiffs who formerly were deemed to need protection from such clauses.[153] Supreme Court cases also enforce consent to jurisdiction[154] and forum selection, both in commercial cases[155] and, more recently, in a case involving a cruise line passenger.[156] Some recent cases have combined these latter two lines of cases by enforcing clauses providing for adjudication in an English forum under English law, although the effect of the clauses was to avoid application of the federal securities laws.[157]

The federal-state difference regarding enforcement of choice-of-law clauses can be explained only by the interest-group hypothesis discussed above. Under that theory, federal courts would be less likely than state courts to enforce state interest-group deals, because federal judges' tenure and salaries are not controlled by state legislatures.[158] Moreover, federal courts have a weaker "prestige" incentive for refusing the enforce choice-of-law clauses, because in diversity cases they must borrow rules from a state court rather than make their own, whatever the effect of the choice-of-law clause.[159] At the same time, there is no reason to expect federal courts to determine the issue differently on efficiency grounds. The fact that federal courts sometimes do not enforce the clauses does not contradict the interest-group explanation, since the federal courts cannot ignore the large body of state precedent on this issue.[160]

Constitutional Protection of Contractual Choice of Law

This chapter has shown that choice-of-law clauses should be enforced in most cases, but that state courts have an incentive to do the legislature's bidding in refusing to allow contractual evasion of mandatory statutes. The courts' deference to fundamental policy and the difference between the results in federal and state courts suggest that the courts are, in fact, upholding interest-group deals. The first subsection below shows how the commerce clause of the U.S. Constitution[161] limits state nonenforcement of choice-of-law clauses. The second subsection also considers and rejects alternative bases of constitutional protection under the due process[162] and full faith and credit[163] clauses.

The Commerce Clause. While the commerce clause explicitly grants power only to Congress, the Court long ago adopted a "negative" version of the commerce clause that inferentially restricts state power.[164] The first three parts of this subsection discuss three theories of the negative commerce clause that justify protecting choice-of-law clauses. These theories, however, pose a danger of potentially invasive judicial review of state legislation. Accordingly, the fourth part proposes adopting a limited theory of commerce clause protection that applies specifically to choice-of-law clauses.

Cost exportation. The Supreme Court has endorsed an exportation-of-costs theory of the commerce clause, which holds that if the costs of state regulation fall mostly on interest groups outside the state while the benefits accrue to those within it, the legislature lacks incentives to consider both costs and benefits in enacting laws.[165] As the Court has said:

> When the regulation is of such character that the burden falls principally upon those without the state, legislative action is not likely to be subjected to those political restraints which are normally exerted on legislation where it affects adversely some interests within the state.[166]

The theory is constitutionally based on the importance of representative government.[167] It also makes sense in efficiency terms: cost exportation subverts interest-group interaction within the enacting jurisdiction that otherwise would cause laws to tend toward Kaldor-Hicks efficiency.[168]

Protecting choice-of-law clauses is appropriate under the cost-exportation theory, because this theory targets a particular type of interest-group statute that benefits concentrated in-state groups while imposing costs on out-of-state firms or interest groups. In the first place, as discussed in the preceding section, courts are most likely to be perversely motivated to invalidate choice-of-law clauses where they are enforcing legislative interest-group deals. Neither courts' personal interests nor interest-group activity in litigation is likely to motivate courts not to enforce these clauses in other cases, such as where the clauses relate to states' common-law rules.

Choice-of-law-clause cases are also likely to involve the specific type of interest-group deals that benefit in-state groups at the expense of out-of-state groups. The courts often refuse to enforce choice-of-law clauses in order to effectuate a statute's fundamental policy to protect a supposedly weaker over a stronger party.[169] This suggests that invalidating choice-of-law clauses generally disfavors politically potent parties, since firms that are strong in commercial markets are also likely to be strong in political markets. While this result is not necessarily either bad policy[170] or unconstitutional, it is reasonable to suspect that state legislators would not disregard politically potent interests unless those powerful interests were based outside the state. This suspicion is confirmed by the facts that choice-of-law clauses are drafted by relatively sophisticated parties, and that they are generally found in elaborate form contracts that are cost justified mainly if used on a national scale rather than within a single state.

The problem with applying the cost-exportation commerce clause theory is that it is potentially open-ended and difficult to apply. In an increasingly national economy, most state laws potentially are net-cost–exporting, and it is not clear when the exportation justifies judicial intervention. One writer has suggested that the courts determine the law's "outside impact percentage,"[171] but this obviously poses difficult factual problems. Moreover, even if courts could identify cost-exporting legislation, it is not clear to what extent such legislation is inconsistent with representative government. Legislators have incentives to take into account costs imposed on nonresidents and to disregard costs imposed on residents.

The benefits may accrue to cohesive out-of-state groups who wield power through contributions, while costs are borne by politically impotent voters inside the state.[172] Or the costs may be ultimately borne inside the state, even if they initially fall on nonresidents. A law that, for example, limits the activities of out-of-state firms has obvious anticompetitive effects that will increase prices and thereby hurt consumers inside the state.[173] Finally, even if the law does not directly hurt consumers or others in the state, it invites retaliation by other states that will have such effects. If the costs are high enough, the affected people will ultimately coordinate their opposition to discriminatory laws.[174]

The indeterminacy of the cost-exportation approach to the commerce clause is illustrated by *Exxon Corp. v. Governor of Maryland*, in which the Court upheld state regulation forbidding oil refiners from owning gas stations.[175] Although the statute directly affected only out-of-state firms, the affected refiners certainly had significant political clout.[176] Moreover, the regulation's anticompetitive effects had a strong impact on consumers in the state.[177]

Consumers usually are too dispersed, however, to be an effective interest group, and the refiners, although undoubtedly a strong group, may not have been as strong as the gas station operators in a given state, who sought to capture the gains from rising gasoline prices. Thus, although statutes that invalidate choice-of-law clauses are clear examples of cost-exporting legislation, applying a cost-exportation theory could open the door to complex questions of judicial review in other cases. This makes it unlikely that the Court will embrace such a theory, and necessary to articulate an alternative constitutional ground for protecting choice-of-law clauses.

Risk of multiple-state regulation. Some commerce clause cases mandate application of a single uniform rule to avoid burdening interstate commerce with multiple, potentially inconsistent regulation.[178] In *Southern Pacific Co. v. State of Arizona*,[179] for example, the Court held, citing the need for national uniformity, that Arizona lacked power to regulate the length of interstate trains. Similarly, the Court has struck down, on commerce clause grounds, state regulation of truck length,[180] as well as a state rule that required a particular type of mudguard that was different from the type required by most other states.[181]

These cases are obviously relevant to contractual choice of law, because applying the parties' selected law solves potential problems of inconsistent regulation.[182] As with the exportation-of-cost theory, however, applying a multiple-state regulation theory of the commerce clause would be potentially open-ended, because multiple-state laws impose burdens that are not clearly distinguishable from many other types of burdens on interstate commerce. Merely because a state law imposes a potential cost in terms of inconsistent regulation it does not necessarily follow that the federal interest outweighs that of the individual states.[183] Moreover, the principle provides little guidance or limitation, since conflicting state rules often apply, and because the conflicting-regulation theory does not provide a basis for choosing which law to apply.[184] Once again, it is necessary to refine the constitutional basis for protecting contractual choice of law.

Discrimination. Facial or overt discrimination against interstate commerce is the most limited, and easiest to defend, basis of commerce clause protection.[185] Invalidating choice-of-law clauses in favor of the fundamental policy of the avoided law, however, does not facially discriminate against interstate commerce, because it applies equally to both in-state and out-of-state transactions. Although such clauses are more likely to be adopted in interstate than intrastate transactions, this approach would stretch the facial discrimination test into a much broader and harder-to-confine balancing test.[186]

Specific protection of choice-of-law clauses. The discussion so far in this subsection shows that three prominent theories of the commerce clause support constitutional protection of choice-of-law clauses. Each of these theories, however, poses a problem of potentially open-ended judicial review of state statutes and decisions. Accordingly, it is arguably inappropriate to base commerce clause protection for choice-of-law clauses solely on one or more of these theories. We instead suggest dealing with the open-endedness problem by creating a separate and limited theory of the commerce clause that specifically invalidates state statutes to the extent that they prevent enforcement of choice-of-law clauses. This limited theory not only is solidly based on accepted theories of the commerce clause, but also, for the reasons discussed in this section, contains the exercise of judicial discretion.

First, upholding the parties' contractual choice of law does not require the Court to weigh the interests of two states that both seek

135

to apply their law. As long as the Court simply enforces the contract, including the parties' choice of applicable law, there is no real choice-of-law question. The Court needs to determine only whether the state that seeks to apply its mandatory law has a sufficiently compelling interest to justify imposing its law on an interstate transaction. Thus, the theory helps nullify interest-group power not by increasing the power of central courts, but rather by intensifying competition among state legal regimes.

Second, by identifying a specific category of cases in which cost-externalization is likely to be a particular concern, the proposed theory avoids the need to make an exportation-of-costs, multiple-regulation, or discrimination determination in each case. This not only conserves judicial resources, but also prevents the theory from becoming an open-ended basis for invalidating state laws.

To understand the limited nature of the proposed theory, we must keep in mind that the theory does not invalidate state legislation merely because of the legislation's effects on interstate commerce, but rather only to the extent that legislation precludes avoidance through choice-of-law clauses. State securities regulation, for example, has been upheld under the commerce clause,[187] although almost certainly it is cost-exporting interest-group legislation.[188] The proposed theory would preclude applying these laws to invalidate contracts that provide for application of the law of another state. Although the internal-affairs rule does not apply the incorporation state's fraud law to stock sales,[189] potential purchasers could conceivably contract with the firm for application of a disclosure regime other than the state securities law that otherwise would apply.[190] In that situation, the proposed theory would constitutionally compel the states to enforce the contract.[191]

The proposed theory is not only theoretically sound, but also helps explain the Court's two state antitakeover law cases. In *Edgar v. Mite Corp.*,[192] a plurality struck down a state law that imposed conditions, including approval by a state agency, on interstate tender offers. The plurality characterized this as an impermissible direct regulation of interstate commerce, and as a burden on interstate commerce that was impermissible in light of the state's weak regulatory interest.[193] Five years later, in *CTS Corp. v. Dynamics Corp. of America*,[194] the Court held that an interstate tender offer could be regulated by the law of the state of incorporation.[195] The Court noted that the Indiana statute involved in *CTS* did not discriminate against interstate commerce,[196] and unlike the statute involved in *Mite*, did not involve a risk of inconsistent state regulation.[197] The Court also reasoned that states that create corporations can control their attributes.[198] Finally, and perhaps most important, the Court specifically relied on the internal-affairs rule, saying: "No principle of corporation law and practice is more firmly established than a State's authority to regulate domestic corporations, including the authority to define the voting rights of shareholders."[199]

The Court failed to rationalize *CTS* and *Mite* in terms of a general theory of the negative commerce clause. Indeed, the Court began its analysis by noting that its interpretation of the negative commerce clause "has not always been easy to follow," and that the Court "has articulated a variety of tests in an attempt to describe the difference between those regulations that the commerce clause permits and those regulations that it prohibits."[200] The Court's discrimination point applies equally to the statutes in both cases. While the statutes did differ in terms of the risk of inconsistent state regulation, as discussed above,[201] this is not a coherent theory of the commerce clause.

That leaves the Court's reliance on corporations as creatures of state law and its emphasis on the corporate internal-affairs rule. This reasoning suggests that the Court intended to apply special rules for corporations, just as it earlier attempted to create a special status for fraternal benefit associations under the full faith and credit clause.[202] If, however, there is any basis for a theory of constitutional protection along the lines suggested in this section, the theory can be justified only as one relating to contracts generally, and not as a special rule dealing only with corporations. The analysis in this chapter makes clear that there is no justification for different rules regarding contractual choice of law in corporations and other contracts.[203]

Mite and *CTS* are best rationalized on the basis that the Court will invalidate regulation of corporate governance if, and only if, it is imposed other than by the state of incorporation. In other words, while the cases do not make sense in terms of any broad theories of the commerce clause, such as the inconsistent-regulation or discrimination theories the Court discussed in *CTS*, they can be explained in terms of the limited theory suggested in this subsection: state tender offer regulation like that involved in *Mite* is unconstitutional under the commerce clause to the extent that it is interpreted as overrriding the parties' contractual choice of law inherent in selecting the state of incorporation.[204]

To be sure, the Court has not necessarily constitutionalized contractual choice of law under the commerce clause.[205] The Court could, for example, uphold regulation by a nonincorporating state if the firm could avoid excessive burdens by complying with one of two inconsistent laws.[206] The Court also could insist on its creature-of-state-law analysis and refuse to analogize corporate and noncorporate contracts, even to the point of invalidating a state law selected by a choice-of-law clause outside the corporate governance context. The Court's future direction, however, is indicated by its enforcement of forum-selection and arbitration clauses.[207] These cases show the Court's sympathy with the general notion of enforcing contractual selection of adjudication rules, and its willingness to mandate enforcement of contracts in state-court cases if it can find the appropriate constitutional grounds.

Other Constitutional Theories. This subsection discusses the full faith and credit and due process clauses as limitations on states' power to invalidate choice-of-law clauses. The subsection shows that these constitutional provisions are very weak constraints on state power. This analysis complements the discussion in the previous subsection by further clarifying the basis of constitutionally protecting choice-of-law clauses.

The following headed sections divide the analysis among principles that the Court and commentators have applied, discussing the constitutional provisions that have been brought to bear in discussing each principle.

Comity. The full faith and credit clause requires states at least to recognize the interstate authority of other states' laws. This mutual recognition is a crucial aspect of the distinction between federalism under the Constitution and the loose confederacy it replaced. In an often-cited article on full faith and credit, Justice Robert Jackson described the clause as protecting against the "disintegrating influence of provincialism."[208] Under this interpretation of full faith and credit, a state must respect the laws of other states at least to the extent of having a principled basis for refusing to follow the law in a particular case.[209]

The scope of the clause, however, is explicitly left to Congress. Congress's failure to act may preclude the courts from choosing among states that have legitimate interests at stake.[210] This is consistent with the Court's approach in *Allstate Insurance Co. v. Hague*,[211] of virtually merging full faith and credit with due process,[212] and letting a court apply its law as long as it has some reasonable basis for doing so.[213] *Hague* held that Minnesota could apply its rule "stacking" uninsured motorist coverage for three vehicles owned by an insured, rather than applying the different rule of Wisconsin, where the policy was issued and the insured resided. The decedent worked in

Minnesota, his widow became a Minnesota resident, and the insurer was doing business in Minnesota.

It follows that the states easily can concoct a constitutional ground for refusing to apply another state's law. Moreover, there is nothing in the comity principle that directly protects individuals' rights. Rather, the principle is based on the states' prerogatives, and it is primarily intended to divide authority within the federal system. This protects individuals only to the extent that it enforces the self-government decisions they make within state units. In other words, comity does not defend freedom of contract.[214]

Enforcing parties' expectations. The cases support using full faith and credit and due process to enforce the parties' expectations. The *Hague* majority noted that Allstate would not be unfairly surprised by the application of Minnesota law.[215] Justice John Paul Stevens, concurring, said that the parties' expectations are significant under the full faith and credit clause,[216] and he suggested that the due process clause would raise fairness concerns if the parties had made their expectations explicit by providing for application of a particular law.[217] Similarly, in *Phillips Petroleum Co. v. Shutts,*[218] the Court noted that the parties' expectations were important in determining the fairness of applying the forum's law, and that the parties did not expect the forum's law to control when they executed the leases that gave rise to the litigation.[219] It follows that full faith and credit and due process require application of a law the parties, at the time of the transaction, expected would apply. This does not, however, prevent a court from overriding the choice-of-law clause, where the parties would expect this result under applicable choice-of-law rules. In other words, an expectations-based test lets states abrogate contracts as long as they do so under clear rules.

Avoiding application of multiple rules. A series of cases decided under the full faith and credit clause involving fraternal benefit associations holds that the association's formation-state law or charter must apply in order to ensure that a single legal regime applies to all association members.[220] This principle is at least superficially compelling in a case like *Supreme Council of the Royal Arcanum v. Green,*[221] in which the choice-of-law question controlled members' assessments. In this situation, applying multiple laws would give different rights to members in different states regarding a particular aspect of their investment.

On closer examination, however, even these cases do not clearly differ from others on choice-of-law clauses.[222] They therefore involve the same problem of limiting the scope of the rule presented by the

139

commerce clause multiple-state regulation cases[223] and the common-law conflicts rule for corporations.[224] In a case like *Green*, it may be important that members have the same obligations when they are claiming against the same fund. The Court, however, later applied *Green* in less compelling circumstances. In *Modern Woodmen of America v. Mixer*,[225] which involved a presumption-of-death rule, Justice Oliver Wendell Holmes cited the "indivisible unity between the members of a corporation of this kind in respect of the fund from which their rights are to be enforced."[226] Applying different state presumption-of-death laws rather than a single association rule, however, would not significantly have altered the members' rights or have misaligned rights and obligations among members.

Similarly, in *Order of United Commercial Travelers v. Wolfe*,[227] differential enforcement of the notice-of-claim provision would not seriously have impeded the national functioning of the organization.[228] Although the notice-of-claim and prolonged-absence rules in *Wolfe* and *Mixer* could affect the association's ability to make payouts to other members, administering multiple rules is not very costly even in the most compelling cases. Differing member assessment obligations in a case like *Green* amount to different classes of shares, which can be differentially priced by state to reflect mandatory rules applying in each state.[229] In other words, the regulatory costs imposed by these rules are not qualitatively different from those imposed by other state regulations on interstate business.

Thus, as Brainerd Currie has argued,[230] there is no clear theory underlying full faith and credit that would justify abandoning the interest-weighing approach of other constitutional conflicts cases. Indeed, the different treatment of fraternal benefit association and other conflicts cases is sometimes striking. The Court has specifically rejected, for example, the argument that a contractual choice-of-law provision in a nonfraternal-benefit insurance case should be enforced as necessary to apply a uniform law to all policyholders.[231]

The Court has rationalized the distinction between fraternal benefit association and other cases partly by saying that membership is "something more than a contract, it is entering into a complex and abiding relation,"[232] and that a fraternal benefit association is a creature of state law and therefore must be construed under the law of the formation state.[233] But fraternal benefit associations, like corporations, are and should be treated as contracts. Moreover, it is not clear why characterizing fraternal benefit associations as something other than contracts entitles them to more protection under the full faith and credit clause. Finally, even if enforcing a uniform law were constitutionally compelled under the commerce or full faith and credit clauses, this would not necessarily result in enforcing the law selected by the parties. A single uniform rule could be applied by enforcing the law of the one state that has overwhelming contacts with the transaction, even if this is not the law the parties selected.[234]

Federal Choice-of-Law Legislation and Judicial Deference. Federal regulation would be an obvious alternative to judicially enforced constitutional constraints on invalidation of choice-of-law clauses.[235] Congress is explicitly empowered under both the full faith and credit clause[236] and the commerce clause[237] to regulate in this area. A federal choice-of-law rule could preserve state power and reinforce private contracts in a manner similar to commerce clause protection of contractual choice of law.

At the same time, perhaps the courts should defer to Congress. Even a "limited" commerce clause rule might not be easily contained, and therefore might unduly broaden central government authority.[238] And judges do not necessarily have either the ability or the incentives to make the right decisions.[239] In particular, there is no guarantee that courts would not seek to increase their own power in interpreting the limited commerce clause theory.

The appropriate scope of judicial review is ultimately a complex matter of comparing the competence and incentives of judges and legislators.[240] Complete judicial deference to Congress is inappropriate, because Congress acts or fails to act according to the same support-maximizing principles that motivate other politicians. Any congressional action in this area would undoubtedly have to emerge from a competition among interest groups. There is probably no group that would gain enough from a general rule validating choice-of-law clauses to organize support for such a law. Congress may fail to act only to avoid negative interest-group pressure, rather than because action would be inefficient.[241] Accordingly, there is no reason to believe either that Congress will act or that its failure to act justifies inaction by the Court. It follows that the Court should take the initiative to lift state burdens on interstate commerce, particularly since Congress can always correct the Court's most serious mistakes.[242]

Federal versus State Law. Congress could attempt to solve the problem of individual states' externalizing costs by refusing to enforce contractual choice of law, through the enactment of a federal substantive law, such as a federal franchise act. Such a law, however, would frustrate a principal objective of enforcing contractual choice of law by subverting beneficial jurisdictional competition. Accordingly, just

141

as commerce clause protection should be expanded to protect contractual choice of law, so federal legislation should be narrowly interpreted to avoid extending federal restrictions on private ordering. That, in fact, was the Court's approach in refusing in *CTS* to hold that the Williams Act precluded the arguably different balance of bidder and management rights under state antitakeover laws.[243] The same general approach of avoiding interference with state corporation law also underlies the Court's decision not to interpret broadly the federal antifraud provision, §10(b) of the Securities Exchange Act of 1934.[244]

Conclusion and Implications

This chapter suggests that enforcement of choice-of-law clauses is efficient in most cases and that the vague qualifications on enforcement in the case law are unwarranted. The difference between results in federal and state courts supports the hypothesis that the courts' refusal to enforce these clauses is based on a desire to protect rent-seeking deals by interest groups rather than on efficiency considerations. Although the courts have some incentives to enforce these contracts, inefficient nonenforcement is a long-run equilibrium position. The courts accordingly should be compelled under the commerce clause to recognize the important contractual values inherent in choice-of-law clauses and to enforce them in most cases.

Wider enforcement of choice-of-law clauses would bring the internal-affairs rule within the contractual theory of the corporation. Corporations have been singled out for an internal-affairs rule only because they have been characterized as creatures of state law. This means that as the price of receiving the benefits of jurisdictional competition, corporations have not been entitled to the benefits of being recognized as full-fledged contracts under the contracts clause and the First Amendment. Recognizing that all contracts are entitled to the same choice-of-law treatment that is now available only to corporations would remove an important reason for limiting the protection of corporate contracts.

6
Conclusion

This chapter offers some general observations on our monograph and its contributions to the analysis of the application of the Constitution to the corporate law.

The modern economic theory of the firm discussed in chapter 1 demonstrates that, from a positive standpoint, the corporation is fundamentally a set of contracts. It also shows that, from a normative efficiency standpoint, the law should permit and enforce these contracts. It follows that the regulatory theory of the corporation is wrong, both as a description of the corporation and as a matter of policy.

Our monograph derives a coherent theory of the application of the Constitution to the corporation from these basic principles. In the first place, the positive characterization of the corporation as a set of contracts rather than as a "creature" of state law is an important basis for protecting corporate contracts to the same extent as other contracts under the First Amendment and the contract and commerce clauses, rather than making them special wards of the state.

The contractual theory of the corporation also provides a normative basis for constitutionally protecting corporate contracts from legal interference. Thus, retroactive changes in the contract should be unconstitutional under the contract clause, and invalidation of contractual choice of law violates the commerce clause. Moreover, interference with corporate political or governance speech cannot be justified under the First Amendment on the supposed ground that such rules are necessary to protect shareholders. Indeed, if corporate contracts are protected under the commerce and contract clauses, this would further strengthen the argument that no further protection in the form of mandatory regulation of corporate speech is necessary.

Our theory of the Constitution and the corporation has implications for other constitutional provisions that we do not discuss. It follows, for example, from the fact that the corporation is a nexus of contracts rather than a creature of state law, that personal rights in the Constitution should be applied to individuals connected with the firm rather than to the firm itself. Thus, just as the state-creation theory and personification of the corporation should not play any role in the determination of corporations' rights under the First Amendment, contract clause, or commerce clause, so they should not determine the application of the privilege against self-incrimination in the corporate context[1] or entitle foreign corporations to the privileges and immunities of citizens.[2] It was therefore, clearly wrong for the Court to deny a sole owner or shareholder the Fifth Amendment privilege of not being forced to incriminate himself by producing business documents, merely because he had incorporated his business.[3]

Also, the normative aspect of the contractual theory plays a role under other constitutional provisions. Just as the commerce clause should ensure that corporations can contractually choose the governing state law, for example, so the supremacy clause[4] should not unduly extend the application of federal law to trump the application of state law. Indeed, in *CTS Corp. v. Dynamics Corp. of America*,[5] the same case in which the Court apparently endorsed constitutional choice of law under the commerce clause,[6] the Court also gave a limited reading to the supremacy clause that ensured application of the selected state law rather than the federal Williams Act.

Our analysis has general implications for constitutional law. We show how, in applying the Constitution, courts should take into account economic principles that relate to the particular context in which the Constitution is being applied. This suggests that courts should not necessarily apply constitutional provisions in the same way to all subjects, but rather should be wary of different considerations that arise in different contexts. We show in chapter 5, for example, that a special theory of the commerce clause relating to contractual choice of law would make more sense than an unmanageable "grand unified theory" of the commerce clause.[7]

Finally, the general economic implications of our analysis should not be ignored. We have shown how constitutionally protecting a particular form of private ordering—that is, the corporate contract—would be efficient. Similar observations apply to other forms of contracting. In general, significant social gains could be realized if the Constitution were applied so as to ensure that the law facilitates rather than frustrates private agreements.

Notes

PREFACE

1. ADOLPH A. BERLE & GARDINER C. MEANS, THE MODERN CORPORATION AND PRIVATE PROPERTY (1932).
2. 17 U.S. (4 Wheat.) 518, 636 (1819).
3. 110 S.Ct. 1391 (1990).
4. 481 U.S. 69 (1987).

CHAPTER 1: THE NATURE OF THE CORPORATION

1. It is fashionable to refer to the corporation under the private contract approach as a "nexus of contracts." See Michael C. Jensen & William H. Meckling, *Theory of the Firm: Managerial Behavior, Agency Costs and Ownership Structure*, 3 J. FIN. ECON. 305, 311 (1976) ("The private corporation or firm is simply one form of legal fiction which serves as a nexus for contracting relationships. . . ."). This terminology is appropriate as long as one clearly understands that it does not necessarily imply that the corporation exists as an entity wholly apart from the contracts among its participants. The entity theory appears to support the approach that the "entity" is brought into being and therefore is subject to extensive regulation (either through direct administrative regulation or litigation) by the state. We will eschew language that lends itself to a priori treatment of corporations as different from other contractual relationships. The corporation may, indeed, be viewed as a bundle of interrelated contractual relationships, but there is no conceptual justification for reifying this interrelationship.

2. We use "firm" here to refer to the economic concept of coordinating productive activity through a process of hierarchical or bureaucratic decision making rather than through the price system and discrete contracts. On the economics of the firm, see Armen Alchian & Harold Demsetz, *Production, Information Costs, and Economic Organization*, 62 AM. ECON. REV. 777 (1972); Ronald Coase, *The Nature of the Firm*, 4 Economica 386 (1937); Benjamin Klein, Stephen Crawford & Armen Alchian, *Vertical Integration, Appropriable Rents, and the Competitive Contracting Process*, J.L. & ECON. 297 (1978); Oliver Williamson, *Transaction Costs Economics: The Governance of Contractual Relations*, J.L. &

ECON. 233 (1979). In a seminal contribution, Professor Ronald Coase explained use of the firm as a way of saving transactions costs, such as those of entering into contracts and discovering prices. Later major contributions on the theory of the firm focused on other problems. Alchian & Demsetz, supra, discussed the shirking problem inherent in team production. Others, including professors Klein, Crawford & Alchian and Williamson, discussed the problems of enforcing contracts, including postcontractual opportunism.

3. Relational contracts are, in very general terms, those in which the parties' obligations are not fully specified at the outset of the relationship as in the "classical" form of contract. The contrast between "classical" and "relational" contracting has formed the basis of the work of Professor Ian MacNeil. See, e.g., IAN MCNEIL, THE NEW SOCIAL CONTRACT (1980); Ian MacNeil, Relational Contract: What We Do and Do Not Know, 1985 WIS. L. REV. 483; Ian MacNeil, Economic Analysis of Contractual Relations: Its Shortfalls and the Need for a "Rich Classificatory Apparatus," 75 NW. U. L. REV. 1018 (1981); Ian MacNeil, Contracts: Adjustment of Long-Term Economic Relations Under Classical, Neoclassical and Relational Contract Law, 72 NW. U. L. REV. 854 (1978); Ian MacNeil, The Many Futures of Contracts, 47 S. CAL. L. REV. 691 (1974). The parties may turn to relational contracts for reasons similar to those leading to the choice of the firm type of organization, such as reduction of postcontractual opportunism. See Charles Goetz & Robert Scott, Principles of Relational Contracts, 67 VA. L. REV. 1089 (1981). In fact, relational-type contracting blends seamlessly with governance within a firm. See Barry Baysinger & Henry N. Butler, Vertical Restraints of Trade as Contractual Integration: A Synthesis of Relational Contracting Theory, Transaction-Cost Economics and Organizational Theory, 32 EMORY L.J. 1009 (1983).

4. The continuum between corporations and other types of contracts is significant throughout this book, particularly in Chapter Five, which concerns Constitutional enforcement of the parties' choice of law.

5. An illustration of how choice of organizational form reflects trade-offs of agency costs against other benefits of the form is the selection of the franchise contract rather than fully integrating the sales network within a single business association. Both theory and evidence support the assertion that brand-name owners select franchises rather than company-owned stores to help solve monitoring problems. For example, firms are most likely to franchise outlets that rely on transient trade, and therefore will attract business primarily on the basis of the franchiser's brand name rather than local repeat business. See James A. Brickley, Frederick H. Dark & Michael S. Weisbach, An Agency Perspective on Franchising, 20 FIN. MGT. 27 (1991); James A. Brickley & Frederick H. Dark, The Choice of Organizational Form: The Case of Franchising, 18 J. FIN. ECON. 401 (1987); Anthony W. Dnes, "Unfair" Contractual Practices and Hostages in Franchise Contracts, 148 J. INST. & THEO. ECON. 484 (1992); Alan Krueger, Ownership, Agency, and Wages: An Examination of Franchising in the Fast Food Industry, 106 Q. J. ECON. 75 (1991); Robert E. Martin, Franchising and Risk Management, 78 AMER. ECON. REV. 954 (1988); G. Frank Mathewson & Ralph A. Winter, The Economics of Franchise Contracts,

28 J.L. & ECON. 503 (1985); Seth W. Norton, *Franchising, Labor Productivity, and the New Institutional Economics*, 145 J. INST. & THEO. ECON. 578 (1989); Seth W. Norton, *An Empirical Look at Franchising as an Organizational Form*, 61 J. BUS. 197 (1988); Paul H. Rubin, *The Theory of the Firm and the Structure of the Franchise Contract*, 21 J. L. & ECON. 221 (1978). Thus, the parties select the contractual form that optimizes the costs and benefits of the relationship.

6. Professor Michael Jensen, a leading efficient market theorist, has said that "there is no other proposition in economics which has more empirical evidence supporting it than the efficient markets hypothesis." Michael Jensen, *Some Anomalous Evidence Regarding Market Efficiency*, 6 J. FIN. ECON. 95, 96 (1978).

7. This does not, of course, apply to close corporations. However, the participants in closely held firms contract with each other directly, and so do not need the protection of the securities markets as a constraint on the development of efficient arrangements. That is not to say that fiduciary duties are irrelevant, or even less relevant, in closely held than in publicly held firms, but only that the absence of an efficient securities market in shares of closely held firms does not present a problem with respect to contracting around such duties. As to the differences between close and public corporations, see Henry G. Manne, *Our Two Corporation Systems: Law and Economics*, 53 VA. L. REV. 259 (1967).

8. It is commonly accepted that market efficiency varies in degree depending on the nature of the information. The "strong form" of the theory holds that market value reflects all relevant information; the "semi-strong" that market value reflects all public information; and the "weak form" that market prices move in relation to information rather than according to established patterns of price movement. See Eugene Fama, *Random Walks in Stock Market Prices*, 21 FIN. ANAL. J. 55 (1965). Professor Fama recently published a revision of his thinking. See Eugene Fama, *Efficient Capital Markets: II*, 46 J. FIN. 1575 (1991). Fama now divides the three efficiency categories, based tests of efficiency, into (1) tests of return predictability; (2) event studies; and (3) tests for private information.

9. For a discussion of the interrelation of methods of disclosure and degrees of market efficiency, see Ronald Gilson & Reinier Kraakman, *The Mechanisms of Market Efficiency*, 70 VA. L. REV. 549 (1984).

10. See Robert E. Verrechia, *On the Theory of Market Information Efficiency*, 1 J.ACCT. & ECON. 77 (1979).

11. For further discussion of the effect and significance of the state competition for corporate charters, see infra Part III.E.

12. See infra Subsection II.C.1.

13. Much recent commentary criticizes the evidence supporting market efficiency. For summaries of criticism of the efficient capital markets hypothesis, see Jeffrey Gordon & Kornhauser, *Efficient Markets, Costly Information, and Securities Research*, 60 N.Y.U. L. REV. 761 (1986); Reinier Kraakman, *Taking Discounts Seriously: The Implications of "Discounted" Share Prices as an Acquisition Motive*, 88 COLUM. L. REV. 891 (1988); Donald Langevoort, *Theories, Assump-*

tions, and Securities Regulation: Market Efficiency Revisited, 140 U. PA. L. REV. 851 (1992). However, even evidence of market inefficiency does not necessarily undermine the argument in support of enforcing corporate contracts. For example, one of the principal arguments against market efficiency is that securities prices do not accurately reflect all available information because they also reflect "noise" or biases of uninformed traders. See Fisher Black, *Noise,* 41 J. FIN. 529 (1986). But even in a generally "noisy" market, "real" information, including information about the contract terms constraining managers, continues to affect stock prices. See Daniel R. Fischel, *Efficient Capital Markets, the Crash, and the Fraud on the Market Theory,* 74 CORNELL L. REV. 907 (1989). While it may be impossible to fully disentangle the effects of "noise" from those of underlying facts, this does not mean that a contract that ignores investor interests will go unpunished in the market. Moreover, none of this recent theory suggests that government regulators can better value firms or governance arrangements than can the market.

14. This view is clearly reflected in Professors Fama's and Jensen's statement: "Absent fiat, the form of organization that survives in an activity is the one that delivers the product demanded by customers at the lowest price while covering costs." Eugene Fama & Michael Jensen, *Separation of Ownership and Control,* 26 J.L. & ECON. 301, 301 (1983).

15. The legal corporate governance debate tends to focus on the internal corporate relationship between managers (a term that includes officers and directors) and shareholders. The contractual theory of the corporation refers to that relationship under which managers are the shareholders' agents. See Jensen & Meckling, supra note # 1, at 305.

16. As discussed in Section III.E, infra, the role of state law in governance of the corporation is consistent with private ordering under conditions of jurisdictional choice in the market for corporate charters. Conversely, federal regulation of the corporation is consistent with the anticontractarian position.

17. ADOLF BERLE & GARDINER MEANS, THE MODERN CORPORATION AND PRIVATE PROPERTY (1932).

18. See Henry G. Manne, *Some Theoretical Aspects of Share Voting: An Essay in Honor of Adolf A. Berle,* 64 COLUM. L.REV. 1427, 1440–42 (1964).

19. Common shareholders generally have one vote per share of stock and may freely transfer this vote, but only in connection with a sale of the stock. This interrelationship of voting rights and financial interests ensures that voting will be exercised consistently with the economic welfare of the firm. See Frank Easterbrook & Daniel R. Fischel, *Voting in Corporate Law,* 26 J.L. & ECON. 395 (1983). However, this does not mean that one-share-one-vote is necessarily optimal in all circumstances. See Daniel R. Fischel, *Organized Exchanges and the Regulation of Dual Class Common Stock,* 54 U. CHI. L. REV. 119 (1987).

20. The seminal article is Henry G. Manne, *Mergers and the Market for Corporate Control,* 73 J. POL. ECON. 110 (1965).

21. For reviews of the evidence, see Gregg A. Jarrell, James A. Brickley & Jeffry N. Netter, The Market for Corporate Control: The Evidence Since 1980,

2 J.ECON. PERSP. 49 (1988); Roberta Romano, *A Guide To Takeovers: Theory, Evidence, and Regulation,* 9 YALE J. ON REG. 119 (1992) (arguing that evidence shows that most regulation of takeovers is unwarranted).

22. For evidence that voting rights have market value, see Ronald C. Lease, John J. McConnell & Wayne H. Mikkelson, *The Market Value of Control in Publicly-Traded Corporations,* 11 J. FIN. ECON. 439 (1983). Also, the mere fact that such voting rights have survived more than fifty years after Berle and Means concluded they were meaningless is of some significance.

23. See ALFRED CHANDLER, STRATEGY AND STRUCTURE: CHAPTERS IN THE HISTORY OF INDUSTRIAL ENTERPRISE (1962); Oliver Williamson, *Markets and Hierarchies* (1975); Oliver Williamson, *The Modern Corporation: Origins, Evolution, Attributes,* 19 J. ECON. LITERATURE 1537 (1981).

24. Fama and Jensen, supra note 14.

25. Teece, *Internal Organization and Economic Performance: An Empirical Analysis of the Profitability of Principal Firms,* 30 J. INDUS. ECON. 173 (1981).

26. Barry D. Baysinger & Henry N. Butler, *Revolution versus Evolution in Corporation Law: The ALI's Project and the Independent Director,* 52 GEO. WASH. L. REV. 557 (1985); Barry D. Baysinger & Henry N. Butler, *Corporate Governance and the Board of Directors: Performance Effects of Changes in Board Composition,* 1 J.L. ECON. & ORGANIZATION 101 (1985); John W. Byrd & Kent A. Hickman, *Do Outside Directors Monitor Managers? Evidence from Tender Offer Bids,* 32 J. FIN. ECON. 195 (1992). Additional internal monitoring to improve financial performance is provided by outside auditors. See Ross L. Watts & Jerold L. Zimmerman, *Agency Problems, Auditing, and the Theory of the Firm: Some Evidence,* 26 J.L. & ECON. 613 (1983).

27. See Douglas W. Diamond & Robert E. Verrechia, *Optimal Managerial Contracts and Equilibrium Security Prices,* 37 J. FIN. 275 (1982).

28. Eugene Fama, *Agency Problems and Theory of the Firm,* 88 J. POL. ECON. 288 (1980). There have been criticism and calls for reform of executive compensation in recent months. The Securities and Exchange Commission recently increased disclosure requirements regarding executive compensation. See Executive Compensation Disclosure, Sec. Act. Rel. 6940, Exchange Act Rel. 30,851, 57 F.R. 29,582 (1992). These revisions came in the wake of proposed congressional action, including a proposed "Corporate Pay Responsibility Act," S. 2030, 102nd Cong., 2d Sess. (1992). The criticism and proposals, in turn, came in the wake of significant curtailment of the takeover market which, as we argued above, is vital in constraining agency costs. Accordingly, excessive compensation may point to the need for less regulation of the corporate contract, not more.

29. See Roger L. Faith, Higgins & Tollison, *Managerial Rents and Outside Recruitment in the Coasian Firm,* 74 ECON. REV. 60 (1984).

30. See generally, Harold Demsetz & Kenneth Lehn, *The Structure of Corporate Ownership: Causes and Consequences,* 93 J. POL. ECON. 1155 (1985).

31. For recent commentary on monitoring by large shareholders, see Bernard Black, *Agents Watching Agents: The Promise of Institutional Investor Voice,* 39 U.C.L.A. L. REV. 811 (1992); Bernard Black, *The Value of Institutional*

Investor Monitoring: The Empirical Evidence, 39 U.C.L.A. L. REV. 895 (1992); Bernard Black, *Shareholder Passivity Reexamined*, 89 MICH. L. REV. 520 (1990); John Coffee, *Liquidity vs. Control: The Institutional Investor as Corporate Monitor*, 91 COLUM. L. REV. 1277 (1991); Ronald J. Gilson & Reinier Kraakman, *Reinventing the Outside Director: An Agenda for Institutional Investors*, 43 STAN. L. REV. 863 (1991); Edward Rock, *The Logic and (Uncertain) Significance of Institutional Shareholder Activism*, 79 GEO. L.J. 445 (1991).

32. Eugene Fama & Michael Jensen, *Organizational Forms and Investment Decisions*, 14 J. FIN. ECON. 101 (1985); Fama & Jensen, supra note 14; Manne, supra note 18.

33. Fama and Jensen, supra note 32, at 107.

34. Franco Modigliani and Merton Miller, *The Cost of Capital, Corporation Finance and the Theory of Investment*, 48 AM. ECON. REV. 261 (1958).

35. See Jensen & Meckling, supra note 15.

36. Among other things, a high-dividend policy may align manager and shareholder interests with regard to the level of risk. See Frank Easterbrook, *Two Agency-Cost Explanations of Dividends*, 74 AM. ECON. REV. 650 (1984). This may explain the long-standing puzzle as to why dividends are paid. See, e.g., Fisher Black, *The Dividend Puzzle*, 2 J. PORTFOLIO MANAGEMENT 5 (1976).

37. See Michael Jensen, *Agency Costs of Free Cash Flow, Corporate Finance and Takeovers*, 76 AM. ECON. Rev. 323 (1986) (explaining that debt, unlike dividends, bonds future payouts). Jensen's theory may explain a substantial portion of the premia paid in leveraged buyouts. Note, however, that the managers may demand to be compensated for taking the insolvency risk inherent in a high debt firm.

38. Technically these risks will be taken on the equity holders' behalf by managers to the extent that the managers' interests are aligned with those of the shareholders. On the other hand, as mentioned above, the managers may also act as subordinated debt holders and therefore contrary to shareholder interests.

39. The choice between secured and unsecured lending may be amenable to a similar type of explanation. See Thomas Jackson & Anthony Kronman, *Secured Financing and Priorities among Creditors*, 88 YALE L.J. 1143 (1979); Robert Scott, *A Relational Theory of Secured Financing*, 86 COLUM. L. REV. 901 (1986); Clifford W. Smith, Jr., & Jerold B. Warner, *On Financial Contracting: An Analysis of Bond Covenants*, 7 J. FIN. ECON. 117 (1979).

40. It is important, however, to note that markets and incentive devices can respond even to final-period problems. See Lee A. Craig & Charles R. Knoeber, *Manager Shareholding, the Market for Managers, and the End-Period Problem: Evidence from the U.S. Whaling Industry*, 8 J.L. ECON. & ORGANIZATION 607 (1992) (discussing evidence that management shareholdings in whaling industry varied with end-period problem).

41. See Oliver Williamson, *The Economic Institutions of Capitalism* 46 (1985).

42. For discussions of the costs of fiduciary duties, see Kenneth Davis, *Judicial Review of Fiduciary Decisionmaking—Some Theoretical Perspectives*, 80 Nw. U. L. REV. 1 (1985); Daniel Fischel & Michael Bradley, *The Role of Liability Rules*

150

and the Derivative Suit in Corporate Law: A Theoretical and Empirical Analysis, 71 CORNELL L. REV. 261 (1986).

43. See Frank H. Easterbrook & Daniel R. Fischel, *Contract and Fiduciary Duty*, 37 J.L. & ECON. 425 (1993).

44. See B & H Warehouse, Inc. v. Atlas Van Lines, Inc., 490 F.2d 818 (5th Cir. 1974); John C. Coffee, Jr., *No Exit: Opting Out, The Contractual Theory of the Corporation, and the Special Case of Remedies*, 53 BROOK. L. REV. 919, 962n.9109 (see fn. 67). Retroactive share transfer restrictions may also be invalid by statute. See Del. Stat. Ann. tit. 8, §202(b) (Michie 1986).

45. It follows that a statute that imposed an opt-out provision in the face of such a qualification would trump the corporate contract, and would accordingly be unenforceable under the Contract Clause. See Chapter Two, infra, text accompanying notes 116–25.

46. See Chapter Two, infra.

47. For statutory definitions of director duties that eliminate negligence liability for corporations chartered in the applicable state, see Ind. Code Ann. §23-1-35-1(e) (Burns Supp. 1987); Va. Code Ann. §13.1-690(A) (1987).

48. See infra text accompanying notes 93–97.

49. For commentary advocating regulation of corporate contracts because shareholders are not adequately protected, see Lucian A. Bebchuk, *Federalism and the Corporation: The Desirable Limits on State Competition in Corporate Law*, 105 HARV. L. REV. 1435 (1992); Jeffrey N. Gordon, *Ties That Bond: Dual Class Common Stock and the Problem of Shareholder Choice*, 75 CAL. L. REV. 1 (1988).

50. For recent discussions of the role of institutional investors, see supra note 31.

51. This "internal affairs" rule is discussed in more detail in Chapter Five supra.

52. William Cary, *Federalism and Corporate Law: Reflections Upon Delaware*, 83 YALE L.J. 663 (1974).

53. See RALPH WINTER, GOVERNMENT AND THE CORPORATION (1978); Daniel Fischel, *The "Race to the Bottom" Revisited: Reflections on Recent Developments in Delaware's Corporation Law*, 76 NW. U. L. REV. 913 (1982); Peter Dodd & Richard Leftwich, *The Market for Corporate Charters: "Unhealthy Competition" Versus Federal Regulation*, 53 J. BUS. 59 (1980).

54. For theory and evidence supporting this point, see Barry Baysinger & Henry N. Butler, *The Role of Corporate Law in the Theory of the Firm*, 28 J.L. & ECON. 179 (1985) (arguing that firms will choose states with "strict" or "liberal" rules in terms of the degree of constraint on managers according to the relative monitoring capacity of the shareholders); Roberta Romano, *Law as a Product: Some Pieces of the Incorporation Puzzle*, 1 J.L. ECON. & ORGANIZATION 225 (1985) (stating that firms tend to reincorporate in Delaware if they intend to engage in a specific transaction that is facilitated in that state).

55. See Jonathan Macey & Geoffrey Miller, *Toward an Interest-Group Theory of Delaware Corporate Law*, 65 TEX. L. REV. 469 (1987). If lawyers are favored in code drafting, one reason why this is not competed away in the corporate chartering market is that lawyers are given substantial power within corpora-

tions to make chartering decisions. This power cannot be withdrawn without losing some of the advantages of the lawyers' expertise. In other words, the charter-selection process involves the same tradeoffs of agency costs and the benefits of using agents that are involved in other elements of the corporate contract.

56. For a discussion of why the efficiency of state law cannot be presumed in the absence of effective competition, see Larry E. Ribstein, *Efficiency, Regulation and Competition: A Comment on Easterbrook & Fischel*, 87 Nw. U. L. Rev. 254 (1992).

57. See David Haddock & Jonathan Macey, *Regulation on Demand: A Private Interest Model, With an Application to Insider Trading Regulation*, 30 J.L. & Econ. 311 (1986).

58. The literature is far too extensive to list. Some of the major contributions to the development of the economic theory of the firm are cited in supra note 2. Legal commentaries reflecting this contractual theory include Nicholas Wolfson, The Modern Corporation: Free Markets versus Regulation (1984); Barry Baysinger & Henry N. Butler, *Antitakeover Amendments, Managerial Entrenchment, and the Contractual Theory of the Corporation*, 71 Va. L. Rev. 1257 (1985); David Haddock, Jonathan Macey & Fred S. McChesney, *Property Rights in Assets and Resistance to Tender Offers*, 73 Va. L. Rev. 701 (1987); Daniel R. Fischel, *The Corporate Governance Movement*, 35 Vand. L. Rev. 1259 (1982).

59. See, e.g., Victor Brudney, *Corporate Governance, Agency Costs, and the Rhetoric of Contract*, 85 Colum. L. Rev. 1403 (1985).

60. 17 U.S. (4 Wheat.) 518 (1819).

61. Id. at 635 (cited with approval in CTS Corporation v. Dynamics Corporation of America, 481 U.S. 69, 89 (1987)).

62. Thus, Justice Marshall described the Dartmouth College charter as "a contract, on the faith of which, real and personal estate has been conveyed to the corporation. It is then a contract within the letter of the Constitution." Id. at 644.

63. Id. at 627.

64. See Chapter Two, infra text accompanying notes 59–65.

65. For a discussion of the evolution of American corporate law from special to general incorporation see Henry N. Butler, *Nineteenth Century Jurisdictional Competition in the Granting of Corporate Privileges*, 14 J. Leg. Stud. 129 (1985).

66. See Austin v. Michigan Chamber of Commerce, 494 U.S. 652 (1990), discussed in Chapter Three, infra text accompanying notes 23–25; CTS Corp. v. Dynamics Corp. Am., 482 U.S. 69 1 (1987), discussed in infra Chapter Five, text accompanying notes 196–98.

67. See Brudney, supra note 59, at 1415; Coffee, supra note 44, at 939–40.

68. See Fred S. McChesney, *Law, Economics, and Law and Economics in the Corporate Field: A Comment on Eisenberg*, 89 Colum. L. Rev. 1530 (1989).

69. For another argument supporting this conclusion, see Bernard S. Black, *Is Corporate Law Trivial?: A Political and Economic Analysis*, 84 Nw. U. L. Rev. 542 (1990).

70. See, e.g., Del. Stat. Ann. tit. 8, §251(c).

71. See, e.g., Del. Stat. Ann. tit. 8, §262(a).

72. See Hariton v. Arco Electronics, Inc., 188 A.2d 123 (S.Ct. 1963). But see Farris v. Glen Alden Corp., 143 A.2d 25 (1958).

73. See, e.g., Del. Stat. Ann. tit. 8, §170(a).

74. See, e.g., id. §244(a)(4) (board allowing to increase surplus by reducing capital amounts in excess of par). See generally BAYLESS MANNING, LEGAL CAPITAL (2d ed. 1985).

75. 328 N.E.2d 505 (1975).

76. For a contrary view on this specific question see Frank Easterbrook & Daniel Fischel, *Close Corporations and Agency Costs*, 38 STAN. L. REV. 271, 294 (1986).

77. To see this point, consider what the result in *Donahue* would have been if all of the parties had explicitly contracted that the corporation could purchase stock owned by controlling shareholders without buying stock owned by the minority.

78. Limited partners have only those voting rights granted them by the partnership agreement. See Uniform Limited Partnership Act, §302 (1985). With respect to opting out of fiduciary duties by disincorporating, see Larry E. Ribstein, *Unlimited Contracting in the Delaware Limited Partnership and its Implications for Corporate Law*, 17 J. CORP. L. 299 (1991).

79. See, e.g., Lewis D. Solomon & Kathleen J. Collins, *Humanistic Economics: A New Model for the Corporate Social Responsibility Debate*, 12 J. CORP. L. 331, 338 (1987). In his recent book, Richard Epstein endorses the basic premise of the regulatory theory that limited liability is a concession of the state, but argues that the doctrine of unconstitutional conditions prevents states from using their concession power to restrict corporate constitutional rights. *See* Epstein, *Bargaining with the State*, 107–26 (1993). The concession theory is no sounder in the hands of an antiregulatory theorist than in those of proregulatory commentators. Corporations should not be relegated to the doubtful protection of the unconstitutional conditions theory when constitutional rights should apply directly. Moreover, application of that broad theory may prevent state law from serving its useful role in defining contract terms. See chapters 3 and 4.

80. For elaboration of this point, see Larry E. Ribstein, *Limited Liability and Theories of the Corporation*, 50 MD. L. REV. 80 (1991).

81. See Uniform Partnership Act, §§6, 7(4) (defining partnership and certain profit-sharing arrangements that are not presumptively partnerships, respectively). Indeed, in several states, even partners may have limited liability by registering as a "limited liability partnership." See Del. Stat. tit. 6, §1515; La. Rev. Stat. §3431 (1993); N.C. Stat. §59–45 (1993); Tex. Rev. Unif. Partnership Act §3.08 (1993).

82. See, e.g., Cislaw v. Southland Corp., 6 Cal. Rptr. 2d 386 (1992).

83. See Henry Hansmann & Reinier Kraakman, *Toward Unlimited Shareholder Liability for Corporate Torts*, 100 YALE L.J. 1879 (1991); David Leebron, *Limited Liability, Tort Victims, and Creditors*, 91 COLUM. L. REV. 1565 (1991); see

NOTES TO PAGES 22–24

also Janet C. Alexander, *Unlimited Shareholder Liability Through a Procedural Lens*, 106 HARV. L. REV. 387 (1992); Henry Hansmann & Reinier Kraakman, *Response: A Procedural Focus on Unlimited Shareholder Liability*, 106 HARV. L. REV. 446 (1992); Theresa A. Gabaldon, *The Lemonade Stand: Feminist and Other Reflections on the Limited Liability of Corporate Shareholders*, 45 VAND. L. REV. 1387–1456 (1992).

84. Joseph Grundfest, *The Limited Future of Unlimited Liability*, 102 YALE L.J. 387 (1992); Larry E. Ribstein, *The Deregulation of Limited Liability and the Death of Partnership*, 70 WASH. U. L.Q. 417 (1992).

85. See, e.g., Brudney, supra note 59.

86. See George Priest, *A Theory of the Consumer Product Warranty*, 90 YALE L.J. 1297 (1981) (explaining how optimal contracts can be produced in the absence of bargaining).

87. See William Bratton, *The Economics and Jurisprudence of Convertible Bonds*, 1984 WIS. L. REV. 667, 686 (arguing that standard bond forms save drafting costs and facilitate efficient market pricing); Charles Goetz & Robert Scott, *The Limits of Expanded Choice: An Analysis of the Interactions Between Express and Implied Contract Terms*, 73 CAL. L. REV. 261, 265–73 (1985) (discussing formulation errors as a primary factor in the development of standard terms); MacNeil, The Many Futures of Contracts, supra note 3, at 771 (asserting that standardization of contract increases confidence of contracting party in the deal). As to reduced information costs, see Broad v. Rockwell Int'l Corp., 642 F.2d 929, 943 (5th Cir.) (en banc), *cert. denied*, 454 U.S. 965 (1981).

A large degree of uniformity in the language of debenture indentures is essential to the effective functioning of the financial markets; uniformity of the indentures that govern competing debenture issues is what makes it possible meaningfully to compare one debenture issue with another, focusing only on the business provisions of the issue (such as the interest rate, the maturity date, the redemption and sinking fund provisions and the conversion rate) and the economic conditions of the issuer, without being misled by peculiarities in the underlying instruments.

88. Public corporation shareholders may superficially resemble consumers of mass-produced products who are protected by substantial legal regulation—dispersed, incapable of bargaining effectively over terms, and uninformed. Indeed, corporate shareholders may seem even more in need of protection than consumers because the "product" they are buying is complex, described in arcane terms, and difficult to fully evaluate. However, even consumer product markets are competitive as long as there are a substantial number of comparison shoppers. See Alan Schwartz & Louis Wilde, *Intervening in Markets on the Basis of Imperfect Information: A Legal and Economic Analysis*, 127 U. PA. L. REV. 630 (1979). Moreover, despite the superficial similarity between consumers and investors, corporate shareholders and consumer product purchasers differ significantly. Efficient securities markets make price information virtually free. Also, securities analysts and the financial press perform the function of comparison shoppers in the

154

consumer context. While in the consumer context information learned by comparison shoppers cannot be readily communicated to non-shoppers, the efficient market facilitates communication of information learned by analysts and others concerning contract terms. It follows that, even if there are only a few informed participants, the efficient securities markets provide pressure toward competitive terms. Shareholders need to look only at the trading price in order to receive a normal rate of return. Moreover, the purchaser of corporate stock is not buying an "unknowable" future risk of managerial misconduct. He is instead buying a detailed package that includes monitoring devices (such as outside boards and auditors), incentive compensation, and managers with substantial reputational investments, and that can be priced in efficient securities markets. As such, the corporate contract cannot be regarded as an "experience" good for which information can be obtained only by using it. See Phillip Nelson, *Information and Consumer Behavior*, 78 J. POL. ECON. 311 (1970); Michael R. Darby & Edi Karni, *Free Competition and the Optimal Amount of Fraud*, 16 J.L. & ECON. 67 (1973). The purchaser of an automobile is, on the other hand, buying an intricately complex machine that he will use under many different circumstances (some of which are unforeseeable) over a period of several years.

89. See Melvin A. Eisenberg, *The Structure of Corporate Law*, 89 COLUM. L. REV. 1461, 1485–88 (1989). For a recent application of the "implicit contract" approach to justify stakeholder (mostly employee) protection, see Katherine Van Wezel Stone, *Policing Employment Contracts within the Nexus-of-Contracts Firm*, 43 U. TORONTO L. J. 353 (1993). This article is cogently criticized in William J. Carney, *Two Modes of Discourse in the Stakeholder Debate*, 43 U. TORONTO L.J. 379 (1993).

90. See Clive Bull, *Implicit Contracts in the Absence of Enforcement and Risk Aversion*, 73 AM. ECON. REV. 658 (1983); Rosen, *Implicit Contracts: A Survey*, 23 J. ECON. LITERATURE 1144 (1985).

91. See George A. Akerloff, *The Market for 'Lemons': Qualitative Uncertainty and the Market Mechanism*, 84 Q.J. ECON. 488 (1970).

92. See Coffee, supra note 44 at 946, 948.

93. Several commentators have expressed a preference for court-made over statutory rules concerning corporate governance. See Ian Ayres, *Judging Close Corporations in the Age of Statutes*, 70 WASH. U. L.Q. 365 (1992); Robert C. Clark, *Contracts, Elites and Traditions in the Making of Corporate Law*, 89 COLUM. L. REV. 1703 (1989); John C. Coffee, Jr., *The Mandatory/Enabling Balance in Corporate Law: An Essay on the Judicial Role*, 89 COLUM. L. REV. 1618 (1989). However, the discussion in the text focuses on the inherent defects of judicial rulemaking as compared with private ordering, rather than as compared with legislation.

94. See Daniel Fischel & Michael Bradley, *The Role of Liability Rules and the Derivative Suit in Corporate Law: A Theoretical and Empirical Analysis*, 71 CORNELL L. REV. 261 (1986).

95. See Alan Schwartz and Louis L. Wilde, *Intervening in Markets on the Basis of Imperfect Information: A Legal and Economic Analysis*, 127 U. PA. L. REV.

630, 678 (1979) (advocating administrative rather than judicial intervention in markets because the stakes in individual cases are seldom sufficient to justify broad inquiry).

96. R. McCormick & R. Tollison, Politicians, Legislation and the Economy: An Inquiry Into the Interest Group Theory of Government 6 (1981). Indeed, no one's motivations are beyond question. Because courts may be subject to various types of legislative pressure, it is no solution to leave most corporate questions for judicial determination, as suggested in the commentary cited supra note 93. The motivation problem underlying mandatory legal rules goes even deeper. Moreover, as Irving Kristol has suggested, law professors proposing broad legal intrusion into corporate governance stand to gain as lawyers, consultants, and outside directors. See Irving R. Kristol, "The War Against the Corporation," Wall St. J., January 24, 1989, at A20. For a more extensive public choice analysis of law professors' role in formulating corporate law, see Larry E. Ribstein, *The Mandatory Nature of the ALI Code*, 61 Geo. Wash. L. Rev. 984 (1993).

97. See Henry N. Butler, *Corporation-Specific Anti-Takeover Statutes and the Market for Corporate Law*, 1988 Wis. L. Rev. 365; Roberta Romano, *The Political Economy of Takeover Statutes*, 73 Va. L. Rev. 1 (1987).

98. See Barry Baysinger & Asghar Zardkoohi, *Technology, Residual Claimants, and Corporate Control*, 1 J.L. Econ. & Organization 339 (1986); Demsetz & Lehn, supra note 30.

99. See Barry Baysinger & Henry Butler, supra note 26.

100. For a discussion noting this problem in the consumer contract area, see Schwartz and Wilde, supra note 95, at 667. Even if limitations on opt-out provisions cannot be completely evaded and therefore are at least partially effective, the substitutability of terms results in considerable confusion and unpredictability, thereby increasing investor uncertainty as brand names necessarily convey less than complete information.

101. See, e.g., Farris v. Glen Alden Corp., 143 A.2d 25 (1958).

102. See, e.g., Pratt v. Ballman-Cummings Furniture Co., 495 S.W.2d 509 (1973).

103. See Larry E. Ribstein, *An Applied Theory of Limited Partnership*, 37 Emory L. J. 837 (1988).

104. See generally, Larry E. Ribstein & Robert Keatinge, Ribstein & Keatinge on Limited Liability Companies (1994).

105. The Uniform Partnership Act, which applies in this respect to both limited and general partnerships, permits a partner to receive an individual benefit from the firm with the consent of the other partners. See U.P.A. §21 (1914), 6 U.L.A. (1969). Thus, a partner may be permitted under the partnership agreement to reap personal benefit from partnership opportunities. See Singer v. Singer, 634 P.2d 766 (Okla.App. 1981). See generally Alan R. Bromberg & Larry E. Ribstein, Bromberg and Ribstein on Partnership, §7.07(h) (1988). See also Ribstein, supra note 78 (discussing Delaware limited partnership statutory provision explicitly making limited partnerships in that state subject to private ordering). Note, however, that a new version of the

Uniform Partnership Act recently has been promulgated which limits waivers of fiduciary duties. See U.P.A. §103(b) (1992). Interestingly enough, Melvin Eisenberg, a leading adherent of the regulatory theory of the corporation, perhaps aware of the potential competition between the partnership and corporate forms, wrote letters to the National Conference of Commissioners on Uniform State Laws on the eve of its adoption of the Revised Uniform Partnership Act, ("RUPA") urging the Commissioners not to permit waiver of fiduciary duties as was provided in the draft presented to the Commissioners for approval. The Commissioners changed RUPA at the last minute to prohibit fiduciary duty waivers. For a discussion of RUPA and the Eisenberg letters, see Larry E. Ribstein, *The Revised Uniform Partnership Act; Not Ready for Prime Time*, 49 Bus. Lawyer 45, 58, n. 102 (1993).

CHAPTER 2: PROTECTION OF THE CORPORATE CONTRACT

1. For an elaboration of this point, see Larry E. Ribstein, *Efficiency, Regulation and Competition: A Comment on Easterbrook & Fischel*, 87 Nw. U. L. Rev. 254 (1992).

2. 290 U.S. 398 (1934). For further discussion of *Blaisdell*, see infra.

3. Id. at 455.

4. Epstein argues that the Contract Clause only applies to state laws because rent-seeking was limited at the federal level through processes such as separation of powers. See Richard Epstein, *Toward a Revitalization of the Contract Clause*, 51 U. Chi. L. Rev. 703, 714 (1984).

5. See Epstein, supra note 4; Kmiec & McGinnis, *The Contract Clause: A Return to the Original Understanding*, 14 Hastings Const. L. Q. 525 (1987); Jonathan R. Macey, *Promoting Public-Regarding Legislation Through Statutory Interpretation: An Interest Group Model*, 86 Colum. L. Rev. 223, 242–250 (1986); Cass Sunstein, *Naked Preferences and the Constitution*, 84 Colum. L. Rev. 1689 (1984).

6. Gordon Tullock, *The Welfare Costs of Tariffs, Monopolies and Theft*, 5 West. Econ. J. 224 (1967).

7. See generally, Sam Peltzman, *Toward a More General Theory of Economic Regulation*, 19 J.L. & Econ. 211 (1976); Richard A. Posner, *Theories of Economic Regulation*, 5 Bell. J. Econ. 335 (1974); George Stigler, *The Economic Theory of Regulation*, 2 Bell J. Econ. 3 (1971).

8. As a result, contract-impairing legislation cannot be Pareto-optimal in the sense of creating winners without making anyone worse off. At best, contract impairment is Kaldor-Hicks efficient, but only if the social benefit from the legislation exceeds losses to impaired parties.

9. See Richard Epstein, Takings 74–92 (1985) (arguing that appropriation of subject of contract that frustrates rights of prospective buyer should be a compensable taking).

10. See Ogden v. Saunders, 25 U.S. (12 Wheat.) 213 (1827); Robert Hale, *The Supreme Court and the Contract Clause*, 57 Harv. L. Rev. 512, 518–33 (1944).

11. See Ogden 25 U.S. at 339; Epstein, supra note 4, at 723–30.

12. The Contract Clause also has not been applied to impairment of

unaccrued remedies (e.g., shortening the statute of limitations) as distinguished from rights under contracts. See Hale, supra note 10, at 533–37. As with prospective limits on contracting, winners and losers cannot necessarily be identified at the time of the regulation. Finally, the Clause does not apply to frustration of the object of the contract. See Hale, supra note 10, at 671–74. Again, winners and losers are less likely to be clearly identifiable here than with contract impairment because frustration of the object of the contract can hurt both contracting parties.

13. Nevertheless, as discussed below, the "reasonable and necessary" qualification of the Contract Clause in effect eliminates the categorical approach in favor of just such a review.

14. 17 U.S. (4 Wheat.) 518 (1819).

15. Id. at 644–45.

16. See generally LAWRENCE TRIBE, CONSTITUTIONAL LAW (2d ed., 1988).

17. 290 U.S. 398 (1934).

18. Id. at 434–35. The reservation of power argument first appeared in Justice Johnson's dissent in Fletcher v. Peck, 10 U.S. (6 Cranch.) 87 (1810). For a discussion of the history of this idea in the Supreme Court see Hale, supra note 10, at 872–83.

19. Id. at 439.

20. Id. at 444–45.

21. After Blaisdell it might have been possible for the Court to put the reserved-power genie back in the bottle by restricting Blaisdell to its special facts. In fact, in some cases the Court seemed to move in that direction. In Worthen Co. v. Kavanaugh, 295 U.S. 56 (1935), in an opinion by Justice Cardozo, the Court struck down under the Contract Clause a statute that impaired the rights of holders of bonds by sharply changing the provisions for enforcing payment of the assessments that backed the bonds. The Court noted that, although the statute declared the existence of an emergency, unlike Blaisdell the bondholders were left without protection and the duration of the statute was not limited. Also, in Treigle v. Acme Homestead Ass'n, 297 U.S. 190 (1936), the Court struck down a statute that limited the withdrawal rights of members of a building and loan association. Although the state supreme court had deemed the statute a valid response to an economic emergency which threatened the survival of building and loan associations, the Court held that the statute merely effected a redistribution among association members.

22. A critical indication of the shift in the Court's approach to the Contract Clause was Veix v. Sixth Ward Ass'n, 310 U.S. 32 (1940), in which the Court upheld a statute limiting the withdrawal rights of building and loan association members, citing the state's power "to safeguard the vital interests of its people" recognized in Blaisdell. The legislation was emergency in nature although not temporary. Treigle was put aside because the statute there was passed after the plaintiff had given notice of withdrawal and was not in the public interest (although it was similar to and motivated by precisely the same concerns as the statute involved in *Veix*).

23. 290 U.S. 398 (1934).

24. See Epstein, supra note 4; Kmiec & McGinnis, supra note 5.

25. The Supreme Court invalidated only two state laws on Contract Clause grounds during this period. See Note, A Process-Oriented Approach to the Contract Clause, 89 YALE L.J. 1623, 1623 (1980).

26. 379 U.S. 497 (1965).

27. Id. at 533.

28. 431 U.S. 1 (1977).

29. Id. at 16.

30. Id. at 25–26. See also infra text accompanying notes 43–51.

31. 438 U.S. 234 (1978).

32. Id. at 438 n.15.

33. Id. at 245.

34. Id. at 246–47.

35. Id. at 247–48.

36. 459 U.S. 400 (1983) (upholding a state statute regulating gas prices that impaired a clause in plaintiff's contract with a utility company that escalated prices up to the state ceiling).

37. 462 U.S. 176 (1983) (upholding a state severance tax statute that prohibited producers from passing the tax through to consumers).

38. 480 U.S. 470 (1987) (upholding a statute providing for liability for subsidence from coal mining that impaired contractual waivers of liability for surface damage). The most recent Contract Clause case, General Motors Corp. v. Romein, 112 S.Ct. 1105 (1992), provides little indication of the Court's direction on the Contract Clause. The case involved a complex and unusual situation in which a state legislature first passed a statute that affected workers' rights to benefits under existing collective bargaining agreements, and then passed another statute retroactively removing the retroactive effect of the first statute. The Court held that the first statute did not give General Motors constitutionally protected contract rights that were impaired by the second statute.

39. See Keystone, 480 U.S. at 505; Exxon Corp., 462 U.S. at 192 n.13; Energy Reserve Group, 459 U.S. at 412–13.

40. Exxon Corp., 462 U.S. at 191–92.

41. Although the Contract Clause is not as prominent a source of Constitutional protection as it once was, it is still being widely applied by the courts to strike down state legislation. See, e.g., In re Walker, 959 F.2d 894 (10th Cir. 1992) (striking down state statute on exemptions for IRAs); Association of Surrogates and Supreme Court Reporters v. N.Y., 940 F.2d 766 (2nd Cir. 1991) (striking down state impairment of public employees' contracts); Northshore Cycles, Inc. v. Yamama Motor Corp., U.S.A., 919 F.2d 1041 (5th Cir. 1990) (striking down law requiring manufacturer to repurchase distributor's inventory).

42. See Kmiec & McGinnis, supra note 5.

43. 438 U.S. 234 (1978).

44. 431 U.S. 1 (1977).

45. Id. at 26 n.25 (citing Perry v. United States, 294 U.S. 330 (1935)).

46. Id. at 53 n.16.

47. Id. at 45 n.13.

48. U.S. Trust, 431 U.S. at 26.

49. This is the teaching of the "public interest" theory of regulation. See generally George Stigler, *The Theory of Economic Regulation*, 2 BELL J. ECON. & MGMT. SCI. 3 (1971).

50. U.S. Trust, 431 U.S. at 62 n.18.

51. Indeed, in light of the obligation to compensate, states may actually have no right to impair their own contracts without paying what amounts to, in effect, damages for breach of contract.

52. 459 U.S. 400 (1983).

53. Id. at 4-17-18, n.25.

54. Id. (citing Note, supra note 25, at 1645).

55. The Court's concern with legislator self-interest is consistent with Richard Epstein's theory of the need for the Contract Clause and other constitutional limits on legislation. See Epstein, supra note 4, at 713–17.

56. See James Buchanan, *Toward Analysis of Closed Behavioral Systems*, in THEORY OF PUBLIC CHOICE: POLITICAL APPLICATIONS OF ECONOMICS (J. Buchanan and R. Tollison eds., 1972).

57. See FRANK H. EASTERBROOK & DANIEL R. FISCHEL, THE ECONOMIC STRUCTURE OF CORPORATE LAW 222–23 (1992) (noting the state-competition constraint on opportunistic antitakeover statutes).

58. See infra text accompanying note 73.

59. See supra text accompanying notes 14–15.

60. 17 U.S. (4 Wheat.) at 708.

61. Del. Gen. Corp. Laws §394.

62. E.g., Looker v. Maynard, 179 U.S. 46 (1900) (requirement of cumulative voting for directors); Miller v. State, 82 U.S. 478 (1872) (change in ratio of city-appointed directors); Adair v. Orrell's Mutual Burial Ass'n, 201 S.E. 2d 905 (N.C. 1974) (requirement that mutual burial association pay benefits in cash to any official funeral director and not merely the association's own funeral director). Mobile Press Register, Inc. v. McGowin, 124 So. 2d 812 (Ala. 1960) (preemptive rights no longer conferred by statute but must be provided for in certificate); But see Coombes v. Getz, 285 U.S. 434 (1932) (statutory reservation of power does not permit impairment of vested property rights or obligations of third parties).

63. There is a superficial analogy to terminable at will franchise or license agreements. However, reserved power provisions actually go farther than terminability at will, since they permit the states not only to terminate, but to alter corporate contracts. The power to terminate is often costly to exercise, since the terminating party loses the benefits of the contract. Thus, a contract including such a power is not completely one-sided. However, because a unilateral power to alter a contract can be used to suit the needs of the altering party, any "contract" including this kind of power would be illusory.

64. See Yoakam v. Providence Biltmore Hotel Co., 34 F.2d 533 (D.R.I.

1929) holding invalid under Delaware law charter amendments which eliminated sinking fund for preferred shareholders); Yukon Mill & Grain Co. v. Vose, 206 P.2d 206 (Okla. 1949) (redemption of preferred stock); State ex rel. Swanson v. Perham, 191 P.2d 689 (Wash. 1948) (alteration of shareholders' right to elect directors by straight rather than cumulative voting); see also A.P. Smith Mfg. Co. v. Barlow, 98 A.2d 581 (N.J. 1953) (enlargement of corporate power to make charitable donations validated as in the public interest but not by reservation of power provision). For a good early discussion of the effect of the contract theory on the application of reservation-of-power provisions see Gustavus Ohlinger, *Some Comments on the Reserved Power to Alter, Amend and Repeal Corporate Charters*, 29 MICH. L. REV. 432 (1931). It is particularly interesting that the most recent Supreme Court opinions on the issue of the application of reserved-power provisions, Coombes v. Getz, 285 U.S. 434 (1932), held that a reserved power provision in the state constitution did not permit alteration of statutory liability of corporate officers to creditors. There is no reason for distinguishing in this respect the contract rights of creditors from those of shareholders.

65. Most partnership acts include specific provisions preventing impairment. See Uniform Partnership Act §4(5), 6 U.L.A. (1969); Uniform Limited Partnership Act §30(2), 6 U.L.A. (1969); Uniform Limited Partnership Act (1985), 6 U.L.A. (Supp. 1988). But see Revised Uniform Partnership Act §107 ("a partnership governed by this [Act] is subject to any amendment or repeal of this [Act]") (1992).

66. See Chapter One, supra text accompanying notes 79–84.

67. See Perry v. Sindermann, 408 U.S. 593, 597 (1972); Littlefield v. City of Afton, 785 F.2d 596 (8th Cir. 1986); Parks v. Watson, 716 F.2d 646 (9th Cir. 1983); Robert L. Hale, *Unconstitutional Conditions and Constitutional Rights*, 35 COLUM. L. REV. 321 (1935); Note, *Unconstitutional Conditions*, 73 HARV. L. REV. 1595 (1960).

68. See Richard Epstein, *Unconstitutional Conditions, State Power and the Limits of Consent*, 102 HARV. L. REV. 4 (1988).

69. See Epstein, supra note 68, at 28–31.

70. 25 U.S. (12 Wheat.) 213 (1827).

71. Id. at 339. For a similar argument see Epstein, supra note 4, at 727–28.

72. LAWRENCE TRIBE, AMERICAN CONSTITUTIONAL LAW 469 (1978).

73. It has been argued that lawmakers are most responsive, in fashioning corporate laws, to the one cohesive interest group that can gain from those laws—the corporate bar. See Jonathan Macey & Geoffrey Miller, *Toward an Interest-Group Theory of Delaware Corporate Law*, 65 TEX. L. REV. 469 (1987).

74. The corporate contract can be impaired by shareholder litigation as well as by legislation. Because the impairing effect of judicial decisions is not widely recognized, however, the reserved power is not perceived as permitting shareholder-induced impairments.

75. At the same time, reserved-power states are unlikely to lose chartering business by shifts to other business forms. That is because the states, as well as the federal tax system, regulate the availability and cost of the limited

liability that is a critical term of the corporate contract. The most common ways to obtain limited liability other than through incorporation involve formation under revenue-producing statutes such as limited partnership. A firm that does not form under such a statute cannot obtain complete immunity from tort liability. Even a firm that does not need such immunity (because it can adequately insure) often cannot contract out of personal liability of owners if it does not comply with statutory formalities. For example, a firm that deals with third parties as a limited liability organization may not be entitled to limited liability even as to such third parties if the parties to the corporation have improperly assumed to act as a corporation. See generally Larry E. Ribstein, *The Deregulation of Limited Liability and the Death of Partnership*, 70 WASH. U. L. Q. 417 (1992); Ribstein, supra note 68.

76. See Roberta Romano, *Law as a Product: Some Pieces of the Incorporation Puzzle*, 1 J.L., ECON. & ORGAN. 225 (1985).

77. This may have been the case, for example, in Greenwood v. Freight Co., 105 U.S. 13 (1881), in which the state revoked the monopoly privileges of a state railroad. See also Calder v. Michigan, 218 U.S. 591 (1910), in which the charter expressly provided that it was subject to later legislation.

78. See Coyne v. Park & Tilford Distillers Corp., 154 A.2d 893 (Del. 1959); See also Weinberg v. Baltimore Brick Co., 108 A.2d 81 (Del. 1954) (statute permitting payment of dividends from current earnings despite impairment of capital where charter specifically permitted payment of dividends out of "net earnings").

79. See Ayers v. Burley Tobacco Growers Cooperative Ass'n, 344 S.W.2d 836 (Ky. App. 1961) (statute permitting directors to convert a 50-year corporation into one with a perpetual term not an impairment when coupled with appraisal right).

80. See William Carney, *Fundamental Corporate Changes, Minority Shareholders, and Business Purposes*, 1980 AM. B. FOUND. RES. J. 69, 95 n.105 (suggesting breach of contract analogy). It is not clear that appraisal rights are constitutionally compelled. Compare MELVIN A. EISENBERG, THE STRUCTURE OF THE CORPORATION 75 (1976) (arguing that appraisal rights have no constitutional basis) with Bayles Manning, *The Shareholder's Appraisal Remedy: An Essay for Frank Coker*, 72 YALE L.J. 223, 246, n.38 (1962) (contra); see also Carney, supra at 94 (suggesting appraisal rights not constitutionally necessary because of reserved-power provisions). However, the availability of appraisal rights does reconcile cases invalidating charter amendments eliminating accrued dividend rights. See Keller v. Wilson & Co., 190 A. 115 (Del. 1936); Morris v. American Public Utilities Co., 122 A. 696 (Del. Ch. 1923), with those permitting loss of such rights in mergers, where appraisal rights were available. See Bove v. Community Hotel, 249 A.89 (R.I. 1900).

81. See Calder v. Michigan, 218 U.S. 591 (1910); Davis v. Louisville Gas & Electric Co., 142 A. 654 (Del.Ch. 1928) (charter permitted any change "now or hereafter prescribed by statute"); cf. Energy Reserves Group v. Kansas Power & Light, 459 U.S. 400 (1983) (upholding statute against Contract Clause challenge where the parties provided in their contract that the terms were subject to present and future federal and state law).

82. This was the situation in Calder, 218 U.S. at 591, involving a water company monopoly.

83. An argument can be made that the Contract Clause also should invalidate judicial impairments of the corporate contract—that is, preclude judicial decisions from being given stare decisis effect that would change existing contracts. This is an important issue in the light of the adoption of the American Law Institute's Principles of Corporate Governance: Analysis and Recommendations (1993) which may lead to judicial adoption of significant changes in corporate law. See Larry E. Ribstein, *The Mandatory Nature of the ALI Code*, 61 Geo. Wash. L. Rev. 984 (1993). Although such an application of the Contract Clause may at first seem surprising, there are strong reasons to support it. Certainly judicial decisions can have the same impairing effect as statutes. For example, in Armstrong v. Marathon Oil Co., 513 N.E.2d 776 (1987), the Ohio supreme court held that a stock's market price was controlling for purposes of determining "fair cash value" under the appraisal statute—a result reached in other jurisdictions only by amending the appraisal statute (see, e.g., Del.Code Ann. tit. 8, §262). Moreover, judicial impairments, like legislative impairments, dissipate resources in zero-sum wealth redistribution—in this case, primarily because of litigation costs rather than rent-seeking. The language of the Contract Clause—"No State shall . . . pass any . . . Law"—seems to preclude application to judicial decisions. This reflects the fact that, at the time of the Constitution, legislatures were the only lawmaking bodies. However, modern courts clearly make law. See John Martinez, *Taking Time Seriously: The Federal Constitutional Right to Be Free From "Startling" State Court Overrulings*, 11 Harv. J.L. & Pub. Policy 297, 324–26 (1988). Interpretation of the Contract Clause arguably should adapt to this institutional change. The case law under the Contract Clause leans against extending the Clause to judicial decisions, but it is not conclusive. For general reviews of the case law see Hale, supra note 10, at 862–67; Martinez, supra, at 318–19. A leading early case supporting application to judicial decisions was Gelpcke v. City of Dubuque, 68 U.S. (1 Wall.) 175 (1863). Later Supreme Court cases have gone the other way. See, e.g., Tidal Oil Co. v. Flanagan, 263 U.S. 444 (1924). Nevertheless, courts have applied the Contract Clause to judicial decisions that change the interpretation of statutes. For a comprehensive review of the law, concluding that the Contract Clause probably no longer applies to judicial impairments, but that legislative and judicial impairments should not be sharply distinguished, see Barton H. Thompson, Jr., *The History of the Judicial Impairment "Doctrine" and its Lessons for the Contract Clause*, 44 Stan. L. Rev. 1373 (1992).

84. Even if the shareholders probably would approve these amendments, management might be unwilling to take the risk that the vote will make the corporation more vulnerable to takeover by advertising its vulnerability or signaling shareholder dissatisfaction with current management.

85. 457 U.S. 624 (1982).

86. 481 U.S. 69 (1987).

87. The Commerce Clause aspect of *CTS* is discussed in Chapter Five, infra text accompanying notes 194–207.

88. See Frank Easterbrook & Daniel Fischel, *The Proper Role of a Target's Management in Responding to a Tender Offer*, 94 HARV. L. REV. 1161 (1981); Ronald Gilson, *A Structural Approach to Corporations: The Case Against Defensive Tactics in Tender Offers*, 33 STAN. L. REV. 819 (1981).

89. See Barry Baysinger & Henry N. Butler, *Antitakeover Amendments, Managerial Entrenchment, and the Contractual Theory of the Corporation*, 71 VA. L. REV. 1257 (1985); David Haddock, Jonathan R. Macey & Fred S. McChesney, *Property Rights in Assets and Resistance to Tender Offers*, 73 VA. L. REV. 701 (1987).

90. See Larry E. Ribstein, *Takeover Defenses and the Corporate Contract*, 78 GEO. L. J. 71 (1989).

91. See Easterbrook & Fischel, supra note 88.

92. Thus, Easterbrook and Fischel argue that permitting management to auction the company may increase premiums but will ultimately not benefit shareholders because they will reduce bids. See Easterbrook and Fischel, supra note 88, at 1175–1182.

93. For a discussion of the problems inherent in this particular situation, see Henry N. Butler, *Corporation-Specific Anti-Takeover Statutes and the Market for Corporate Law*, 1988 WIS. L. REV. 365.

94. See Roberta Romano, *The Political Economy of Takeover Statutes*, 73 VA. L. REV. 1 (1987). This is supported by the fact that Delaware, which does not have a dominant home corporation, lagged the trend in adopting such a statute and finally adopted one of the weaker statutes.

95. See Michael W. Miller, "How Indiana Shields a Firm and Challenges the Takeover Business," Wall St. J., July 1, 1987, at A1 (Arvin sought to avoid takeover by the Belzberg family of Canada; Bob Garton, president of the Indiana Senate, and Arvin chairman James Baker had been friends since junior high school).

96. Examples include North Carolina, at the request of Burlington Industries which was fighting a bid from Asher Edelman and others, see Paul Richter, "Company Pressures; States Act to Stem Tide of Takeovers," L. A. Times, Sept. 15, 1987, at A1; Arizona, at the request of Greyhound, see id.; Minnesota, at the request of Dayton Hudson, which was fighting a bid by the Dart Group, see id.; World News Digest; "Minnesota Blocks Dayton Hudson Bid," Facts on File, July 10, 1987, 496; Massachusetts, at the request of Gillette, the governor signing the bill in front of the Gillette Building (Richter, above this note); Wisconsin, at the request of Heileman, which was defending against a bid by Bond Corporation Hodings, Ltd. (Rose & Burrough, "Heileman Snubs Bond's Offer of $1.2 Billion," Wall St. J., Sept. 18, 1987, col. 1); Florida, at the request of Harcourt, Brace, Jovanovich, which was fighting a bid by British publisher Robert Maxwell (U.P.I., Wire Release, "Corporate Takeovers Denounced," (September 1, 1987); Washington, responding to rumors that T. Boone Pickens sought Boeing Corporation (Richter, above this note; Boeing is the only corporation to which the statute applies).

97. Professor Romano argues that smaller shareholders would be more likely to favor control share-type provisions in order to reduce their informa-

tion costs and ensure that they get the best price. But control-share type provisions also may hurt small, dispersed, passive shareholders by denying them the benefit of the disciplinary effects of the market for corporate control. It may be that the information and price advantages of the control share provisions outweigh their effects on the market for control. See Romano, supra note 94, at 170. On the other hand, perhaps high-concentration-ratio firms lobby for control share statutes because, while these provisions hurt all types of shareholders, they are more likely to be rejected by corporations controlled by institutional investors for whom it is cost-effective to be informed about the effects of the provisions.

98. CTS Corp. 481 U.S. at 91.

99. Justice Scalia wrote separately, declining to join in the last part of the majority's discussion of the Commerce Clause issue, from which the above quote is taken.

100. See supra text accompanying notes 59–65.

101. Ohlinger, supra note 64, at 445.

102. See supra text accompanying notes 89–90.

103. See supra text accompanying notes 28–30.

104. See United States Trust, 431 U.S. at 29 n.27; Epstein, supra note 4.

105. For a recent discussion and analysis of these statutes, see Symposium, *Corporate Malaise-Stakeholder Statutes: Cause or Cure?*, 21 STETSON L. REV. 1 (1991).

106. Minn. Stat. Ann. §302A.251(5) (West 1994 Supp.).

107. See Robert Hansen, *Other Constituency Statutes: A Search for Perspective*, 46 Bus. Law. 1355 (1991) (comparing statutes to common law business judgment standard). Note that the question is not whether the statute is inconsistent with the contract between the directors and the abstraction called the "corporation," but whether it impairs one of the contracts that comprise the corporation—i.e., the contract between the directors and shareholders. It is significant in this regard that although the above statute requires the directors to consider "the best interests of the corporation," it clearly implies that the directors may, in doing so, disregard shareholder interests.

108. See, e.g., Herald Co. v. Seawell, 472 F.2d 1081, 1095 (10th Cir. 1972) (upholding defensive stock issuance by management of newspaper partly on ground that newspaper was a "quasi-public institution" whose management had obligations to the public).

109. See Paramount Communications v. Time, 571 A.2d 1140 (Del. 1989).

110. As discussed above, if the nonshareholder-constituency statutes alter the corporate contract, there is clearly impairment despite the shareholders' ability to opt out by sale or reincorporation.

111. See Ind. Code Ann §§23-1-35-1(d), (f) (Burns 1989); 15 Pa. Cons. Stat. Ann. §§515(a)–(b), 516 (a) (Purdon Supp. 1992); Conn. Gen. Stat. Ann. §33-313(e) (West Supp. 1992). For commentary critical of these provisions, see Hansen, supra note 107; James J. Hanks, Jr., *Playing with Fire: Nonshareholder Constituency Statutes in the 1990s*, 21 STETSON L. REV. 97 (1991).

112. See A.P. Smith Mfg. Co. v. Barlow, 97 A.2d 186, aff'd, 98 A.2d 581

(N.J. 1953) (sustaining statute permitting charitable contributions up to one percent of capital in any year on "public interest" grounds).

113. While the statutes arguably enhance the directors' ability to resist takeovers, they do so by defining how directors may exercise powers they have under other elements of the contract rather than, as with control share acquisition statutes, giving the directors a power they did not have before.

114. Moreover, the impairment is arguably not a serious one, which would lighten the scrutiny level with respect to justification. Directors have wide leeway in defensive moves under the business judgment rule even if they are required to consider only shareholder interests. Thus, it is unlikely that permitting directors to consider nonshareholder interests would change any results.

115. See Epstein, supra note 4.

116. See Fla. Stat. Ann. §607.164(2); Ind. Code Ann. §23-1-35-1(a) (Burns 1989); Ohio Rev. Code Ann. §1701.59(D); Va. Code Ann. §13.1-690(A); Wis. Stat. Ann. §180.307.

117. See, e.g., infra text accompanying notes 121–22.

118. See Va. Code Ann. §13.1-690(A) (1985).

119. See Joseph Bishop, *Sitting Ducks & Decoy Ducks: New Trends in the Indemnification of Corporate Directors and Officers*, 77 YALE L.J. 1078, 1099 (1968) ("The search for cases in which directors of industrial corporations have been held liable in derivative suits for negligence uncomplicated by self-dealing is a search for a very small number of needles in a very large haystack.")

120. 488 A. 2d 858 (Del. 1985). Smith arguably changed the contracts of Delaware corporations by, in effect, increasing the directors' standard of care from gross negligence to ordinary care. For an argument that the Contract Clause should prevent such a holding from being given stare decisis effect, see supra note 83.

121. Va. Code Ann. §13.1-692.1 (1987). Because the Virginia provision on the standard of care, Va. Code Ann. §13.1-690(A) (1985), requires managers to exercise "good faith business judgment," the Virginia limitation of liability primarily applies to reckless conduct that would otherwise be covered by section 13.1-690(A).

122. Wis. Stat. Ann. §180.044 (West 1990). The statute does not permit indemnification in cases involving willful misconduct, improper personal profit, criminal conduct unless the manager had no reasonable basis to believe the conduct was unlawful, or a material conflict of interest.

123. For a discussion of the Maryland statute, see Henry N. Butler & Larry E. Ribstein, *Free at Last? The Contractual Theory of the Corporation and the New Maryland Officer-Director Liability Provisions*, 18 U. BALT. L. REV. 352, 365–67 (1989).

124. See, e.g., Shlensky v. Wrigley, 237 N.E. 2d 776 (Ill. 1968); Dodge v. Ford Motor Co., 170 N.W. 668 (Mich. 1919).

125. See State ex rel. Swanson v. Perham, 191 P.2d 689 (Wash. 1948). The court distinguished Looker v. Maynard, 179 U.S. 46 (1900), which permitted imposition of cumulative voting, on the ground that Looker involved a

mutual life insurance company in which the rights of the public—i.e., the policy holders—were affected by the change.

126. See supra Chapter 1, part III.D.

127. This is a theory underlying appraisal rights. See supra note 80.

128. See Federal United Corp. v. Havender, 11 A.2d 331 (Del. 1940).

129. 488 A.2d 858 (Del. 1985).

130. See generally Butler & Ribstein, supra note 123; Harvey Gelb, *Director Due Care Liability: An Assessment of the New Statutes*, 61 Temp. L. Q. 13 (1988); Thomas Hazen, *Corporate Directors' Accountability: The Race to the Bottom—The Second Lap*, 66 N.C. L. Rev. 171 (1987).

131. Del. Code Ann. tit. 8, §102(b)(7). Section 102(b)(7) affects the amendment power through §242(a), which permits amendment to include only those provisions that might be contained in the original certificate. Del. Code. Ann. tit. 8, §242(a).

132. Del. Code Ann. tit. 8, §242(a).

133. Id. §102(b)(1).

134. For a case outside Delaware, see Irwin v. West End Development Co., 342 F. Supp. 687, 701 (D.Colo. 1972) (holding that broad exculpatory provision permitting self dealing could not validate unfair director compensation).

135. See Piccard v. Sperry Corp., 48 F. Supp. 465, 469 (S.D.N.Y. 1943), aff'd mem., 152 F.2d 462 (2d Cir.), cert. denied, 328 U.S. 845 (1946) (validating charter provision that permitted interested director to be counted for quorum purposes); Sterling v. Mayflower Hotel Corp., 93 A.2d 107 (Del. 1952).

136. See, e.g., Del. Code Ann. tit. 8, §242(c)(2).

Chapter 3: Corporate Campaign Activities

1. See John Stuart Mill, On Liberty ch. 2 (1st ed. 1859). Another famous early source of First Amendment theory is John Milton, Areopagitica—A Speech for the Liberty of Unlicensed Printing (1644): "An though all the winds of doctrine were let loose to play upon the earth, so Truth be in the field, we do injuriously, by licensing and prohibiting to misdoubt her strength. Let her and Falsehood grapple: who ever knew Truth put to the worst, in a free and open encounter."); see also Thomas I. Emerson, *Toward a General Theory of the First Amendment*, 72 Yale L.J. 877 (1963) (stating that "attainment of truth" is one of four fundamental values underlying the right to freedom of expression, along with "self-fulfillment," "participation in decision-making," and achieving a "balance between stability and change").

2. Abrams v. U.S., 250 U.S. 616, 630 (1919).

3. See Alexander Meiklejohn, Free Speech and its Relation to Self-Government (1948); Vincent Blasi, *The Checking Value in First Amendment Theory*, 1977 Am. Bar. Found. Res. J. 521 (arguing that freedom of speech is important in checking the abuse of official power); Robert H. Bork, *Neutral Principles and Some First Amendment Problems*, 47 Ind. L.J. 1 (1971) (arguing that the First Amendment was intended to protect constitutional processes of government and should not be extended beyond this sphere).

4. See Martin H. Redish, *The Value of Free Speech*, 130 U. Pa. L. Rev. 591 (1982) (advocating a "self-realization" theory of the First Amendment).

5. For an articulation of some interests relevant to the balancing process see Emerson, supra note 1, at 920–55. This book therefore rejects a deontological approach that would elevate a particular value, such as self-expression, above all others. Such an analysis is both difficult to defend and inconsistent with the Court's own approach. For an analysis comparing ontological and deontological approaches to First Amendment analysis see Ronald A. Cass, *Commercial Speech, Constitutionalism Collective, Choice*, 56 U. Cin. L. Rev. 1317 (1988). For an article discussing corporate governance speech from a noninstrumentalist perspective on the need to protect self-expression, see Aleta G. Estreicher, *Securities Regulation and the First Amendment*, 24 Ga L. Rev. 223 (1990). The best articulation of such an approach is Richard A. Posner, *Free Speech in an Economic Perspective*, 20 Suffolk U. L. Rev. 1 (1986). Posner builds on Judge Hand's rule in United States v. Dennis, 183 F.2d 201, 212 (2d Cir. 1950), aff'd, 341 U.S. 494 (1951), that a court should determine the constitutionality of a speech restriction by asking "whether the gravity of the 'evil', discounted by its improbability, justifies such invasion of free speech as is necessary to avoid the danger."

6. See infra text accompanying note 22.

7. For examples of the ideological slant inherent in the commercial/noncommercial distinction, see Chapter Four, infra text accompanying notes 46–47.

8. 494 U.S. 652 (1990).

9. 435 U.S. 765 (1978).

10. See Bellotti, 435 U.S. at 778–80.

11. See id. at 791 n.30.

12. See id. at 791–95.

13. Id. at 805 (White, J., dissenting).

14. See id. at 812–21. Justice White analogized the situation in Bellotti to cases holding that employees could not be compelled to have their union dues support political causes they opposed. See id. at 813–19 (discussing Abood v. Detroit Board of Education, 431 U.S. 209 [1977]); Machinists v. Street, 367 U.S. 740 (1961). Justice White also noted that the Court had construed the Corrupt Practices Act as having the purpose of ensuring minority shareholder or union consent to corporate and union political views. See Bellotti, 435 U.S. at 819–20 (discussing United States v. CIO, 335 U.S. 106 (1948)). White also reasoned that the state has an interest in ensuring that shareholders will not be deterred from investing in corporations because of unwillingness to support corporate political views. See id. at 818–19.

15. 17 U.S. (4 Wheat.) 518 (1819).

16. Id. at 636 (quoted in Bellotti 435 U.S. at 823).

17. Bellotti 435 U.S. at 825 (Rehnquist, J., dissenting). Like Justice White, Justice Rehnquist distinguished corporations organized "for explicitly political purposes." Id. at 825 n.5.

18. See id. at 826–27 n.6.

19. 459 U.S. 197 (1982).
20. Id. at 207–08.
21. See id. at 210 n.7.
22. 479 U.S. 238 (1986).
23. 494 U.S. 652 (1990).
24. Id. at 1397.
25. 110 S. Ct. at 1398. Along similar lines, the Court upheld the statute's distinction between all corporations and all unincorporated associations against an Equal Protection argument because of the state's interest in protecting against "political 'war chests' amassed with the aid of advantages given to corporations." 110 S.Ct. at 1401.

26. As discussed, Justice White made this argument in Bellotti. See supra note 14. In NWRC, Justice Rehnquist, writing for a unanimous Court, said that one of two purposes of federal restrictions on campaign contributions is to protect corporate shareholders or union dues contributors "from having that money used to support candidates to whom they may be opposed." 459 U.S. at 208 (citing U.S. v. CIO, 335 U.S. 106 (1948)). And Justice Brennan's Austin concurrence emphasized the state's "compelling interest in preventing a corporation it has chartered from exploiting those who do not wish to contribute to the Chamber's political message." Austin, 494 U.S. at 652 (Brennan, J., dissenting). Like White, Brennan also relied in part on Street.

27. For the view that corporate speech should be constitutionally protected only to the extent necessary to protect the rights of individuals connected with the corporation, see Victor Brudney, *Business Corporations and Stockholders' Rights under the First Amendment*, 91 YALE L.J. 235 (1981) (arguing that state may protect the speech rights of minority shareholders); Charles R. O'Kelley, *The Constitutional Rights of Corporations Revisited: Social and Political Expression and the Corporation after First National Bank v. Bellotti*, 67 GEO. L.J. 1347 (1979) (stating that the Supreme Court's initial recognition of constitutional rights of corporations was based on rationale of protecting incorporators' property invested in the firm); David L. Ratner, *Corporations and the Constitution*, 15 U.S.F. L. REV. 11 (1981).

28. This was also an important basis of Justice White's Bellotti dissent. See Bellotti, 435 U.S. at 805.

29. This point is recognized even by a prominent critic of corporate speech rights. See C. EDWIN BAKER, HUMAN LIBERTY AND FREEDOM OF SPEECH 219–20 (1989).

30. For a contrary view, see Brudney, supra note 27; Schneider, supra note (seq rat ratner) at 1266; see also CHARLES E. LINDBLOM, POLITICS AND MARKETS 192–94 (1977) (discussing the unconstrained ability of businessmen to draw on corporate resources to support their political activities).

31. The business judgment rule provides broad latitude for corporate political activity. See Shlensky v. Wrigley, 237 N.E. 2d 776 (Ill. 1968) (sustaining a business decision motivated partly by nonbusiness objectives); see also A.P. Smith Mfg. Co. v. Barlow, 98 A.2d 581, app. dismissed, 346 U.S. 861 (1953) (holding charitable gift not ultra vires). Since control changes are

costly, they will be employed to constrain only very costly corporate speech. Perhaps as large institutional shareholders become more active in corporate governance, corporate speech can be more closely identified with specific shareholders. For a comprehensive reexamination of the passive-shareholder view of public corporation governance see Black, *Shareholder Passivity Reexamined*, 89 MICH. L. REV. 520 (1990). It is sufficient to note at this point that new trends in shareholder monitoring have not developed to the point where large shareholders can be identified with specific corporate activities.

32. See Armen A. Alchian & Harold Demsetz, *Production, Information Costs, and Economic Organization*, 62 AM. ECON. REV. 777, 788 (1972). Most individuals either hold diversified portfolios of investments or invest in corporations indirectly through institutions such as mutual funds. Accordingly, they care little about the internal affairs of individual companies or statements or expenditures made by their managers. Because shareholders are residual claimants, while creditors and others rely on the corporation's performance of specific contractual obligations, the shareholders' contracts seem to differ from those of other corporate claimholders in a way that arguably makes shareholders uniquely responsible for managers' speech. Other claimants, however, can check managerial conduct. For example, creditors may have significant monitoring rights, particularly in insolvent or nearly insolvent firms. See NICHOLAS WOLFSON, THE FIRST AMENDMENT AND THE SEC 111, 123 (1990) (questioning whether creditors should be distinguished from shareholders since both groups are investors who differ only regarding the form of their contracts). Workers may have considerable say through their power to strike or quit. Indeed, the regulatory theory of the corporation even supports legal rules requiring managers to represent the interests of nonshareholder "stakeholders." See Herald Co. v. Seawell, 472 F.2d 1081 (10th Cir. 1972) (upholding defensive stock issuance partly on ground that the target, a large urban newspaper, was a "quasi-public institution"); Wieboldt Stores, Inc. v. Shottenstein, Fed. Sec. L. Rep. (CCH) ¶94,812 (N.D. Ill. 1989) (holding that corporation, acting on behalf of unsecured creditors, could sue directors for approving an LBO on ground that the board had a duty to determine whether the LBO was in the best interests of the corporation as well as the shareholders); GAF Corp. v. Union Carbide Corp., 624 F. Supp. 1016 (S.D.N.Y. 1985) (upholding "pension parachute" that vests "excess" funds in pension plan to assure workers that such funds will not be used by bidder); John C. Coffee, Jr., *The Uncertain Case for Takeover Reform: An Essay on Stockholders, Stakeholders and Bust-Ups*, 1988 WIS. L. REV. 435, 448 (arguing that the board should be viewed as a "mediator" to enforce implicit contracts among shareholders and other constituencies).

33. See John R. Bolton, *Constitutional Limitations on Restricting Corporate and Union Political Speech*, 22 ARIZ. L. REV. 373, 377 (1980) (noting early characterization of corporate speech as "embezzlement").

34. See supra note 26.

35. See supra note 14.

36. Bellotti, 435 U.S. at 794.

37. More recently, in Barnes v. State Farm Mutual Automobile Ins. Ass'n, 20 Cal.Rptr.2d 87 (1993), the court held that Bellotti and its reasoning applied to a policy holder in a mutual insurance company who claimed to have First Amendment right to object to the company's use of funds for political activities. The court rejected the plaintiff's attempted distinction of Bellotti based on compulsory automobile insurance, reasoning that plaintiff still had the option to choose his insurer.

38. See ROBERT G. HANSEN & JOHN R. LOTT, JR., EXTERNALITIES AND CORPORATE OBJECTIVES IN A WORLD WITH DIVERSIFIED SHAREHOLDER/CONSUMERS OR, WHY DO WE CONTINUE TO TEACH VALUE MAXIMIZATION AS THE PROPER CORPORATE OBJECTIVE? (Working Paper, January 1993).

39. Id. at 1412.

40. See CTS Corp. v. Dynamics Corp. of America, 481 U.S. 69, 91 (1987) (upholding state antitakeover statute against Commerce Clause and Supremacy Clause attack).

41. See id. at 1412.

42. Id. at 1405.

43. The sale price reflects at least all current public information concerning the stock. Although there may be undisclosed inside information that is not reflected in stock price, there is no reason to believe that the expected value of undisclosed information at the time of a speech-motivated trade is anything other than zero.

44. See Stern v. General Electric Co., 921 F.2d 296 (2d Cir. 1991) (holding that shareholder action for corporate waste not preempted by FECA but complaint failed to state a cause of action for breach of fiduciary duty).

45. See ALBERT O. HIRSCHMAN, EXIT, VOICE AND LOYALTY: RESPONSES TO DECLINE IN FIRMS, ORGANIZATIONS, AND STATES (1970). As shareholder dissatisfaction with managers' speech increases, "exit" becomes less satisfactory and "voice" becomes more satisfactory. "Voice" is more likely than "exit" to result in discipline of the managers as distinguished merely from relief for shareholders.

46. See Henry G. Manne, Insider Trading and the Stock Market 111–158 (1966); Dennis W. Carlton & Daniel R. Fischel, Regulation of Insider Trading, 35 STAN. L. REV. 857, 870–78 (1983); David D. Haddock & Jonathan R. Macey, A Coasian Model of Insider Trading, 80 Nw. U. L. REV. 1449 (1986).

47. See LARRY SABATO, PAC POWER (1984) (showing that only 17% of corporate PACs do any shareholder solicitation); Bernadette A. Budde, Business-Related Political Action Committees, 3 J. L. & POLITICS 440, 456 (1987).

48. See Sabato, supra note 47, at 34 (asserting that corporate CEOs normally have significant influence on activities of corporate PACs); Archibald Cox, Constitutional Issues in the Regulation of the Financing of Election Campaigning, 31 CLEV. ST. L. REV. 395, 410–11 (1982) (noting that it is PAC leadership—primarily corporate executives—who obtain influences through PACs).

49. Shareholders could, of course, form their own interest groups to oppose those of managers. But the shareholders' groups, unlike "corporate" PACs, would have to bear their own organization costs. These costs, together with the free-rider problem inherent in collective action, would inhibit such efforts.

50. For this reason, one could regard state corporate law provisions as not really "mandatory." See Bernard Black, *Is Corporate Law Trivial?: A Political and Economic Analysis*, 84 Nw. Univ. L. Rev. 542 (1990).

51. For commentary favoring mandatory federal rules on this basis see Lucian A. Bebchuk, *Federalism and the Corporation: The Desirable Limits on State Competition in Corporate Law*, 105 Harv. L. Rev. 1435 (1992); Jeffrey N. Gordon, *Ties That Bond: Dual Class Common Stock and the Problem of Shareholder Choice*, 75 Cal. L. Rev. (1988).

52. Cf. Cort v. Ash, 422 U.S. 66 (1975) (refusing to recognize a shareholder right of action against managers under federal election law on ground that statute was not intended to provide for such relief).

53. Nor is there any basis for distinguishing "ideological" and for-profit corporations from the standpoint of the need for shareholder protection. As discussed below, members of ideological corporations face high costs of exit, and therefore the same or greater agency costs that are faced by members of for-profit corporations. For a discussion of the essential similarities between ideological and for-profit corporations from the standpoint of organization theory see Wolfson, supra note 32.

54. Austin, 110 S.Ct. at 1398 (emphasis added).

55. Justice White's Bellotti dissent articulated a rationale for limited constitutional protection of corporate speech that is at least superficially similar to Rehnquist's state-creation theory. White reasoned that states ought to be able to prevent corporations from using their state-conferred advantages to dominate the political process. This could be described as the "Frankenstein" theory of corporate speech: The state should be able to build limits into its creatures to prevent them from destroying their creators. See Carl E. Schneider, *Free Speech and Corporate Freedom: A Comment on First National Bank of Boston v. Bellotti*, 59 S. Cal. L. Rev. 1227, 1257 (1986) (comparing corporate privileges to state's creation of nuclear power). "Frankenstein" was used in another sense by Ratner, supra note 27, at 29 (referring to the Court's recognition of corporate free speech rights as endowing the corporation with human characteristics).

56. See Bellotti, 435 U.S. at 778–80 nn.14–15.

57. The state-privilege argument was an important basis for the state court decision upholding more than seventy years earlier the constitutionality of the Michigan statute involved in Austin. See People v. Gansley, 158 N.W. 195 (Mich. 1916).

58. See Flint v. Stone Tracy Co., 220 U.S. 107, 162 (1911):
[T]he tax is laid upon the privileges which exist in conducting business with the advantages which inhere in the corporate capacity of those taxed, and which are not enjoyed by private firms or individuals . . . the continuity of the business, without interruption by death or dissolution, the transfer of property interests by the disposition of shares of stock, the advantages of business controlled and managed by corporate directors, the general absence of individual liability, these and other things inhere in the advantages of business thus conducted, which do not exist when the same business is conducted by private individuals or partnerships.

59. See CTS Corp. v. Dynamics Corp. of Am., 481 U.S. 69, 91 (1987) ("It is thus an accepted part of the business landscape in this country for States to create corporations, to prescribe their powers, and to define the rights that are acquired by purchasing their shares.").

60. This point was made by Justice Scalia in his dissenting opinion in Austin 494 U.S. at 680: Those individuals who form that type of voluntary association known as a corporation are, to be sure, given special advantages—notably, the immunization of their personal fortunes from liability for the actions of the association—that the State is under no obligation to confer. But so are other associations and private individuals given all sorts of special advantages that the State need not confer, ranging from tax breaks to contract awards to public employment to outright cash subsidies. It is rudimentary that the State cannot exact as the price of those special advantages the forfeiture of First Amendment rights.

This point is also made in Richard Epstein, *Bargaining with the State,* 112–14 (1993) (arguing that it is unconstitutional to make privilege of incorporation conditional on limiting corporations' First Amendment rights). As discussed in Chapter Two, however, the argument that incorporation is a state-conferred privilege makes no more sense when used by proponents of economic rights than when used by those who favor regulation. Moreover, basing corporate First Amendment rights on the unconstitutional conditions doctrine would go beyond the protection that is warranted under the contract theory of the corporation in that it would prohibit states even from providing default rules limiting agents' speech rights.

61. Justice Powell's position in Bellotti that a corporation, as a "person," is entitled to First Amendment protection, see Bellotti, 435 U.S. at 780, is related to the state-creation theory. This holding seems hospitable to the corporation. While the First Amendment straightforwardly protects speech, the Fourteenth Amendment protects only a "person" from denial of liberty without due process, including denial of First Amendment rights. It has long been clear that "person" includes corporations. See Santa Clara County v. Southern Pacific R. Co., 118 U.S. 394 (1886). Yet this characterization does not help clarify the scope of constitutional protection of corporate political speech. In the first place, the characterization unfortunately links constitutional protection of the corporation to the outmoded "state-creation" theory. In any event, because a corporation has the legal attributes of a "person" only by operation of law, the policies underlying the law ultimately do and should determine the extent to which a corporate person has particular attributes for purposes of constitutional protection. See I. Alan R. Bromberg & Larry E. Ribstein, Bromberg and Ribstein on Partnership §1.03 (1988). Thus, characterizing the corporation as a "person" can result in denial of as well as endowment with constitutional rights. The Court has held that the self-incrimination clause protects only individuals, and so cannot be used to protect a custodian of corporate records from having to produce those records. See United States v. White, 322 U.S. 694 (1944); Wilson v. United States, 221 U.S. 361 (1911). In Braswell v. United States, 487 U.S. 99 (1988),

the Court unfortunately carried the legal personification of the corporation to the extreme of denying the self-incrimination privilege to production of documents by the sole shareholder of a corporation. Nevertheless, some commentators continue to argue that legal abstractions like concepts of the corporation have legal significance. See Morton J. Horowitz, *Santa Clara Revisited: The Development of Corporate Theory*, 88 W. VA. 1. REV. 173, 175–76 (1985); David Millon, *Theories of the Corporation*, 1990 DUKE L.J. 201, 243. For an attempt to explain application of the First Amendment to the corporation in terms of these abstractions, see Charles D. Watts, Jr., *Corporate Legal Theory under the First Amendment: Bellotti and Austin*, 46 U. MIAMI L. REV. 317 (1991) (distinguishing "fictional entity," "natural entity," and "aggregate" theories of the corporation, and defending Supreme Court's adoption of the "natural entity" theory in its corporate political speech cases).

62. See Daniel A. Farber & Phillip P. Frickey, *The Jurisprudence of Public Choice*, 65 TEX. L. REV. 873 (1987) (suggesting redressing this problem by eliminating "economic" PACs).

63. In fact, the "capture" theory resembles the first primitive approaches by political scientists to explain regulation as a narrow function of influence solely by regulated firms. See ARTHUR F. BENTLEY, THE PROCESS OF GOVERNMENT (1908); DAVID B. TRUMAN, THE GOVERNMENT PROCESS: POLITICAL INTERESTS AND PUBLIC OPINION (1951). This theory has long since been replaced by a broader theory that considers all of the relevant interest groups. See sources cited supra note. For a comparison of the "capture" theory and the modern economic theory of regulation see RICHARD A. POSNER, ECONOMIC ANALYSIS OF LAW 341–44 (1992).

64. Buckley v. Valeo, 424 U.S. 1, 26 (1976).

65. See Bolton, supra note 33, at 417.

66. See Cox, supra note 48, at 417 (analogizing such restrictions to Roberts' Rules of Order).

67. See U.S. v. United States Brewers' Ass'n, 239 F. Supp. 163 (W.D. Pa. 1916) (citing this justification in rejecting First Amendment challenge to campaign financing law); John R. Bolton, *Constitutional Limitations on Restricting Corporate and Union Speech*, 22 ARIZ. L. REV. 373, 376 (1980) (discussing role of this justification in early campaign financing laws).

68. See CHARLES LINDBLOM, POLITICS & MARKETS 194 (1977); Cox, supra note 48; see also Schneider, supra note 55, at 126; Note, *The Corporation and the Constitution: Economic Due Process and Corporate Speech*, 90 YALE L.J. 1833 (1981).

69. See Buckley, 424 U.S. at 48–49 ("[T]he concept that government may restrict the speech of some elements of our society in order to enhance the relative voice of others is wholly foreign to the First Amendment.").

70. See Bellotti, 435 U.S. at 788–92. Justice Powell wrote that there was no evidence that "corporate advocacy threatened imminently to undermine democratic processes," see id. at 789, and did not find the argument "inherently persuasive or supported by the precedents of this Court" see id. at 790. He also quoted the above language from Buckley in opposition to the

argument that corporate speech may "drown out" other viewpoints, see id. at 790–91, and noted that the equality argument had been accepted only in the "special context of limited access to channels of communication," id. at 791 n.30 (citing Red Lion Broadcasting Co. v. FCC, 395 U.S. 367 (1969)), and had been rejected even in the more persuasive context of candidates' access to newspaper space, see id. (citing Miami Herald Publishing Co. v. Tornillo, 418 U.S. 241 (1974). The Court may revisit this argument in the context of a First Amendment challenge to the "must-carry" provisions of the Cable Television Consumer Protection and Competition Act of 1992. See Turner Broadcasting System Inc. v. F.C.C., 819 F.Supp. 32 (D.D.C.) (upholding provisions), 114 S.Ct. 38 (1993) (noting probable jurisdiction).

71. Bellotti, 435 U.S. at 809–12.

72. NRWC, 459 U.S. at 208–10 (discussing the early history of restrictions on union and corporate contributions and noting that such restrictions may be necessary to protect "the integrity of our electoral process") (quoting U.S. v. CIO, 352 U.S. 567, 570 (1957)).

73. The Court never clarifies how disproportionate influence might be a problem. One commentator notes that the Supreme Court's shift in positions from Buckley to Austin on "corruption" indicates the Court's ambivalence about whether voters are "civic smarties" who are capable of sorting out the information for themselves, or irrational "civic slobs" who are irrational and likely to be misled by heavy campaign spenders. See Daniel R. Ortiz, The Rationality of Politics: Individual Political Decisionmaking under the First Amendment (University of Virginia School of Law Legal Studies Workshop Working Paper No. 93-3, 1993). We would agree with Ortiz that voters may be "civic slobs" to some extent and swayed by campaign spending although, whereas Ortiz attributes this to voter irrationality, we would argue that the voters are making rational judgments about how much time and other resources to invest in finding political information. But, as Ortiz himself suggests, see id. at 52, the Supreme Court is probably not applying inconsistent political theories about voter behavior, but rather intended all along to favor individual over corporate speakers. Accordingly, we focus on this issue, rather than the voter rationality point, and consider whether there is any justification for a corporate/individual distinction based on ability to amass resources with which to sway voters.

74. See Austin, 494 U.S. at 660 ("[T]he corrosive and distorting effects of immense aggregations of wealth that are accumulated with the help of the corporate form and that have little or no correlation to the public's support for the corporation's political ideas.").

75. For commentary critical of applying an equality principle under the First Amendment see Baker, supra note 29, at 37–46; Lillian R. Bevier, *Money and Politics: A Perspective on the First Amendment and Campaign Finance Program*, 73 CAL. L. REV. 1045 (1985). Nicholas Wolfson, *Equality in First Amendment Theory*, 38 ST. LOUIS U. L. J. 379 (1993). The Austin Court attempted to reconcile limiting corporate speech with the Court's rejection of the "equality" principle by reasoning that it is not corporate wealth in itself that justifies

regulation, but rather the fact that this wealth is accumulated by means of "the unique state-conferred corporate structure," Austin, 494 U.S. at 660. But this simply returns to the argument based on supposedly state-conferred corporate privileges. Justice Scalia colorfully described this attempt to bolster the invalid "inequality" justification with the equally invalid "special privileges" argument: When the vessel labeled "corruption" begins to founder under weight too great to be logically sustained, the argumentation jumps to the good ship 'special privilege'; and when that in turns begins to go down, it returns to 'corruption.' Thus hopping back and forth between the two, the argumentation may survive but makes no headway towards port, where its conclusion waits in vain. Id. at 685.

76. Under an important extention of interest group theory, politicians function as active participants rather than mere brokers, receiving payments by threatening regulation. See Fred S. McChesney, Rent Extraction and Rent Creation in the Economic Theory of Regulation, 16 J. LEG. STUD. 1 (1987).

77. An interest group that receives $1 worth of benefit from a wealth transfer will pay $1 less the cost of receiving the benefit. This cost includes resources expended to learn the effects of legislation and identifying and communicating with other potential group members who may be affected. See ROBERT A. MCCORMICK & ROBERT D. TOLLISON, POLITICANS, LEGISLATION AND THE ECONOMY 17 (1981); George J. Stigler, The Theory of Economic Regulation, 2 BELL J. ECON. & MGT. SCI. 3, 10–13 (1971). The "free rider" problem is an important constraint on interest group activity: while benefits are shared by all members of the group, the costs may be incurred by a few organizers who cannot cheaply force the other group members to bear their share. This problem was emphasized in the pioneering work on group formation, MANCUR OLSON, THE LOGIC OF COLLECTIVE ACTION (1965). For some other discussions of the importance of free riding in interest group theory see R. McCormick & R. Tollison, supra note 77, at 17–18; Gary S. Becker, A Theory of Competition Among Pressure Groups for Political Influence, 98 Q. J. ECON. 371, 377 (1983); Robert D. Tollison, Public Choice and Legislation, 74 VA. L. REV. 339 (1988). Thus, although total benefits to large groups may increase quickly with the size of the group, the costs of overcoming the free rider problem rise rapidly with increasing size of the group. That is why relatively small interest groups, such as those consisting of producers, often can outbid much larger groups with more voters. Mancur Olson refers to the latter as "latent" groups. See Olson, supra, at 48–52. For example, if group A can gain a gross marginal benefit of $1 from a wealth transfer at a total marginal organizational cost (including the costs of overcoming the free rider problem) of $.50, and group B will lose $1 from the transfer and has organizational costs of $.60, group A can "bid" $.50 to effect the transfer, while group B can bid no more than $.40. There may be no "free rider" costs if a single member will incur a substantial loss or gain from a wealth transfer without any organizational effort to devise incentives or penalties. Also note that marginal organizational costs of seeking a wealth transfer normally will be lower for existing than for forming groups.

This graph assumes wealth transfers worth \$1. The horizontal line at \$1 is what all groups would pay in the absence of organizational costs to effect and avoid transfers. Under this zero-organizational-cost assumption there would be no wealth transfers. More generally, wealth transfers depend on heterogeneous organization costs. See id. at 25–27.

The graph reflects that groups with more than \$1 of organization costs would "pay" less than 0 for \$1 of wealth transfers. The downward sloping demand curve (D) reflects what interest groups with different organization costs would pay for \$1 of wealth transfers. Groups with demand prices between P^* and P^*-f cannot outbid groups with demand prices higher than P^* but, given the costs (f) of running the system, they can bid enough to resist the transfer. The upward sloping supply curve (S) is simply the demand curve turned around and increased at every point by a constant amount (f) which represents the direct costs of operating the political transfer system. The intersection of S and D (P) is a transfer point: groups with organization costs less than (above and to the left of) this point will pay for wealth transfers provided by interest groups with organization costs more than (below and to the right of) P^*-f.

78. See Olson, supra note 77, at 132–67 (first describing this as a "byproduct" effect); see also McCormick & Tollison, supra note 77, at 17; Tollison, supra note 77, at 342–43.

79. See Austin, 494 U.S. at 660–61; Bellotti, 435 U.S. at 807–09 (White, J., dissenting). Restrictions on corporate campaign expenditures and contributions also leave corporations free to engage in other political activity such as lobbying, but this is clearly not a full substitute for the restricted activity.

80. The Court held that statutory limits on PAC expenditures were unconstitutional in Federal Election Comm'n v. National Conservative Political Action Comm., 470 U.S. 480 (1985). The activities of such business-oriented groups as the Business Roundtable (consisting of chief executives of large corporations) and United Shareholders of America might be sufficiently "expressive" of underlying member views to be protected under the MCFL rationale. This result is, of course, somewhat doubtful in light of Austin's refusal to protect the activities of the Michigan Chamber of Commerce.

81. See 2 U.S.C. §441b (b)(2)(C) (exempting from restrictions on corporate and union expenditures and contributions amounts paid for "the establishment, administration, and solicitation of contributions to a separate segregated fund to be utilized for political purposes").

82. For reports and studies of corporate PAC activities see III Federal Election Commission Reports on Financial Activity, Final Report, Party and Non-Party Political Committees (Non-Party Detailed Tables (Corporate and Labor)) (1987–88); Federal Election Commission, Report on 1990 Congressional Election Spending (Feb. 22, 1991); Sabato, supra note 47.

83. The relevant provision of the election law, 2 U.S.C. §441b(a), has been interpreted as prohibiting corporations from using general revenues to engage in "express advocacy" of particular candidates, as distinguished from advocacy of issues. See Massachusetts Citizens for Life, 479 U.S. at 249; Buckley, 424 U.S. at 44 & n.52; Faucher v. F.E.C., 928 F.2d 468 (1st Cir. 1991).

84. See Austin, 110 U.S. at 1425 (Kennedy, J., dissenting); see also Michael J. Malbin, *Looking Back at the Future of Campaign Finance Reform, in* MONEY AND POLITICS IN THE UNITED STATES, 247 n.21 (M. Malbin ed., 1984) (noting low contribution ratios for employees solicited by corporate PACs).

85. See Sabato, supra note 47, at 126–28.

86. See infra text accompanying notes 110–114.

87. See Michael E. Levine & Jennifer L. Forrence, *Regulatory Capture, Public Interest and Public Agenda,* 6 J. L., ECON. & ORG. 167, 186–87 (1990). Among other things, unconstrained legislators may act consistently with ideological preferences that are not shared by their constituents. See Joseph P. Kalt & Mark A. Zupan, *The Apparent Ideological Behavior of Legislators: Testing for Principal-Agent Slack in Political Institutions,* 33 J. L. & ECON. 103 (1990) (showing evidence that ideological voting of politicians is partly a function of ability of voters to form coalitions, measured in the study by the degree to which voters in the state conform to the national political norm as indicating their heterogeneity).

88. For data showing the effects of challenger and incumbent spending see GARY C. JACOBSON, MONEY IN CONGRESSIONAL ELECTIONS 48–49 (1980); Gary C. Jacobson, *Practical Consequences of Campaign Finance Reform: An Incumbent Protection Act?* 24 PUB. POL. 1 (1976).

89. For evidence that corporate political action committees tend to support incumbents see Jacobson, Money in Congressional Elections, supra note 88; Budde, supra note 47, at 455; Gary C. Jacobson, *Money and Votes Reconsidered: Congressional Elections, 1972–82,* 47 PUB. CHOICE 7 (1985); Gerald Keim & Asghar Zardkoohi, *Looking for Leverage in PAC Markets: Corporate and Labor Contributions Considered,* 58 PUB. CHOICE 21 (1988). On the other hand, corporate PACs do give significant support to challengers. See Theodore J. Eismeier & Phillip H. Pollock III, *Political Action Committees: Varieties of Organization and Strategy, in* Money and Politics in the United States, 131 (Michael Malbin ed., 1984). Also, irrespective of general tendencies, the fact remains that incumbents would be constrained by challengers' potential for tapping corporate money. See Jacobson, *Money and Votes Reconsidered* supra, at 53.

90. Justice Scalia quoted de Tocqueville: " 'Governments . . . should not be the only active powers; associations ought, in democratic nations, to stand in lieu of those powerful private individuals whom the equality of conditions has swept away.' " Austin, at 693–94 494 U.S. (quoting Alexis de Tocqueville, Democracy in America 109 (Bradley ed., 1948); see also JAMES COLEMAN, THE ASYMMETRIC SOCIETY 51–55 (1982) (arguing that private organizations protect individuals from state power). Note that these arguments focus on private associations' ability to protect individuals from the "state." The more important point concerns protection of constituents from government agents. This point also accords with a positive economic theory of the First Amendment. If people think they can win a race for political favor, they may oppose restrictions on lawmaking if their expected gross gains exceed their rent-seeking costs. But the constitution reflects the fact that most people know in

advance, at the time constitutional restrictions are set in place, that they will be hurt by laws that favor incumbent politicians. See Fred S. McChesney, *A Positive Regulatory Theory of the First Amendment*, 20 CONN. L. REV. 355, 366–67 (1988).

91. See generally ANTHONY DOWNS, AN ECONOMIC THEORY OF DEMOCRACY (1957); see also Daniel A. Farber, *Free Speech Without Romance: Public Choice and the First Amendment*, 105 HARV. L. REV. 554 (1991) (arguing that First Amendment protection offsets public goods aspects of information that could cause underinvestment in lobbying against regulation).

92. See Phillip Nelson, *Political Information*, 91 J. L. & ECON. 315, 327–29 (1976) ("Even though contributions are being made for the most pernicious of purposes, the majority benefits. The payoff to other minorities is reduced more than the gain of the new contributors. . . . One . . . expects limits on campaign financing to strongly favor minority interests against the majority.") For an example of this phenomenon, see Don Phillips, "Bringing Truck Lobby to Screeching Halt," Wash. Post, June 15, 1991, at A1 (reporting that railroads' advertising campaign showing danger of triple-trailer trucks offsets power of trucking lobby).

This is true whether the expenditures are in a referendum campaign as in Bellotti or in a candidate election as in Austin. Indeed, expenditures by interest groups may be more important in the latter context as a way of exposing candidate contributions by other interest groups. Justice Scalia's Austin dissent makes the point that the information that the corporation is behind the expediture is relevant to voters:

Why should the Michigan voters in the 93d House District be deprived of the information that private associations owning and operating a vast percentage of the industry of the State, and employing a large number of its citizens, believe that the election of a particular candidate is important to their prosperity? Austin, 494 U.S. at 694.

93. MCFL, 479 U.S. at 256–60.

94. The first such restriction, the federal Corrupt Practices Act, was passed in 1907. Corrupt Practices Act, ch. 420, 34 Stat. 864 (1907). The Michigan statute involved in Austin descended from the Michigan Corrupt Practices Act, 193 Mich. Pub. Acts 109 (1913).

95. For a discussion linking this distrust to control of the power of financial institutions see Mark J. Roe, *A Political Theory of American Corporate Finance*, 91 COLUM. L. REV. 10, 32–36 (1991).

96. The Sherman Antitrust Act was passed in 1890, following antitrust statutes or constitutional amendments by 18 states in 1889–1890. See WILLIAM LETWIN, LAW AND ECONOMIC POLICY IN AMERICA: THE EVOLUTION OF THE SHERMAN ANTITRUST ACT, (1965).

97. See TERRY M. MOE, THE ORGANIZATION OF INTERESTS 47–50, 65–70 (1980) (noting some ways that organizers of interest groups can manipulate selective incentives to maximize support).

98. See RUSSELL HARDIN, COLLECTIVE ACTION 32 (1982) (stating that outings were major early motivation for joining Sierra Club); id. at 105 (stating that

Sierra Club's political activities supported by contributions rather than by members' dues).

99. See Moe, supra note 97, at 61 (noting importance of union shop rules in increasing union membership); id. at 168–76 (discussing importance of economic incentives in American labor unions); id. at 181–91 (discussing economic incentives in farm group membership); id. at 205–18 (summarizing results of questioning members of various interest groups). As an example of the importance of selective incentives to attracting members to these groups, Moe reports that in 1971 the Farm Bureau had 7,000 members in Cook County, Illinois, where Chicago and only 1000 farms were located, and that Indiana had 50% more Farm Bureau members than farms.

100. See generally, Hardin, supra note 98.

101. Imperfectly disciplined managers may overinvest surplus in political activities if they will personally gain from doing so. But there is no reason to believe that for-profit managers will systematically gain more from political investments than from nonpolitical investments given their ability to divert financial gain from nonpolitical investments to themselves through excessive compensation and the like. Indeed, managers in for-profit firms are less likely to prefer political investments for selfish reasons than those in ideological firms given the for-profit managers' significant opportunities for financial gain. Indeed, one commentator has argued that nonprofits are organized as such precisely in order to prevent managers from engaging in undetectable diversion of profits. See Henry Hansmann, *Ownership of the Firm*, 4 J. L., Econ. & Org. 267 (1988).

102. See Hardin, supra note 98, at 35–37.

103. Id. at 106; Moe, supra note 97, at 113–19.

104. For studies of the effect of geographic concentration on interest group formation see Gilbert Becker, *The Public Interest Hypothesis Revisited: A New Test of Peltzman's Theory of Regulation*, 49 Pub. Choice 223 (1986); Sally C. Kilbane & John H. Beck, *Professional Associations and the Free Rider Problem: The Case of Optometry*, 65 Pub. Choice 181 (1990); Sharon M. Oster, *An Analysis of Some Causes of Interstate Differences in Consumer Regulations*, 18 Econ. Inquiry 39 (1980); George J. Stigler, *The Theory of Economic Regulation*, in The Citizen and the State, 114 (George J. Stigler ed., 1975).

105. See Moe, supra note 97, at 113–19; Hardin, supra note 98, at 32–33 (explaining this as important explanation for women's organizations); Carole J. Uhlaner, *"Relational Goods" and Participation: Incorporating Sociability Into a Theory of Rational Action*, 62 Pub. Choice 253 (1989).

106. See Hardin, supra note 98, at 223.

107. Id. at 110.

108. Id. at 225.

109. See Gerald Keim & Asghar Zardkoohi, *Looking for Leverage in PAC Markets: Corporate and Labor Contributions Considered*, 58 Pub. Choice 21 (1988). The authors argue that corporate PACs face bigger coordination problems because they are more numerous and represent more disparate interests. The authors present data that labor PACs are better able than corporate PACs

to contribute to candidates consistent with ideology, rather than mostly, as is the case with corporate PACs, as "protection money" to more powerful incumbents.

110. See *Federalist* 10 (James Madison).

111. See Gary S. Becker, *Public Policies, Pressure Groups, and Dead Weight Costs*, 28 J. Pub. Econ. 329 (1985); Gary S. Becker, *A Theory of Competition Among Pressure Groups for Political Influence*, 98 Q. J. Econ. 371 (1983).

Effective interest groups also can offset the tendency toward redistribution of wealth among districts. Powerful politicians may maximize votes in their own district by securing legislation that benefits their districts at the expense of nonresident voters. But money is more mobile than votes. Thus, legislators may be disciplined by the threat of losing contributions from outside the district. See W. Mark Crain, Robert D. Tollison & Donald R. Leavens, *Laissez-Faire in Campaign Finance*, 56 Pub. Choice 201 (1988) (showing that in states that do not regulate campaign finance there are fewer government transfers than in states that do regulate campaign finance). The authors also show that there are more laws in such states, indicating that regulation of campaign finance involves a trade-off between, on the one hand, "off-budget" wealth transfers to corporations and labor from less organized interest groups and, on the other, "on-budget" wealth transfers directly from government.

112. See Becker, Public Policies, supra note 111. Note that even if subsidies measured by corporate profits are less than the transferees' costs, there still may be a net gain taking into account redistributions by the benefitting firms, including increased wages. See id. at 338.

113. Id. For example, law efficiency may have increased as environmentalists and customers became more organized, and therefore more able to counteract the power of polluters and producers. See Paul H. Rubin, *Common Law and Statute Law*, 11 J. Leg. Stud. 205 (1982); see also Terry L. Anderson & Robert D. Tollison, *Ideology, Interest Groups and the Repeal of the Corn Laws*, 141 J. Inst. & Theor. Econ. 197 (1985) (arguing that corn tariffs were repealed as a result of affiliation of interest groups motivated by economic self interest).

114. See W. Mark Crain, Robert D. Tollison & Donald R. Leavens, supra note 111.

115. Indeed, not only is redistributing power among groups not sufficiently desirable to justify interfering with a First Amendment right, but it may perversely influence the results of political competition. The reason is that differences among firms concerning their surplus available for political activity are not random, but in fact are correlated to some extent with organizational efficiency. In other words, the success of efficiently organized firms succeed in financial and product markets is transferred to political markets.

116. See Hardin, supra note 98, at 122–23 (stating that whether group works toward ideological goals depends in part on extent to which members have ideological commitment to organization); Moe, supra note 97, at 74:

What the by-product theory asserts, in other words, is a disjunction between member goals and group goals. There is no necessary connection between the two in latent groups. As long as members are tied into the group by means of selective incentives, it is to their advantage to continue contributing even if they disagree with associational policy, and even if the group is entirely unsuccessful in achieving goals they agree with. The leadership can pursue an independent course without fear of losing either members or their contributions and is set free of member pressure in respect to political issues and activities. An example of this disjunction is the Farmers Union, which Moe characterizes, see id. at 188, as far more liberal than its membership.

117. For a recent humorous survey of the disproportionate political strength of the farm lobby relative to the number of farmers, and how this has translated into massive wealth transfers to farmers, see P. J. O'ROURKE, PARLIAMENT OF WHORES 142–53 (1991).

118. Where the optimal size of the organization is large (because marginal benefits of increased size exceed the marginal cost of additional members) compared to the number of people sharing a given ideology, any competing club would be inefficiently small. In this situation, the member of an existing organization would not be able to viably threaten exit for purposes of forming a competing organization. See DENNIS C. MUELLER, PUBLIC CHOICE 150–54 (2d ed. 1989); James M. Buchanan, *An Economic Theory of Clubs*, 32 ECONOMICA 1 (1965).

119. See Rothenberg, *Putting the Puzzle Together: Why People Join Public Interest Groups*, 60 PUB. CHOICE 241 (1989) (giving cost benefit explanation of membership in Common Cause); Hardin, supra note 98, at 223 (arguing that Sierra Club overcomes collective action problem partly by being a "prominent" choice toward which environmentally conscious people gravitate).

120. See Malbin, supra note 84, at 259–60.

121. See Hardin, supra note 98, at 88–89 (noting that government programs tend to benefit the more affluent).

122. See Chapter Two, supra text accompanying notes 4–5.

123. To use Gordon Tullock's colorful example, nepotism may be good because it reduces the number of people competing for a job: if Mayor Richard Daley had confined all of the more lucrative appointments to his close relatives, the social savings might have been considerable." Gordon Tullock, *Rent Seeking as a Negative-Sum Game and Efficient Rent Seeking*, in TOWARD A THEORY OF THE RENT SEEKING SOCIETY 103 (James M. Buchanan. et al. eds., 1980). Tullock was referring to Richard J. Daley, not the son, Richard M. Daley, who took office after a costly election campaign some time after the father's death.

124. See Jonathan R. Macey, *Transaction Costs and the Normative Elements of the Public Choice Model: An Application to Constitutional Theory*, 74 VA. L. REV. 471 (1988): see also Jonathan R. Macey, *Promoting Public-Regarding Legislation Through Statutory Interpretation: An Interest Group Model*, 86 COLUM. L. REV. 223 (1986) (suggesting a rent-seeking-minimizing approach to statutory interpretation).

125. See supra note 89 (noting corporations' support of incumbents).

126. It might seem that large firms would oppose restrictions on corporate speech because they will consistently be winners. In an industry consisting of many firms, the industry as a whole may act collectively to obtain a particular law, but only because a few firms in the industry (perhaps the bigger firms) receive sufficiently large benefits to incur the costs of seeking collective action. These firms will influence the content of the regulation to benefit them, possibly at the expense of other companies in the industry. For example, regulation that increases costs may help an industry by providing an entry barrier, but because of scale economies the regulation may help large firms more than small firms. See Ann P. Bartel & Lacy G. Thomas, *Direct and Indirect Effects of Regulation: A New Look at OSHA's Impact*, 28 J. L. & Econ. 1 (1985); Michael T. Maloney & Robert A. McCormick, *A Positive Theory of Environmental Quality Regulation*, 25 J. L. & Econ. 99 (1982); B. Peter Pashigian, *The Effect of Environmental Regulation on Optimal Plant Size and Factor Shares*, 27 J. L. & Econ. 1 (1984). For discussions of the effect of assymmetry in resolving collective action problems see Hardin, supra note 98, at 67–89; Posner, supra note 62; George J. Stigler, *Free Riders and Collective Action: An Appendix to Theories of Economic Regulation*, 5 Bell J. Econ. 359 (1974). Accordingly, while large firms in large industries may favor corporate political activity, a much larger number of small firms which would be significant net losers from rent-seeking costs may have enough at stake to oppose corporate political activity. But small firms are not necessarily losers, and they can form effective organizations such as the Michigan State Chamber of Commerce involved in Austin.

127. See Sabato, supra note 47, at 3–5 (discussing the Tillman Act of 1907 following flagrant "assessments" of business on behalf of McKinley's 1896 campaign, and the 1974 amendments to the Federal Election Campaign Act following Watergate).

Certainly, however, there are other forces at work. Incumbents may be net gainers from corporate speech restrictions if this political capital would flow disproportionately to challengers. Also, as noted at text supra notes 94–96, there was popular support for restrictions on large corporations. And managers may have selfish reasons for favoring the combination of permitting PAC activity while restricting direct corporate activity. See supra text accompanying notes 48–49.

128. See David D. Haddock, Jonathan R. Macey & Fred S. McChesney, *Property Rights in Assets and Resistance to Tender Offers*, 73 Va. L. Rev. 701 (1987) (noting possibility of solving analogous problem in takeover resistance through private contracting).

129. For a discussion of litigation as rent-seeking conduct see Rubin supra note 113.

130. This was an important point of contention in Austin, since the Michigan statute did make that distinction. See Austin, 494 U.S. at 666–68.

131. See Michael C. Munger, *On the Political Participation of the Firm in the Electoral Process: An Update*, 56 Pub. Choice 295 (1988) (showing evidence that

firms' PAC contributions are not correlated with industry concentration); Asghar Zardkhoohi, *On the Political Participation of the Firm in the Electoral Process*, 51 S. ECON. J. 804 (1985) (reaching similar conclusion); George J. Stigler, supra note 126 (showing evidence that industry association size is not correlated with industry concentration).

132. Moreover, these justifications for corporate speech restrictions discussed in this Article are based on untested assertions. State regulation of corporate campaign contributions might be tested by interstate comparisons. The rent-seeking justification might be tested by comparing the law output of regulating and non-regulating states. For a study applying this approach, see Crain, Tollison & Leavens, supra note 114. The "corruption" argument could be supported by comparing the types of laws found in regulating and nonregulating states. But the shareholder-protection hypothesis is difficult to test: because campaign finance laws apply irrespective of state of incorporation, and therefore apply to most large companies, it is probably impossible to do meaningful stock-price comparisons between regulated and non-regulated firms. Nevertheless, it might be useful to learn the extent of any injury to shareholders from permitting corporate PAC activity by investigating a possible correlation between PAC contributions and promanagement legislation.

CHAPTER 4: CORPORATE GOVERNANCE SPEECH

1. For discussions of this doctrine and applications to securities law, see generally Symposium, *The First Amendment and Federal Securities Regulation*, 20 CONN. L. REV. (1988); Symposium, *Commercial Speech and the First Amendment*, 56 CINN. L. REV. (1988); Symposium, *Constitutional Protections of Economic Activity: How They Promote Individual Freedom*, 11 GEO. MASON U. L. REV. 81-114 (1988); Note, *The Federal Securities Laws, The First Amendment and Commercial Speech: A Call For Consistency*, 59 ST. JOHN'S L. REV. 57 (1984).

2. See Chapter One.

3. See Bernard S. Black, *Is Corporate Law Trivial?: A Political and Economic Analysis*, 84 NW. U. L. REV. 542 (1990).

4. See infra text accompanying notes 63–64.

5. See infra text accompanying notes 72–81.

6. Voiding of the securities laws would be analogous to the commercial speech doctrine itself discussed in Part 1, infra, in the sense that it imposes appropriate First Amendment constraints on special interest legislation that seeks to limit business-related speech.

7. 316 U.S. 52 (1942).

8. 425 U.S. 748 (1976).

9. Id. at 770.

10. See NICHOLAS WOLFSON, CORPORATE FIRST AMENDMENT RIGHTS AND THE SEC (1991); Ronald H. Coase, *The Market for Goods and the Market for Ideas*, 64 AM. ECON. REV. 384 (1974); Ronald H. Coase, *Advertising and Free Speech*, 6 J. LEG. STUD. 1 (1977) ("Advertising"); see also Aaron Director, *The Parity of the Economic Market Place*, 7 J. L. & ECON. 1 (1964).

11. Such advertising has been characterized as commercial. See National Commission on Egg Nutrition v. FTC, 570 F.2d 157 (7th Cir. 1977), cert. denied, 439 U.S. 281 (1978) (upholding FTC order prohibiting an egg industry trade association from making certain statements about the health value of eggs and characterizing speech as commercial); In re R.J. Reynolds Tobacco Co., 111 F.T.C. 539 (1988) (administrative agency ruling that RJR's attacks on the federal government's position that there is a link between smoking and heart disease were commercial speech); Quinn v. Aetna Life & Casualty Co., 409 N.Y.S.2d 473 (Sup. Ct. 1978) (holding that insurer's advertisements blaming high insurance premiums on large tort damage awards were commercial speech). For an analysis of this cases criticizing the commercial-noncommercial distinction, see Alan Howard, *The Constitutionality of Deceptive Speech Regulations: Replacing the Commercial Speech Doctrine with a Tort-Based Relational Framework*, 41 Case W. Res. L. Rev. 1093 (1991).

12. Central Hudson Gas & Elec. Corp. v. Public Service Comm'n of New York, 447 U.S. 557, 561 (1980).

13. See Board of Trustees of State Univ. of New York v. Fox, 492 U.S. 469, 473–74 (1989); Bolger v. Youngs Drug Prods. Corp., 463 U.S. 60, 66–67 (1983); see also City of Cincinnati v. Discovery Network, Inc., 1993 WL 79631 (1993) (assuming but not deciding that this is the test).

14. See Justice Blackmun's concurring opinions in Edenfield v. Fane, 113 S.Ct. 1792 (1993); City of Cincinnati v. Discovery Network, Inc., 1993 WL 79631 (1993); Central Hudson Gas & Elec. Corp. v. Public Service Comm'n of New York, 447 U.S. 557, 561 (1980).

15. See, e.g., Bates v. Arizona, 433 U.S. 350 (1977).

16. See In re Primus, 436 U.S. 112 (1978).

17. See Edenfield v. Fane, 113 S.Ct. 1792 (1993).

18. See Ohralik v. Ohio State Bar Ass'n, 436 U.S. 447, 456 (1978); see also Fred S. McChesney, *Commercial Speech in the Professions: The Supreme Court's Unanswered Questions Questionable Answers*, 134 U. Pa. L. Rev. 45 (1985) (criticizing this distinction between advertising and other promotional activities).

19. 447 U.S. 557, 566 (1980).

20. There is an interaction between the "definition" of commercial speech discussed in subpart I.A and the test applied to regulation of "commercial" speech. At least the first two parts of the Central Hudson test could be characterized as defining categories of speech—i.e., speech that is unlawful, misleading, or whether there is otherwise a "substantial" government interest to regulate—that are similar to Justice Blackmun's suggested categories of unprotected commercial speech. See supra text accompanying note 14. The principal difference between these parts of Central Hudson and Justice Blackmun's approach is one between rules and standards. See generally, Colin S. Diver, *The Optimal Precision of Administrative Rules*, 93 Yale L.J. 65 (1983; Isaac Ehrlich & Richard A. Posner, *An Economic Analysis of Legal Rulemaking*, 3 J. Leg. Stud. 257 (1974); Louis Kaplow, *Rules vs. Standards: An Economic Analysis*, 42 Duke L. J. 557 (1992); Carol M. Rose, *Crystals and Mud in Property Law*, 40 Stan. L. Rev. 577 (1988).

21. 492 U.S. 469 (1989). See Alfred P. Mauro, Jr., *Comment, Commercial Speech after Posadas and Fox: A Rational Basis Wolf in Intermediate Sheep's Clothing*, 66 TUL. L. REV. 1931 (1992).

22. 1993 WL 79631 (1993).

23. 113 S.Ct. 1792 (1993).

24. As noted supra at note 18, the Court in prior cases had sustained bans on lawyer solicitations. In Edenfield, the Court distinguished CPA solicitations on the ground that CPAs lack lawyers' peresuasive skills and deal with sophisticated business people. See Edenfield, 113 S.Ct. at 1797–98. For a similar, more recent case, see Ibanez v. Florida Board of Accountancy, 1994WL249528 (1994) (striking down the Board's censure of a CPA for using a "Certified Financial Planner" designation, reasoning that the Board failed to show that using the designation without a required disclaimer was either inherently or potentially misleading).

25. See infra Part IV.

26. See supra text accompanying notes 12–13. Moreover, the economic interest of the speaker is not a sound basis for distinction since even the most public-oriented "political" rhetoric often masks interest group legislation sponsored by legislators who seek to maximize contributions to their campaigns. Indeed, Jon Macey has advocated a mode of interpretation of legislation that is designed specifically to flush out the real motivations for legislation. See Jonathan R. Macey, *Promoting Public-Regarding Legislation Through Statutory Interpretation: An Interest Group Model*, 86 COLUM. L. REV. 223 (1986).

27. 779 F.2d 793 (2d Cir. 1985).

28. For another case in which the court held that a newspaper advertisement in connection with a politically-tinged proxy contest was held not to be a solicitation, see Brown v. Chicago, Rock Island & Pacific Railroad, 328 F.2d 122 (7th Cir. 1964); see also Comment, *Solicitation under the Proxy Rules: The Need for a More Precise Definition of Solicitation*, 8 Sw. U. L. REV. 1019 (1976).

29. 472 U.S. 181 (1985).

30. 851 F.2d 365 (D.C. Cir. 1988).

31. 15 U.S.C. §77q(b).

32. This approach is consistent with that of Ronald Cass, who has developed a pragmatic basis for distinguishing categories of speech for which First Amendment protection is most appropriate. See Ronald A. Cass, *Commercial Speech, Constitutionalism, Collective Choice*, 56 U. CIN. L. REV. 1317 (1988); Ronald Cass, *The Perils of Positive Thinking: Constitutional Interpretation and Negative First Amendment Theory*, 34 UCLA L. REV. 1405 (1987).

33. See ALEXANDER MEIKLEJOHN, FREE SPEECH AND ITS RELATION TO SELF-GOVERNMENT (1948); Vincent Blasi, *The "Checking Value" in First Amendment Theory*, 1977 AM. B. FOUND RES. J. 521; Robert Bork, *Neutral Principles and Some First Amendment Problems*, 47 IND. L. J. 1 (1971); Thomas H. Jackson & John C. Jeffries, *Commercial Speech: Economic Due Process and the First Amendment*, 65 VA. L. REV. 1 (1979).

34. See Wolfson, supra note 10, at 117.

35. See generally Mark Roe, *A Political Theory of American Corporate Finance*, 91 COLUM. L. REV. 10 (1991); see also Chapter Three, Section D.

36. See, e.g., Barnes v. Glen Theatre, Inc., 111 S.Ct. 2456 (1991) (involving nude dancing ban).

37. See Wolfson, supra note 10, at 114–15; Martin Redish, *The First Amendment in the Marketplace: Commercial Speech and the Values of Free Expression*, 38 GEO. WASH. L. REV. 429 (1971). Other commentators who advocate that the First Amendment generally protects self-expression or self-realization would not, however, protect commercial speech. See C. EDWIN BAKER, HUMAN LIBERTY AND FREEDOM OF SPEECH (1989); Thomas I. Emerson, *Toward a General Theory of the First Amendment*, 72 YALE L.J. 877, 105 n.46 (1963); Thomas Emerson, *First Amendment Doctrine and the Burger Court*, 68 CAL. L. REV. 422, 458–61 (1980).

38. Virginia Pharmacy, 425 U.S. at 765.

39. For an articulation of a pragmatic cost-benefit approach to the First Amendment, see Richard A. Posner, *Free Speech in an Economic Perspective*, 20 SUFFOLK U. L. REV. 1 (1986). Posner analyzes speech restrictions under the First Amendment by using a version of the Learned Hand formula: B < PL, where B is the cost of regulation, and PL is the discounted probability of the harm from speech. Posner builds on Judge Hand's rule that a court should determine the Constitutionality of a speech restriction by asking "whether the gravity of the 'evil', discounted by its improbability, justifies such invasion of free speech as is necessary to avoid the danger." Posner reduces this to the formulation that the regulation should be sustained only if B < PL, where B is the social loss from suppressing the information (V) plus error costs (E) of trying to distinguish valuable from undesirable information, and L is discounted to present value. Thus, the formula becomes $V + E < P \times L/(1 + i)n$, where n is the number of periods between the speech and the expected harm and i is the discount rate. For another discussion and application of the Posner formula, see Larry E. Ribstein, *Corporate Political Speech*, 49 WASH. & LEE L. REV. 109 (1992).

40. See Chapter Three, supra notes 76–77 and accompanying text.

41. See Gary S. Becker, *A Theory of Competition Among Pressure Groups for Political Influence*, 98 Q. J. ECON. 371, 377 (1983).

42. See JOSEPH A. SCHUMPETER, CAPITALISM, SOCIALISM, AND DEMOCRACY (3d ed. 1950).

43. See J. P. Kalt & M. A. Zupan (1988); J. P. Kalt & M. A. Zupan, *Capture and Ideology in the Economic Theory of Politics*, 74 AM. ECON. REV. 279 (1984); James B. Kau & Paul Rubin, *Self-Interest, Ideology, and Logrolling in Congressional Voting*, 22. J.L. & ECON. 365 (1979). These discussions focus on the existence of "slack" in politicians' voting. By contrast, the argument in the text focuses on politicians' incentives to maximize this "slack" by insulating themselves from electoral constraints. The two ideas arguably merge regarding preferences for anti-regulatory speech in that these preferences could be explained as politicians' use of slack.

44. See Fred S. McChesney, *A Positive Regulatory Theory of the First Amendment*, 20 CONN. L. REV. 355 (1988).

45. See Blasi, supra note 33; Cass, supra note 32; Frederick A. Schauer, *Commercial Speech and the Architecture of the First Amendment*, 56 U. CIN. L. REV. 1181 (1988); Steven Shiffrin, *The First Amendment and Economic Regulation: Away from a General Theory of the First Amendment*, 78 NW. U. L. REV. 1212 (1984).

46. In other words, although the majority group's collective benefits from being informed may outweigh its costs, individuals' benefits from being informed might outweigh the potential gains to the individual unless some of their information costs were, in effect, defrayed by advertisers.

47. See supra note 10 and accompanying text.

48. Virginia Pharmacy, 425 U.S. at 771 n.24.

49. See Posner, supra note 39 (endorsing the chilling effect argument).

50. See Chapter Three, supra text accompanying notes 97–100.

51. See Wolfson, supra note 10, at 99.

52. See George J. Bentson, *Government Constraints on Political, Artistic and Commercial Speech*, 20 CONN. L. REV. 303, 308–09 (1988); Posner, supra note 39, at 36–39.

53. One indication of the advantages of incumbency is that PAC spending heavily favors incumbents. See text accompanying Chapter Three, notes 87–90.

54. See Coase ("Advertising"), supra note 10, at 29.

55. See Jonathan R. Macey & Geoffrey Miller, *The Fraud on the Market Theory Revisited*, 77 VA. L. REV. 1001 (1991).

56. There is overwhelming evidence that securities markets incorporate new information rapidly in stock prices is overwhelming, and at the same time also evidence that stock prices are somewhat "noisy" in that they react to forces other than new information. For reviews of the evidence on stock market efficiency, see Eugene Fama, *Efficient Capital Markets: II*, 46 J. FIN. 1575 (1991); Jeffrey Gordon & Kornhauser, *Efficient Markets, Costly Information, and Securities Research*, 60 N.Y.U.L. REV. 761, 781–86 (1985); Donald Langevoort, *Theories, Assumptions, and Securities Regulation: Market Efficiency Revisited*, 140 U. Pa. L. REV. 851 (1992). We need not settle this issue, because the point in the text is only that active stock markets limit the potential damage from securities fraud, not that they eliminate it.

57. See Posner, supra note 39, at 39–40.

58. See Wolfson, supra note 10, at 64–65.

59. See id. at 135–36.

60. For example, bans on attorney solicitation may help certain lawyers compete with others while hurting consumers of legal services. See Ohralik v. Ohio State Bar Ass'n, 436 U.S. 447, 472–77 (1978) (Marshall, J., dissenting); McChesney, supra note 44.

61. This is consistent with Ronald Cass' "negative" theory of the First Amendment, which seeks to identify certain categories of cases in which government regulation of speech may be a problem. See Cass, Positive Thinking, supra note 32.

62. See supra text accompanying note 14.

63. See Larry E. Ribstein, *Private Ordering and the Securities Laws: The Case of General Partnerships*, 42 CASE RES. L. REV. 1 (1991) (discussing avoidance of the securities law by choosing the general partnership form).

64. See Bonny v. The Society Of Lloyd's, 1993 WL 292345 (7th Cir. 1993) (enforcing choice of English law and forum in securities case); Larry E. Ribstein, *Efficiency, Regulation and Competition: A Comment on Easterbrook & Fischel*, 87 NW. UNIV. L. REV. 254 (1992) (discussing the effect of jurisdictional competition on the securities laws).

65. See Lochner v. New York, 198 U.S. 45 (1905). For arguments that the commercial speech distinction is necessary to avoid a return to substantive due process review, see Michael P. Dooley, *The First Amendment and the SEC: A Comment*, 20 CONN. L. REV. 335, 352 (1988); Jackson & Jeffries, supra note 33 (arguing that Virginia Pharmacy was actually based on the same sort of concerns for economic efficiency that underly substantive due process challenges).

66. See, e.g., Richard A. Epstein, Takings (1985).

67. 478 U.S. 326 (1986). For an argument that Posadas should not be interpreted to "overrun the constitutional protection of commercial speech generally," see Richard A. Epstein, Bargaining with the State, 209–10 (1993); Richard A. Epstein, *The Supreme Court, 1987 Term: Foreword-Unconstitutional Conditions, State Power, and the Limits of Consent*, 102 HARV. L. REV. 4, 66–67 (1988).

68. See Virginia Pharmacy, quoted supra note 9.

69. See Central Hudson Gas & Elec. Corp. v. Public Serv. Comm'n, 447 U.S. 557, 574–75 (1980).

70. See supra text accompanying notes 41–47.

71. See Securities Exchange Act of 1934, 15 U.S.C. §77(n).

72. 17 C.F.R. §240.14a-8.

73. See Wolfson, supra note 10, at 122–24 (noting the political nature of proxy proposals).

74. 795 F. Supp. 95 (S.D.N.Y. 1992), dismissed as moot, 969 F.2d 1430 (2d Cir. 1992).

75. Amalgamated Clothing and Textile Workers Union, v. Wal-Mart Stores, Inc., 1993 WL 134134 (S.D.N.Y. 1993).

76. See United Paperworkers Int'l v. Int'l Paper Co. 985 F.2d 1190 (2d Cir. 1993).

77. See RALPH NADER, ET AL. TAMING THE GIANT CORPORATION (1976); CHRISTOPHER STONE, WHERE THE LAW ENDS (1975); Lewis Solomon & Kathleen J. Collins, *Humanistic Economics: A New Model for the Corporate Social Responsibility Debate*, 12 J. CORP. L. 331 (1987).

78. See SEC v. Joseph Schlitz Brewing Co., 452 F. Supp. 824 (E.D. Wis. 1978) (requiring disclosure of corporate misconduct); LARRY E. RIBSTEIN, BUSINESS ASSOCIATIONS 340–41 (2d ed. 1990); Stevenson, *The SEC and the New Disclosure*, 63 CORNELL L. REV. 50 (1976); Stevenson, *The SEC and Foreign and Foreign Bribery*, 32 Bus. Law. 53 (1976).

79. See generally Chapter One.

80. There is a close connection between what have been termed "relational" contracts and the governance of firms. See Chapter One, supra text accompanying notes 2–4.

81. For other arguments that the politicization of the corporate form justifies applying First Amendment protection, see Wolfson, supra note 10, at 145–46; Henry N. Butler, *Edited Transcript of Symposium on the First Amendment and Securities Regulation*, 20 CONN. L. REV. 383, 454 (1988) (quoting Wolfson to the effect that "from the [American Law Institute's and SEC's] standpoint, full first amendment protection of proxy speech is a hoisting of their petard with a vengeance"). Note that proxy regulation is probably more accurately explained by interest group or legislative agency costs considerations than on public interest grounds. However, it makes sense to apply a "public regarding" construction in assessing the validity of the statute to force the underlying motivations into the open. See Macey, supra note 26.

82. See Mark J. Roe, Foundations of Corporate Finance: *The 1906 Pacification of the Insurance Industry*, 93 COLUM. L. REV. 639 (1993); Mark J. Roe, *Political Elements in the Creation of a Mutual Fund Industry*, 139 U. PA. L. REV. 1469 (1991); Mark J. Roe, supra note 35.

83. Roe, supra note 35, at 49–50.

84. Business and financial institutions have been characterized as an intermediating force between the government and the individual. See Wolfson, supra note 10, at 138.

85. Id. at 50.

86. With respect to politicians' acting as entrepreneurs to threaten regulation in order to increase support from the would-be subjects of the regulation, see Fred S. McChesney, *Rent Extraction and Rent Creation in the Economic Theory of Regulation*, 16 J. LEG. STUD. 1 (1987).

87. See Roberta Romano, *Public Pension Fund Activisim in Corporate Governance Reconsidered*, 93 COLUM. L. REV. 795 (1993).

88. Id. at 812.

89. See supra text accompanying notes 75–76.

90. See Grimes v. Ohio Edison Co., 1993 WL 137801 (2d Cir. 1993) (holding that proposal to require approval of capital spending over $300 million excluded because it could apply even to trivial items over the threshold); Grimes v. Centerior Energy Corp., 909 F.2d 529 (D.C. Cir. 1990), cert. denied, 111 S. Ct. 799 (1991) (holding that proposal to amend utility company's articles to generally limit capital spending was within ordinary business exclusion). The SEC also at one time excluded executive compensation proposals, but has recently changed its position because of the "widespread public debate" See Fed. Sec. L. Rep. (CCH), -‖ 76,101 - 76,110 ("no action" letters); id. at -‖ 84,926 (Chairman Breeden's statement).

91. 475 U.S. 1 (1986).

92. See First National Bank of Boston v. Bellotti, 435 U.S. 765 (1978) (discussed in Chapter Three, supra text accompanying notes 8–12).

93. See Pacific Gas, 475 U.S. at 14 n.10. Justice Stevens, dissenting, concluded that the two situations could not be distinguished. See id. at 39–40.

94. Cf. Wolfson, supra note 10 at 128–32 (analogizing the Belotti line of cases and proxy speech on the ground that all involve the question of who makes political speech for corporation).

95. Conversely, managers can use "external" "political" speech to alter their relationships with shareholders. See Henry N. Butler & Larry E. Ribstein, *State Anti-Takeover Statutes and the Contract Clause,* 57 U. Cin. L. Rev. 611 (1988); Roberta Romanno, *The Political Economy of Takeover Statutes,* 73 Va. L. Rev. 1 (1987) (discussing lobbying by managers for state antitakeover statutes).

96. See infra text accompanying notes 110–14 (discussing regulation of "solicitations"). For criticism of this aspect of proxy regulation, see Black, supra note 106; John Pound, *Proxy Voting and the SEC: Investor Protection Versus Market Efficiency,* 29 J. Fin. Econ. 241 (1991). The SEC has responded to this criticism with new proxy rules that reduce, but do not eliminate, this regulation. See Regulation of Communications among Shareholders, S.E.C. Release No. 34-31326, 1992 WL 301258 (Oct. 16, 1992).

97. It is not clear whether rules requiring preclearance present more of a problem than rules imposing damages after the transaction. Wolfson, supra note 10, at 154–56, notes a potentially serious First Amendment problem with SEC preliminary review disclosures, particularly because of potential delay and limited judicial review. However, as Wolfson says, see id. at 156–57, mandatory restraint may not have a larger chilling effect than a large ex post damage award. Although Wolfson is concerned about the use of preliminary review to impose a "government orthodoxy," ex post damages could have the same effect. Moreover, preliminary screening may actually support mandatory federal regulation by helping to solve the problem of unpredictability that is inherent in fraud cases. See Frank Easterbrook & Daniel Fischel, *Mandatory Disclosure and the Protection of Investors,* 70 Va. L. Rev. 669 (1984).

98. Cass, Commercial Speech, supra note 32, at 1369, distinguishes corporate managers from politicians on the ground that managers' compensation reflects their contributions to the firm, although perhaps imperfectly. This questionably ignores politicians' significant intangible compensation through power and prestige.

99. See SEC v. Wall Street Publishing Inst., 851 F.2d 365, 373–74 (D.C.Cir. 1988) (upholding regulation under First Amendment in part because it only required additional disclosure rather than prohibiting disclosure).

100. See SEC Rule 408, 17 C.F.R. §230.408.

101. See Wolfson, supra note 10, at 36 (noting that mandatory disclosure rules can impose a "straitjacket" on permissible speech).

102. See the discussion of Pacific Gas, supra notes 91–93.

103. See supra text accompanying note 93 (comparing the two situations). The shareholder proposal rule arguably helps shareholders overcome the free rider problem and therefore encourages speech by shareholders at the

same time as it chills speech by managers. However, rather than refuting the chilling effect argument, it only shows the extent to which regulators are able to slant the debate through regulation that favors one side over the other.

104. See United Paperworkers Int'l v. Int'l Paper Co. 985 F.2d 1190 (2d Cir. 1993); supra text accompanying note 76.

105. Evidence of market efficiency is discussed in Chapter One, *supra*, at notes 6–13. It has been argued that the social value of market efficiency may not be enough to justify some regulation that promotes this efficiency. See Lynn Stout, *The Unimportance of Being Efficient: An Economic Analysis of Stock Market Pricing and Securities Regulation*, 87 MICH. L. REV. 613 (1988). However, even if this is true, the point in the text is only that delay of disclosure is more costly in capital than in political markets. More importantly, Professor Stout's argument undercuts a principal rationale for securities regulation based on efficient allocation of resources. Accordingly, if she is correct, there may be too little benefit associated with securities regulation to offset the potential cost.

106. See Wolfson, supra note 10, at 151 (questioning government's ability to review tender offer disclosures); Bernard S. Black, *Disclosure, Not Censorship: The Case for Proxy Reform*, 17 J. CORP. L. 49, 55 (1991) (criticizing "silliness" of government review of proxy material submitted by an institutional investor service).

107. See Easterbrook & Fischel, supra note 97.

108. See Jonathan Macey & Geoffrey Miller, *The Fraud-on-the-Market Theory Revisited*, 77 VA. L. REV. 1001 (1991).

109. See Benston, supra note, at 319 (making a similar point about First Amendment constraints on proxy regulation).

110. See supra text accompanying notes 106–107.

111. SEC Rule 14a-1(1), 17 C.F.R. §240.14a-1(1); see also Studebaker Corp. v. Gittlin, 360 F.2d 692 (2d Cir. 1966) (stating that "solicitation" includes solicitation to join in request for shareholder list).

112. See supra note 96.

113. See supra text accompanying notes 96–97.

114. Indeed, it is not clear these changes went far enough to make the solicitation rules constitutional. Among other things, the amended rules still require shareholders to comply where they are seeking proxy authority and where they have an interest in the matter subject to vote, and require even disinterested large shareholders who are not seeking proxy authority but are engaging in any kind of a written "solicitation" (including a letter) to give public notice to the Commission. See SEC Rule 14a-2(b), 17 C.F.R. §§240.14a-2(b).

115. 15 U.S.C. §77a et seq.

116. More precisely, the statute forbids the use of a "prospectus," which is broadly defined in the Act to include most written communications. Securities Act of 1933, 15 U.S.C. §77b(10).

117. Securities Act of 1933. 15 U.S.C. §77e.

118. Id. §§77k, 77l(2), 77q(a).

119. Some state laws operating on a principle of "merit" regulation permit administrators to bar the sale of securities even if full disclosure is made. See, e.g., Mo. Rev. Stat. §409.306(a).

120. See Chapter Five, infra, text accompanying notes 186–190.

121. See Note, supra note 1 (distinguishing third party communications and prospectuses advertising securities on the ground that latter are less likely to be chilled by government regulation). For an argument that prospectus regulation involves regulation of the conduct of issuing securities, see Allen D. Boyer, *Free Speech, Free Markets, and Foolish Consistency,* 92 COLUM. L. REV. 474, 484–86 (1992). This is simply wrong: issuance of securities is clearly governed by state corporate law. Securities law governs only disclosures on public offerings of stock.

122. One writer has argued that the First Amendment should be applied in this context because prospectus regulation inhibits freedom of association. See Wolfson, supra note 10, at 144. However, the securities of ordinary for-profit firms are not analogous to membership in private clubs. Under the Capital Assets Pricing Model, securities involve fungible packages of risk-return tradeoffs. Cf. Frank Easterbrook & Daniel Fischel, *Optimal Damages in Securities Cases,* 52 U. CHI. L. REV. 611 (1985) (discussing this as a reason why investors should not be entitled to benefit-of-the-bargain damages in securities fraud cases).

123. See Securities Act of 1933, 15 U.S.C. §77k.

124. See supra text accompanying notes 106–107.

125. See Forms S-1, S-2 and S-3 under the Securities Act of 1933.

126. See infra text accompanying notes 129–132.

127. Indeed, one writer argues that market efficiency is most important regarding new issues and financing generally because in this context it has a direct impact on resource allocation. See Stout, supra note 105.

128. See SEC Rule 135, 17 C.F.R. §230.135 (setting forth the information issuers can disclose about their offerings); Securities Act Release No. 3844 (Oct. 8, 1957) (giving examples of permissible and impermissible disclosures); Carl M. Loeb, Rhoades & Co., 38 S.E.C. 843 (1959) (holding that disclosures during registration about an impending offering violated the 1933 Act). The clearest indication of the problems publicly held issuers face under the 1933 Act is Chris-Craft Industries, Inv. v. Bangor Punta Corp., 426 F.2d 569 (2d. Cir. 1970) (en banc), rev'd on other grounds, 430 U.S. 1 (1977), which held that a company making an exchange offer, and therefore required to make certain disclosures to the target shareholders under the 1934 Act about the offer, violated the 1933 Act by saying too much.

129. It might also be argued that the Act helps reduce litigation costs by forcing investors to rely on easily provable written statements. See Easterbrook & Fischel, supra note 97, at 679. However, the Act also imposes liability for oral statements whether or not the investor has received a statutory prospectus. See Securities Act of 1933, 15 U.S.C. §§77l(2), 77q(a). In this respect the Act actually impedes the private market solution to the litigation cost problem of binding the investor to a reliance solely on the prospectus.

130. See Michael E. Schoeman, *The First Amendment and Restrictions on Advertising of Securities Under the Securities Act of 1933*, 41 Bus. Law. 377 (1986) (also concluding that the 1933 Act is unreasonably broad and therefore unconstitutional under Central Hudson).

131. See Homer Kripke, *The SEC, the Accountants, Some Myths and Some Realities*, 45 N.Y.U. L. Rev. 1151 (1970).

132. See Edenfield v. Fane, 113 S.Ct. 1792 (1993); discussed supra text accompanying notes 123–124.

133. See supra note 19.

134. See supra text accompanying notes 8–9.

135. See supra text accompanying notes.

136. See Securities Exchange Act of 1934, 15 U.S.C. §78l (requiring issuers with more than a certain number of holders to register); id. 15 U.S.C. §78m (requiring issuers registered under id. §12 to file regular reports).

137. See United Paperworkers Int'l, 985 F.2d at 1190 (holding that company could not rely on information in these filings for an argument that the company's proxy statement was not misleading in the light of the "total mix" of available information).

138. See supra text accompanying notes 106–108.

139. See supra text accompanying notes 19–20.

140. See Wolfson, supra note 10, at 154 (arguing that the First Amendment would permit regulation of lying but not of timing).

141. See generally Comment, *Disclosure of Socially Oriented Information under the Securities Acts*, 2 U. Haw. L. Rev. 557 (1981).

142. See generally Larry E. Ribstein, *The Scope of Federal Securities Law Liability for Corporate Transactions*, 33 Sw. L. J. 1129 (1980).

143. See Securities Exchange Act of 1934, 15 U.S.C. §§78m(d)–(e), 78n(d)–(e).

144. See, e.g., Securities Exchange Act of 1934, 15 U.S.C. §78n(d) (requiring disclosures in connection with tender offers and acquisitions of large blocks).

145. 15 U.S.C. §78j(b).

146. 17 C.F.R. §240.10b-5.

147. See Basic Inc. v. Levinson, 485 U.S. 224, 239 n.17 (1988) (stating that "[s]ilence, absent a duty to disclose, is not misleading under Rule 10b-5").

148. See Jordan v. Duff & Phelps, Inc., 815 F.2d 429 (7th Cir. 1987) (finding such a duty under state law).

149. See Chapter One, supra, text accompanying notes 51–57.

150. 15 U.S.C. §78p(b).

151. Nor do the insider trading reporting requirements imposed by section 16(a) of the 1934 Act, id. §78p(a), present a significant First Amendment problem, since they can be viewed more as a precondition for engaging in the conduct of insider trading than as speech regulation. The regulation simply requires disclosure of trades. Unlike other mandatory disclosure rules, it does not involve government prescription of the content of what firms or individuals tell the markets about themselves. They are, in effect, no

different from the application required to obtain a drivers' or marriage license.

CHAPTER 5: CHOOSING LAW BY CONTRACT

1. See Restatement (Second) of Conflicts, §302(2) (1971) (stating general rule). For other rules recognizing the applicability of the law of the state of incorporation concerning particular matters, see id. §296 (requirements for incorporation); id. §297 (states recognize foreign incorporations); id. §303 (determination of who are shareholders); id. §304 (participation in management and profits); id. §305 (who votes shares of voting trust); id. §306 (liability of majority shareholder); id. §307 (shareholder liability to the corporation and creditors). Note that the parties may create ambiguity by providing that a shareholders' agreement (or other contract related to the corporation) is governed by a law other than the law of the state of incorporation. Perhaps this specific choice of law should override the more general choice inherent in selecting the incorporating state. On the other hand, to the extent that the agreement affects nonparty shareholders, the parties to the agreement should not be able on their own to override the earlier unanimous choice of the chartering state's law. For a recent case applying the law of the incorporating state in this situation, see Rosenmiller v. Borden (Del. Ch. 1991).

2. For some leading cases see Mansfield v. Hardwood Lumber Co. v. Johnson, 268 F.2d 317 (5th Cir. 1959); Wilson v. Louisiana-Pacific Resources, Inc., 187 Cal. Rptr. 852 (1982); Western Air Lines, Inc. v. Sobieski, 12 Cal. Rptr. 719 (1961). Restatement (Second) of Conflicts, section 302(2) provides that "[t]he local law of the state of incorporation will be applied to determine such issues, except in the unusual case where, with respect to the particular issue, some other state has a more significant relationship to the occurrence and the parties, in which event the local law of the other state will be applied" (emphasis added). Id. Comment g states that this will happen only in "the extremely rare situation where a contrary result is required by the overriding interest of another state in having its rule applied" (emphasis added).

3. See id. Comment e; P. John Kozyris, *Corporate Wars and Choice of Law*, 1985 DUKE L.J. 1, 50; Willis L.M. Reese & Edward M. Kaufman, *The Law Governing Corporate Affairs: Choice of Law and the Impact of Full Faith & Credit*, 58 COLUM. L. REV. 1118 (1958).

4. See cases cited supra note 2.

5. See Restatement (second) of Conflicts, §302(2), Comment e (noting that such matters as corporate torts and ownership of property and share transfer rights did not have to be subject to a single state's law). In particular, the law of the incorporating state may not be applied regarding shareholder inspection rights. See id. §304, Comment d; Sadler v. NCR Corporation, 928 F.2d 48 (2d Cir. 1991); Valtz v. Penta Investment Corp., 188 Cal. Rptr. 922 (1983) (holding that shareholder's inspection right not an "internal affair" and therefore could be regulated by state [California] where corporation had significant contact, including maintenance of principal executive office);

Jefferson Industrial Bank v. First Golden Bancorporation, 762 P.2d 768 (Colo. App. 1988); McCormick v. Statler Hotels Delaware Corp., 203 N.E.2d 697 (Ill. 1964).

6. See 2 JOSEPH BEALE, CONFLICT OF LAWS, §332.2 (1935); HERBERT F. GOODRICH HANDBOOK ON THE CONFLICT OF LAWS 325–33 (3d ed. 1949); RALPH C. MINOR, CONFLICT OF LAWS, 401–02 (1901); ERNEST C. LORENZEN, *Validity and Effects of Contracts in the Conflict of Laws*, 30 YALE L. J. 655, 658 (1921).

7. See WALTER W. COOK, THE LOGICAL AND LEGAL BASES OF THE CONFLICT OF LAWS 392 (1949).

8. See Seeman v. Philadelphia Warehouse Co., 274 U.S. 403 (1927) (holding that Pennsylvania law rather than New York usury law governed loan to be repaid in Pennsylvania involving Pennsylvania corporation doing business in Pennsylvania); Siegleman v. Cunard White Star Ltd, 221 F.2d 189 (2d Cir. 1955) (holding in admiralty case that English law governed as provided in steamship ticket); Duskin v. Pennsylvania-Central Airline Corp., 167 F.2d 727 (6th Cir. 1948) (holding that Pennsylvania law governed contract executed in the District of Columbia between employee domiciled in Oklahoma, temporarily residing in Tennessee, and Delaware corporation with principal office in the District of Columbia, where flying service was strongly connected with Pennsylvania); Hal Roach Studios, Inc. v. Film Classics, Inc., 156 F.2d 196 (2d Cir. 1946) (holding that New York law governed contract with which many jurisdictions had contact).

9. See Restatement (Second) of Conflicts, §187 (1971). The parties can indicate their choice of law by such means as including terms of art in their contract. See id. Comment a.

10. Id. §188.

11. Id. §187(1). See also id. §204(1) (stating that words in contract should be construed "in accordance with the local law of the state chosen by the parties").

12. Id. §187(2).

13. See Adam P. Weinberger, *Party Autonomy and Choice-of-Law: The Restatement (Second), Interest Analysis and the Search for a Methodological Synthesis*, 4 HOFSTRA L. REV. 605, 612–13 (1976). The Restatement identifies the following contacts as relevant to contracts:

(a) the place of contracting,

(b) the place of negotiation of the contract,

(c) the place of performance,

(d) the location of the subject matter of the contract, and

(e) the domicile, residence, nationality, place of incorporation and place of business of the parties. Restatement (Second) of Conflicts, §188(2) (1971).

14. See id. §188(1).

15. Id. §6 lists these factors:

(a) the needs of the interstate and international systems, (b) the relevant policies of the forum, (c) the relevant policies of other interested states and the relative interests of those states in the determination of the particular issue, (d) the protection of justified expectations, (e) the basic policies underlying the particular field of law, (f) certainty, predictability and uniformity of result, and (g) ease in the determination and application of the law to be applied.

16. See RUSSELL J. WEINTRAUB, COMMENTARY ON THE CONFLICT OF LAWS 377 (3rd ed. 1986) (arguing that such an interest should be necessary).

17. See Restatement (Second) of Conflicts (1971); §187(2) referring to the general contracts-conflicts rule in id. §188.

18. See id. §187, Comment g at 568.

19. Id. (referring to id. §90 which provides that a forum will not entertain a foreign cause of action enforcement of which would contravene its "strong public policy").

20. Id.

21. Compare, e.g., Sutter Home Winery, Inc. v. Vintage Selections, Ltd. 1992 WL 179458 (9th Cir. 1992) (holding that California law chosen subject to "applicable" law, which court interpreted to be local liquor franchise law of Arizona) with Tele-Save Merchandising v. Consumers Distributing, 814 F.2d 1120 (6th Cir. 1987) (applying selected N.J. law over Ohio statute where Ohio has policy of enforcing choice of law, contacts were divided and it was not clear fundamental policy would be thwarted because contractual state, New Jersey, had common law remedies); George F. Carpinello, *Testing the Limits of Choice of Law Clauses: Franchise Contracts as a Case Study*, 74 MAR. L. REV. 57 (1990); Thomas M. Pitegoff, *Choice of Law in Franchise Agreements*, 9 FRANCH L.J. 1 (1989) (concluding that most cases do not enforce the choice of law clause on fundamental policy grounds); Larry E. Ribstein, *Choosing Law by Contract*, 18 J. CORP. L. 245 (1993).

22. Compare Broadway & Seymour, Inc. v. Wyatt, 944 F.2d 900 (4th Cir. 1991) (applying selected law and enforcing noncompetition) with Great Fame Up Systems, Inc. v. Jazayeri Enterprises, Inc. 789 F. Supp. 253 (N.D. Ill. 1992) (applying nonselected statute that restricted enforcement but nevertheless enforcing covenant under selected state's law because covenant did not clearly violate the statute).

23. Compare Kronovet v. Lipchin, 415 A.2d 1096 (Md. App. 1980) (enforcing law selected by parties deliberately to avoid nonselected state's usury limit) with North American Bank, Ltd. v. Schulman, 474 N.Y.S.2d 383 (N.Y. Co. Ct. 1984) (refusing to enforce parties' selection of foreign law and applying usury statute).

24. See Restatement (Second) of Conflicts 568 (1971).

25. Id.; see Donald T. Trautman, *Some Notes on the Theory of Choice of Law Clauses*, 35 MERCER L. REV. 535 (1984) (discussing these qualifications on the "fundamental policy" rule).

26. See Restatement (Second) of Conflicts, §294 (1971). Moreover, the court need not apply the organization state's characterization of the firm as a corporation, but rather may make an independent characterization based on the firm's attributes. See id. §298; see also Hemphill v. Orloff, 277 U.S. 537 (1928) (holding that Michigan could require a firm chartered in Georgia as a Commercial Investment Trust to register as a foreign corporation in Michigan in order to do business there).

27. See Greenspun v. Lindley, 330 N.E.2d 79 (1975) (holding that Massachusetts law does not necessarily control Massachusetts business trust but applying it in present case in the absence of a showing concerning the firm's contacts with New York); Means v. Limpia Royalties, 115 S.W.2d 468 (Tex. Civ. App. 1938) (holding that Texas law controls limited liability of Oklahoma trust). Cf. Abu-Nassar v. Elders Futures, Inc., 1991 U.S. Dist. LEXIS 3794 (S.D.N.Y. Mar. 28, 1991) (applying Lebanese law to determine the compliance of limited liability company with formalities of organization but New York law to determine whether veil should be pierced).

28. See Restatement (Second) of Conflicts, §307 (1971).

29. Id. §295(3) (referring to general rule stated in id. §294). Note, however, that Comment d to section 295 states that a limited partner should be compared to a corporate shareholder, indicating that a court should apply the same choice-of-law rule despite the difference in black letter.

30. For a discussion of interstate recognition of noncorporate firms, see Larry E. Ribstein & Robert Keatinge, Ribstein & Keatinge on Limited Liability Companies, §13.04 (1992).

31. See Restatement (Second) of Conflicts, §294, Comment b.

32. If the parties to partnerships have no expectations concerning the applicable law, that is probably only because there has long been a high degree of uniformity in state partnership law. The Uniform Partnership Act has been adopted in substantial part by 49 states. Note, however, that the recent promulgation of the Uniform Partnership Act (1992) may cause substantial disuniformity in partnership law, thereby increasing the importance of the conflicts issues. Section 106 provides that the law of the firm's chief executive office controls but, interestingly enough, that provision is subject to contrary agreement. Id. §106 This may signal a movement of partnership law toward a corporate-type internal affairs rule.

33. See, e.g., Lucian Bebchuk, Limiting Freedom of Contract In Corporate Law: The Desirable Constraints on Charter Amendments, 102 HARV. L. REV. 1820 (1989); Melvin A. Eisenberg, The Structure of Corporate Law, 89 COLUM. L. REV. 1461 (1989); Jeffrey N. Gordon, The Mandatory Structure of Corporate Law, 89 COLUM. L. REV. 1549 (1989).

34. This argument is, in fact, the core of a recent attack on the race to the top. See Bebchuk, supra note 33, at 1458-85.

35. See Reese & Kaufman, supra note 3, at 1121.

36. For criticism of this use of the entity theory, see Latty, supra note 60, at 140 (characterizing personification as "highly nonfunctional dogma").

37. For a more detailed discussion of the benefits of jurisdictional competition, see infra Part II.A.2.

38. Roberta Romano has used the "product" analogy to describe the choice-of-law process in corporate law. See Roberta Romano, Law as a Product: Some Pieces of the Incorporation Puzzle, 1 J. L. ECON. & ORG. 225 (1985) (showing that states do compete to provide corporate contract terms, and that franchise tax revenues provide an important incentive to do so).

39. See infra Part IV.A (discussing interest group theory of legislation).

40. About half the states have statutes forbidding termination other than for "good cause," which includes franchisee breach or withdrawal from the business. For discussions of these statutes, see E.S. Bills, Inc. v. Tzucanow, 700 P.2d 1280 (1985) (Mosk, J., concurring) (discussing rationales for the statutes); James A. Brickley, Frederick H. Dark & Michael S. Weisbach, *The Economic Effects of Franchise Termination Laws*, 34 J. L. & ECON. 101 (1991); Robert W. Emerson. *Franchising and the Collective Rights of Franchisees*, 43 VAND. L. REV. 1503, 1523–32 (1990). Although most of these statutes add little to the "good faith" requirement that already existed under the Uniform Commercial Code and the common law of contract, more recent statutes attempt to regulate franchising more aggressively. A prominent example is 1992 Ia. HF 2362, Ia. Stat. §532H.1 et. seq., which regulates in detail such manners as sale of franchises, encroachment, renewal and termination.

41. There is significant theory and evidence that brand-name owners select franchises rather than company-owned stores to help solve monitoring problems. For example, firms are most likely to franchise outlets that rely on transient trade and therefore will attract business primarily on the basis of the franchisor's brand name rather than local repeat business. See James A. Brickley, Frederick H. Dark & Michael S. Weisbach, *An Agency Perspective on Franchising*, 20 FIN. MGT. 27 (1991); James A. Brickley & Frederick H. Dark, *The Choice of Organizational Form: The Case of Franchising*, 18 J. FIN. ECON. 401 (1987); Anthony W. Dnes, *'Unfair' Contractual Practices and Hostages in Franchise Contracts*, 148 J. INST. & THEO. ECON. 484 (1992); Alan Krueger, *Ownership, Agency, and Wages: An Examination of Franchising in the Fast Food Industry*, 106 Q. J. ECON. 75 (1991); Robert E. Martin, *Franchising and Risk Management*, 78 AM. ECON. REV. 954 (1988); G. Frank Mathewson & Ralph A. Winter, *The Economics of Franchise Contracts*, 28 J.L. & ECON. 503 (1985); Seth W. Norton, *Franchising, Labor Productivity, and the New Institutional Economics*, 145 J. INST. & THEO. ECON. 578 (1989); Seth W. Norton, *An Empirical Look at Franchising as an Organizational Form*, 61 J. BUS. 197 (1988); Paul H. Rubin, *The Theory of the Firm and the Structure of the Franchise Contract*, 21 J.L. & ECON. 221 (1978).

42. Indeed, one writer concludes that, because of the risk of opportunistic appropriation by the franchisor, firm-specific investments by the frachisee, are rarely used in franchising as a way of motivating the franchisee. Instead, they are used largely for other reasons, including screening franchisees and offsetting specific costs franchisors may incur from of transferring franchises. See Dnes, supra note 41.

43. One writer has argued that relatively strict enforcement of termination is a mistake because it does not adequately take into account the "norms" of the relationship, including franchisee's vulnerability and expectation of forbearance from the franchisor. See Gillian K. Hadfield, *Problematic Relations: Franchising and the Law of Incomplete Contracts*, 42 STAN. L. REV. 927 (1990). Even assuming the courts have gotten the contract wrong, however, it does not follow that the courts, or the parties themselves in future contracts, would not do a better job of fixing the problem than the legislature. A general legislative rule certainly would not be appropriate based on Professor

Hadfield's analysis, which emphasizes the fact-specific relational quality of franchise contracts.

44. Richard Posner has advocated application of the First Restatement's "territorial" approach to choice of law partly on the ground that the jurisdiction local to the transaction has a comparative regulatory advantage in determining the appropriate rules. See RICHARD A. POSNER, ECONOMIC ANALYSIS OF LAW 587 (4th ed. 1992). While the territorial approach may be a suitable default rule, enforcing the parties' contract would be superior under this analysis because the question of which law is most appropriate for a particular transaction can best be determined by the parties themselves.

45. For data on how this competition has worked to spread efficient new corporate law terms, see Romano, supra note 38, at 233–35. For a discussion of the conditions necessary to produce competition and an application to Canadian corporate law, see Ronald J. Daniels, *Should Provinces Compete? The Case for a Competitive Corporate Law Market*, 36 McGILL L.J. 130 (1991).

46. See Daniel R. Fischel, *From MITE to CTS: State Anti-Takeover Statutes, the Williams Act, the Commerce Clause, and Insider Trading*, 1987 SUP. CT. REV. 47, 85.

47. For a discussion of the effect of tax classification rules on statutory flexibility, see Larry E. Ribstein, *The Deregulation of Limited Liability and the Death of Partnership*, 70 WASH. U. L.Q. 417, 465–67 (1992).

48. See, e.g., Del. Code. Ann. tit. 6, §18-704; Tex. Rev. Civ. Stat. Ann. tit. 32, art. 1528n, art. 4.07 (allowing the members to provide for free transferability of management rights).

49. LLC statutes provide that foreign LLCs, like foreign limited partnerships, are subject to the law of their formation state. See Ribstein & Keatinge, supra note 30, §13.03.

50. See Ian Ayres, *Making a Difference: The Contractual Contributions of Easterbrook and Fischel*, 59 U. CHI. L. REV. 1391 (1992).

51. For a discussion of the trade-offs involved in selecting specific rules or general standards, see Isaac Ehrlich & Richard A. Posner, *An Economic Analysis of Legal Rulemaking*, 3 L. LEG. STUD. 257 (1974).

52. A related benefit from enforcing choice of law is utilizing the state's reliable application, as distinguished from formulation, of standards. This is a function not merely of the rules being applied but also of who is applying them. Thus, the parties would want their disputes decided by judges who understand the business background of the transaction and who have experience deciding similar cases. This is primarily a function of contractual selection of the forum and adjudicator. The enforcement of such clauses is largely beyond the scope of this Article, although they are discussed infra Part IV.F.1 in terms of how they relate to enforcement choice-of-law clauses.

53. It is also not clear whether, even if arbitrators did prepare opinions, these opinions are binding. The parties presumably could agree to application of stare decisis rules. However, the binding effect of arbitrators' opinions could be expected to correlate with the care with which they are prepared.

54. Enforcement of arbitration is discussed generally infra Part IV.F.1.

55. Federal law ensures enforcement of some arbitration agreements, although it does not necessarily provide the specific rules that apply to arbitration proceedings that are enforced in state court. See infra notes 150–157 and accompanying text.

56. It also may be the case that shareholders who are not "protected" by "proshareholder" local laws may seek to be compensated for the agency and other costs resulting from the extra weighting of their co-shareholders' votes. But this is not so much a cost of nonuniformity as it is the sort of cost that, as discussed supra I.A.1, may be imposed by any inappropriate mandatory rule.

57. For a discussion of different judicial approaches to the question of bad faith termination of franchisees, see T. Mark McLaughlin & Caryn Jacobs, *Termination of Franchisees: Application of the Implied Covenant of Good Faith and Fair Dealing*, 7 FRANCH. l. j. 1 (1987). This problem may become more acute if legislatures promulgate more statutes like the Iowa statute discussed supra note 40. That statute replaces the general "good faith" standard applicable in most states with specific duties. For example, the Iowa statute includes specific rules against "encroachment" by franchisors on existing territories of franchisees. See Iowa Stat. §523H.6. By comparison, courts have not gone further than simply recognizing the application of "good faith" standards in this situation. See Scheck v. Burger King Corp., 798 F.Supp. 692 (S.D. Fla. 1992).

58. See Carlock v. Pillsbury Co., 719 F.Supp. 791 (D. Minn. 1989) (stressing need for national franchise to be subject to a single law).

59. See Bibb. v. Navajo Freight Lines, Inc., 359 U.S. 520 (1959); infra note 180.

60. See Richard M. Buxbaum, *The Threatened Constitutionalization of the Internal Affairs Doctrine in Corporation Law*, 75 CAL. L. REV. 29 (1987); Elvin R. Latty, *Pseudo-Foreign Corporations*, 65 YALE L.J. 137 (1955); Alan R. Palmiter, *The CTS Gambit: Stanching the Federalization of Corporate Law*, 69 WASH. U. L.Q. 445 (1991).

61. See supra text accompanying note 57.

62. See Latty, supra note 60, at 141. (making a similar point about choice-of-law clauses generally).

63. See Buxbaum, supra note 60, at 51.

64. In the first place, only specific issues are adjudicated, meaning that multiple litigation may be necessary. Second, it is not clear when the forum's law may be applied. The Supreme Court has held that although a state may adjudicate nationwide claims in a single class action involving plaintiffs who lack minimum contacts with the forum, if the jurisdiction lacks a sufficient interest in the full faith and credit and due process grounds preclude it from applying its law to nonresidents. See Phillips Petroleum Co. v. Shutts, 472 U.S. 797 (1985); infra note 216.

65. Currie's theories emerge from his writings collected in BRAINARD CURRIE, SELECTED ESSAYS ON THE CONFLICT OF LAWS (1963). For a good description of interest analysis and a comparison with the earlier more rule-oriented approach, see LEA BRILMAYER, CONFLICT OF LAWS: FOUNDATIONS AND FUTURE

DIRECTIONS (1991). For an analysis of the extent to which interest analysis has been adopted by the courts, see Michael E. Solimine, *An Economic and Empirical Analysis of Choice of Law*, 24 GA. L. REV. 49 (1989). For criticisms of the indeterminacy of modern choice-of-law rules, see RICHARD A. POSNER, PROBLEMS OF JURISPRUDENCE 430 (1991); Michael H. Gottesman, *Draining the Dismal Swamp: The Case for Federal Choice of Law Statutes*, 80 GEO. L.J. 1 (1991).

66. See M/S Bremen v. Zapata Off-Shore Co., 407 U.S. 1, 14 (1972) (dealing with a forum selection clause, citing "strong evidence that the forum clause was a vital part of the agreement, and [that] it would be unrealistic to think that the parties did not conduct their negotiations, including fixing the monetary terms, with the consequences of the forum clause figuring prominently in their calculations") (footnote omitted).

67. See George Priest & Benjamin Klein, *The Selection of Disputes for Litigation*, 13 J. LEG. STUD. 1, 13–17 (1984). The Supreme Court recently recognized this point in Carnival Cruise Lines, Inc. v. Shute, 111 S.Ct. 1522, 1527 (1991): [A] clause establishing ex ante the forum for dispute resolution has the salutary effect of dispelling any confusion about where suits arising from the contract must be brought and defended, sparing litigants the time and expense of pretrial motions to determine the correct forum, and conserving judicial resources that otherwise would be devoted to deciding those motions.

68. See Restatement Conflict of Laws, §332 (1934).

69. See infra Part II.B.2.

70. See Michael Gruson, *Governing-Law Clauses in International and Interstate Loan Agreements—New York's Approach*, 1982 U. ILL. L. REV. 207, 226.

71. See articles cited infra note 194.

72. See Romano, supra note 38 (reasoning that investors can rely on Delaware not to tamper with its statute because of Delaware's reliance on franchise tax revenue and side benefits from incorporation).

73. See Carpinello, supra note 21 (asserting that parties should not be able to evade mandatory rules through choice-of-law clauses).

Note that enforcement of contractual choice of law can result in application of a mandatory rule. Courts ordinarily should enforce such a choice. See Michael Gruson, *Forum-Selection Clauses in International and Interstate Commercial Agreements*, 1982 U. ILL. L. REV. 133, 218–22. The parties' choice of a mandatory rule may very well be a deliberate decision to deal in a particular way with unforeseeable problems in long term contracts. For example, the parties may select a law that forbids "bad faith" terminations of franchises because they agree that such a term is appropriate. For a discussion of the analogous issue of rules prohibiting amendment, see Chapter 1, Part III; Chapter 2, Part IV.D. Jurisdictional competition helps ensure the survival of the most efficient of these "mandatory" terms. However, it is important to distinguish a contractual choice of law that would result in invalidating the contract, since the parties obviously intended that their contract should be enforced. For a recent example of a case in which the court's enforcement of the parties' contractual choice of law clearly frustrated the parties' expectations, see Gregory Milanovich v. Costa Crociere, 954 F.2d 763 (D.C. Cir. 1992) (applying contractual choice of Italian law to invalidate cruise line's contract with passenger as one of "adhesion").

74. See, e.g., Woods-Tucker Leasing Corp. of Georgia v. Hutcheson-Ingram Dev. Co. 642 F.2d 744 (5th Cir. 1981) (stating that parties were free to contract for choice of law solely to avoid application of usury statute). For other cases in which courts enforced choice-of-law clauses to override mandatory terms, see supra note 21.

75. See Restatement (Second) of Conflicts, §203, Comment b (1971).

76. A prominent example is the famous case of United Commercial Travelers v. Wolfe, 331 U.S. 586 (1949), discussed infra Part V.B.3, in which the Court enforced a limitations provisions in the contract against the plaintiff's claim that such terms were not enforceable under the law of his state of residence.

77. See generally Benjamin Klein, Stephen Crawford & Armen Alchian, *Vertical Integration, Appropriable Rents, and the Competitive Contracting Process*, J.L. & Econ. 297 (1978).

78. See Alan Schwartz & Louis A. Wilde, *Intervening in Markets on the Basis of Imperfect Information: A Legal and Economic Analysis*, 127 U. Pa. L. Rev. 630, 638 (1979).

79. Exhaustion of remedies is required for both joint and several liability under the law of some states. See Alan R. Bromberg & Larry E. Ribstein, Bromberg & Ribstein on Partnership §§5.08(d)–(g) (1988 & Supp.) Exhaustion is also now required by Uniform Partnership Act (1992), §307(d).

80. Note, however, that the parties may not even know that the partnership law of any state applies. An informal partnership may exist if the parties intend the elements of partnership, even if neither the parties to the firm nor third parties are subjectively aware that the firm is a partnership. See generally Bromberg & Ribstein, supra note 79 at §2.05.

81. See Larry E. Ribstein, *Limited Liability and Theories of the Corporation*, 50 Md. L. Rev. 80 (1991). Even the law of general partnerships may be moving toward increased filings. See Uniform Partnership Act, §303 (1992) (permitting central filing of statements of partnership authority).

82. See supra Part I.B.2 (discussing the possible need for affirmative disclosure rules regarding choice of law).

83. For market inefficiency arguments concerning initial public offerings see, e.g., Victor Brudney, Corporate Governance, *Agency Costs, and the Rhetoric of Contract*, 85 Colum. L. Rev. 1403, 1411–27 (1985); Melvin A. Eisenberg, *The Structure of Corporation Law*, 89 Colum. L. Rev. 1461, 1516–18 (1989).

84. See Elliott Weiss & Lawrence J. White, *Of Econometrics and Indeterminacy: A Study of Investors' Reactions to "Changes" in Corporate Law*, 75 Calif. L. Rev. 551 (1987).

85. See supra Part I.B.3.

86. This argument also has been used to justify broad regulation of corporate governance. See, e.g., Melvin A. Eisenberg, *Contractarianism With-*

out Contracts: A Response to Professor McChesney, 90 COLUM. L. REV. 1321, 1322, 1328–29, 1331 (1990); Melvin A. Eisenberg, *The Structure of Corporate Law*, 89 COLUM. L. REV. 1461, 1486–87 (1989).

87. For a standard legal rule on unconscionability, see Uniform Commercial Code, §2-302.

88. That is particularly so where the contract chooses the entire local law of a particular jurisdiction, since a state's entire law as to a complex contract probably will not operate unfairly against one of the parties on all or most of the many issues that could arise in the future.

89. The most important recent example is the Iowa franchise law first discussed and cited supra note 40. That act invalidates provisions that restrict jurisdiction to a forum outside the state (e.g., Ia. Stat. §523H.3) or that require application of the law of another state (id. §14).

90. See, e.g., W. John Moore, "Franchisees are Sizzling," 17 Nat. J., §340 (Feb. 8, 1992).

91. Romano, supra note 38, at 233–42, shows that franchise tax revenues are an important factor in generating jurisdictional competition regarding corporations.

92. See infra text accompanying note 101 (discussing interest group theory).

93. Jonathan R. Macey & Geoffrey Miller, *Toward an Interest-Group Theory of Delaware Corporate Law*, 65 TEX. L. REV. 469 (1987).

94. For a discussion of other interests of judges, legislators and lawyers relating to enforcement of choice of law clauses, see infra Part IV.

95. The existence of such specialized communities, such as the Delaware bar, partly explains why lawyers in a particular state can capture the benefits of an efficient state law even though the law can be applied in other states. See Larry E. Ribstein, *Efficiency, Markets and Competition: A Comment on Easterbrook & Fischel*, 87 Nw. U. L. REV. 254 (1992). Another explanation is the use of forum selection clauses to restrict the states in which cases are tried. See infra Part IV.F.1.

96. See Macey & Miller, supra note 93 (reaching this conclusion about Delaware corporation law).

97. See Larry E. Ribstein, *The Mandatory Nature of the ALI Code*, 61 GEO. WASH. L. REV. 985, 1023 (1993).

98. However, lawyers might prefer a reduced-competition regime that favored litigation. See Ribstein, supra note 97 (attributing the prolitigation bias of the ALI's Restatement of Corporate Governance to lawyers' role in drafting the Code).

99. See Larry E. Ribstein, *Delaware, Lawyers' Choice of Law*, forthcoming 1994 DEL. J. CORP. LAW. A prominent example is the following recent Delaware statute. H.B. 291, 69 Del. Laws Ch. 127, adding Delaware Code, tit. 6, §2708:

(a) The parties to any contract, agreement or other undertaking, contingent or otherwise, may agree in writing that the contract, agreement or other undertaking shall be governed by or construed under the laws of this State, without regard to principles of conflict of laws, or that the laws of this State shall govern, in whole or in part, any or all of their rights, remedies, liabilities, powers and duties if the parties, either as provided by law or in the manner specified in such writing are, (i) subject to the jurisdiction of the courts of, or arbitration in, Delaware and, (ii) may be served with legal process. The foregoing shall conclusively be presumed to be a significant, material and reasonable relationship with this State and shall be enforced whether or not there are other relationships with this State.

(b) Any person may maintain an action in a court of competent jurisdiction in this State where the action or proceeding arises out of or relates to any contract, agreement or other undertaking for which a choice of Delaware law has been made in whole or in part and which contains the provision permitted by subsection (a) of this section.

(c) The provisions of this section shall not apply to any contract, agreement or other undertaking, (i) to the extent provided to the contrary in Section 1- 105(2) of Title 6 of the Code or, (ii) involving less than $100,000.

(d) In the event that any provision hereof shall be held to be invalid or unenforceable, such holding shall not invalidate or render unenforceable any other provision hereof. Any provision hereof which is held to be invalid or unenforceable only in part or degree or under specific facts, shall remain in full force and effect to the extent, and with respect to facts in connection with which, it has not been held to be invalid or unenforceable.

(e) The provisions of this section shall not limit any jurisdiction otherwise existing in a court sitting in the State of Delaware and shall not affect the validity of any other choice of law provisions in any contract, agreement or other undertaking.

100. See Larry E. Ribstein, *Takeover Defenses and the Corporate Contract*, 78 GEO. L.J. 71 (1989). There is a potential problem in this situation if it is costly for the "third party" to determine the applicable law. This problem is discussed supra Part II.B.2.

101. For a discussion of interest group theory, see Chapter Three, Part IV.A.

102. Over the long run, however, this inefficiency may spur corrective action by injured interest groups. See Gary Becker, *A Theory of Competition Among Pressure Groups for Political Influence*, 98 Q.J. ECON. 371 (1983).

103. See, e.g., the Iowa provisions discussed supra note 40.

104. This insight underlies much of the data supporting the monitoring theory of franchising. See articles cited supra note 41.

105. See Robert E. Martin, *Franchising and Risk Management*, 78 AM. ECON. REV. 954 (1988).

106. See supra Part I.A.5.

107. See Brickley, Dark & Weisbach, supra note 41, at 115–16.

108. See Reinders Brothers, Inc. v. Rain Bird Eastern Sales Corp., 627 F.2d 44 (7th Cir. 1980).

109. The International Franchise Association has 850 members, including the largest franchisors. See W. John Moore, "Policy and Politics in Brief," 17 Nat'l. J. 340 (Feb. 8, 1992).

110. See Michael Hartnett, Franchisors Miffed at Iowa action: Fear Further Empowerment of Franchisees Nationally, Restaurant Business, May 20, 1992, at 20 (quoting reaction of counsel for franchisors to Iowa franchise protection law: "If these changes were limited to Iowa, we would put a fence around the state and quarantine it, but there may be states that are considering it right now that we don't know about").

111. The original statement of this point is Charles M. Tiebout, *A Pure Theory of Local Expenditures*, 64 J. Pol. Econ. 416 (1956).

112. For additional evidence supporting the interest group story, see infra Part IV.F (discussing data on federal enforcement of choice-of-law clauses).

113. See Brickley, Dark & Weisbach, supra note, 41; discussed supra at notes 107–108.

114. See Brickley, Dark & Weisbach, supra note 41.

115. See Richard Martin, *McD Fights to Overturn Iowa Franchise Law*, Restaurant News, at 1 (legislation was drafted by a Des Moines attorney, Douglas Gross, on behalf of a franchisee coalition including Burger King, Pizza Hut, KFC, Taco Bell, and Dairy Queen operators). The Iowa statute is summarized supra note 40.

116. See Chapter Two, supra, text accompanying notes 93–97.

117. See Hartnett, supra note 110, at 20: Gross [attorney for Iowa franchisees' association] says he was advised by Washington, D.C., supporters of the Iowa legislation that it would actually be easier to amend franchise regulations one state at a time than pursue a single piece of federal legislation. "The closer the decision making is to home, the more impact people living at home can have on the legislation," says Gross. "These franchisees are the local business leaders in their community. If they get organized, they can be very powerful."

118. See supra Part II.C.

119. See H. Hart & Albert Sacks, The Legal Process: Basic Problems in the Making and Application of Law 1415 (Tenth Ed. 1958) (stating that a court "should assume, unless the contrary unmistakably appears, that the legislature was made up of reasonable persons pursuing reasonable purposes reasonably"); Richard A. Posner, *Legal Formalism, Legal Realism, and the Interpretation of Statutes and the Constitution*, 37 Case W. Res. L. Rev. 179 (1986); Richard A. Posner, *Statutory Interpretation—in the Classroom and in the Courtroom*, 50 U. Chi. L. Rev. 800 (1983).

120. See Kenneth A. Shepsle; *Congress is a "They," Not an "It": Legislative Intent as Oxymoron*, 12 Int. Rev. L. & Econ. 239 (1992).

121. See Frank H. Easterbrook, *The Supreme Court, 1983 Term-Foreword: The Court and the Economic System*, 98 Harv. L. Rev. 4, 15–18 (1984); William N. Eskridge, Jr., *Politics Without Romance: Implications of Public Choice Theory for Statutory Interpretation*, 74 Va. L. Rev. 275 (1988). For a criticism of this approach on the ground that it may simply shift rent-seeking activity to litigation or make it more difficult to undo interest group deals, see Einer R. Elhauge, *Does Interest Group Theory Justify More Intrusive Judicial Review*, 101 Yale L.J. 31 (1991).

122. See Jonathan Macey, *Promoting Public-Regarding Legislation Through Statutory Interpretation: An Interest Group Model*, 86 COLUM. L. REV. 223 (1986).

123. For example, courts could enforce choice-of-law clauses consistent with the jurisdiction's general policy of enforcing contracts, rather than holding that non-enforcement was compelled by the state's "fundamental policy."

124. See Gary M. Anderson et al., *On the Incentives of Judges to Enforce Legislative Wealth Transfers*, 32 J.L. & ECON. 215 (1989); W. Mark Crain & Robert D. Tollison, *Constitutional Change in an Interest Group Perspective*, 8 J. LEGAL STUD. 165 (1979); William M. Landes & Richard A. Posner, *The Independent Judiciary in an Interest Group Perspective*, 18 J.L. & ECON. 875 (1975).

125. See Posner, supra note 44, at 534–36 (4th ed. 1992) (noting that judges may act to impose personal preferences); RICHARD A. POSNER, *What Do Judges Maximize? (The Same Thing Everybody Else Does)*, Supreme Court Economic Review (1993) (asserting that judges value the power to decide cases); Robert D. Cooter, *The Objecties of Private and Public Judges*, 41 PUB. CHOICE 107, 129–30 (1983). It is not clear, however, that judges do seek to maximize prestige. They may, instead, seek to maximize leisure by adopting rules that minimize their work load. See Posner, *What Do Judges Maximize?*, supra. Or they might prefer above all to maximize the quality, rather than the quantity, of their case load. However, they may find that impossible to accomplish by fashioning general legal rules.

126. See Bruce H. Kobayashi & John R. Lott, Jr., Judicial Reputation and the Efficiency of the Common Law (unpublished manuscript) (Sept. 7, 1993).

127. See Eskridge, supra note 121.

128. See John A. Ferejohn and Barry R. Weingast, *A Positive Theory of Statutory Interpretation*, 12 INT. REV. L. & ECON. 263 (1992) (maintaining that how judges interpret statutes depends partly how they will expect current legislature to react).

129. As to the last two points, see Frank H. Easterbrook, *Some Tasks in Understanding Law through the Lens of Public Choice*, 12 INT. REV. L. & ECON. 284 (1992).

130. Avoidance of choice-of-law clauses through forum-selection, federal litigation, and arbitration is discussed infra Part IV.F.

131. This may be the situation in products liability cases, in which the courts' proliability rules tend to attract business. See Ferens v. John Deere Co., 110 S.Ct. 1274, 1282 (1990) (noting Mississippi's incentive to attract litigation through long statute of limitations).

132. See George L. Priest, *The Common Law Process and the Selection of Efficient Rules*, 6 J. LEG. STUD. 65 (1977); Paul H. Rubin, *Why is the Common Law Efficient?* 6 J. LEG. STUD. 51 (1977).

133. See PAUL H. RUBIN & MARTIN J. BAILEY, *A POSITIVE THEORY OF LEGAL CHANGE* (unpublished manuscript) (1992); Paul H. Rubin, *Common Law and Statute Law*, 11 J. LEG. STUD. 205 (1982).

134. See supra note 21.

135. See Rubin and Bailey, supra note 133 (asserting that the likelihood of

litigation depends on stream of costs of inefficient rules borne by loser, probability of loser's getting rule overturned, and court costs).

136. See supra note 117 and accompanying text. This suggests, ironically, that as a group's power to effect legal rules ignoring contracts grows, the public interest justification for these laws—the group's supposed need for protection from oppressive bargains—diminishes.

137. See supra note 109.

138. See supra note 115 and accompanying text.

139. See Rubin & Bailey, supra note 133.

140. See Michelle J. White, *Legal Complexity and Lawyers' Benefit from Litigation*, 12 Int. Rev. L. & Econ. 381 (1992) (asserting that litigation is increased by rules that are complex but not so complex as to cause more cases to be settled).

141. See Gary Taylor, *Franchise Reform to Yield Feast*, Nat'l Law J., Jan. 20, 1992, at 1: ("Experts predict lawyers will feast on the litigation and legislative reform campaigns already under way as a maturing population of franchisees strives to redefine its foggy relationship with the franchisors who breathed life into their ventures just a few years ago.").

142. See supra Part II.B.4.

143. For a discussion of the role of such clauses in enforcing contractual choice of law, see Ribstein, supra note 21, at 283.

144. This follows from Klaxon Co. v. Stentor Elec. Mfg. Co., 313 U.S. 487 (1941), which requires federal courts in diversity cases to apply the forum state's choice of law rule.

145. See Van Dusen v. Barrack, 376 U.S. 612 (1964).

146. See Ferens v. John Deere Co., 494 U.S. 516 (1990).

147. See Modern Computer Systems, Inc. v. Modern Banking Systems, Inc., 871 F.2d 734 (8th Cir. 1989); Tele-Save Merchandising v. Consumers Distributing, 814 F.2d 1120 (6th Cir. 1987); Pitegoff, supra note 21. In both cases, there were strong dissents noting that the majority's interpretation was contrary to the broad express language of the statute.

148. See Macey, supra note 122.

149. Although final results are likely to divide about equally in the cases in which both parties decide to litigate to judgment rather than to settle, the choice-of-law clause issue is only one of several in most cases. Accordingly, the numbers indicate that some parties who might lose on the choice-of-law issue are taking their chances of succeeding on other grounds. The greater number of federal opinions on this issue arguably suggests that parties who gain from these clauses are bringing their cases in federal court. These numbers are particularly striking in light of the fact that federal circuit courts published only 6631 opinions in 1990, compared to 9632 opinions by the highest state courts. See Director of the Administrative Office of the United States Courts, Annual Report 78 (1990); National Center for State Courts, State Court Caseload Statistics: Annual Report, 1990, Table 6 at 102–06. But this explanation fails to explain why these numbers are not offset by state court actions brought by parties who lose from enforcement. Moreover,

parties who could control the forum presumably would benefit from adjudication in the contractual state even more than from federal adjudication. In fact, the higher number of federal cases may be due simply to the fact that litigants prefer the higher quality of adjudication in federal court. Federal courts are particularly likely to be accessible in cases like this, which involve relatively large contracts and are, almost by definition, multi-state. Under this explanation, the seemingly low number of state court opinions may actually be larger than it otherwise would have been because plaintiffs who stood to lose from choice-of-law clauses avoided federal court.

150. 9 U.S.C. §1 et seq.

151. See id. §92:

A written provision in any maritime transaction or a contract evidencing a transaction involving commerce to settle by arbitration a controversy thereafter arising out of such contract or transaction, or the refusal to perform the whole or any part thereof, or an agreement in writing to submit to arbitration an existing controversy arising out of such a contract, transaction, or refusal, shall be valid, irrevocable, and enforceable, save upon such grounds as exist at law or in equity for the revocation of any contract.

152. See Southland Corp. v. Keating, 465 U.S. 1 (1984).

153. See Gilmer v. Interstate/Johnson Lane Corp., 111 S.Ct. 1647 (1991) (employment discrimination); Rodriguez de Quijas v. Shearson/American Express, Inc., 490 U.S. 477 (1989) (securities law claim); Shearson/American Express, Inc. v. McMahon, 482 U.S. 220 (1987) (securities law claim); Perry v. Thomas, 482 U.S. 483 (1987) (employee).

154. See National Equipment Rental, LTD. v. Szukhent, 375 U.S. 311 (1964).

155. See M/S Bremen v. Zapata Off-Shore Co., 407 U.S. 1 (1972).

156. See Carnival Cruise Lines, Inc. v. Shute, 111 S.Ct. 1522 (1991).

157. See Bonny v. The Society of Lloyd's, 1993 WL 92345 (7th Cir. 1993); Hugel v. Corproation of Lloyd's, 999 F.2d 206 (7th Cir. 1993); Roby v. Corporation of Lloyd's, 996 F.2d 1353 (2d Cir. 1993).

158. Congress has the same reasons as state legislators to preclude contracting parties from opting out of federal law. Nevertheless, as is clear from the federal securities law and employment discrimination cases cited supra notes 153, federal courts have permitted contracting parties to avoid federal as well as state law. Although the life tenure of federal judges leaves them somewhat less subject to legislative discipline than state court judges, this is not a complete explanation because Congress controls federal courts' salary and jurisdiction and can reverse federal court decisions by legislation. However, perhaps Congress is not as concerned as state legislatures about this problem, since the Supremacy Clause of the Constitution, U.S. Const. art. VI, cl. 2, makes clear that the parties cannot easily avoid federal statutes by choosing to be governed by inconsistent state law. Accordingly, federal courts may not fear retaliation to the same extent as state courts. At the same time, federal judges may have an incentive to maximize use of the federal courts. See Kobayashi & Lott, supra note 126 (arguing that courts have an

incentive to decide cases so as to maximize citations, and that this incentive may, among other things, lead federal courts to enlarge their removal jurisdiction).

159. The strongest remaining reason for federal courts to refuse to enforce choice-of-law clauses is simply a desire to avoid the heavier workload that would result if beneficiaries of choice-of-law clauses seek refuge in federal courts. This evidence in the text indicates that the federal courts' relative impartiality appears to dominate any incentive they might have to reduce their workload.

160. The federal cases on contractual choice of law are significant not only by differing from state cases, but in their ability to influence state law. First, the federal courts compete with state courts within the limits of diversity jurisdiction. Accordingly, state courts may lose litigation business to federal courts to the extent that they refuse to enforce contractual choice of law. Second, federal diversity cases provide a significant body of precedents for state courts that may sway courts in marginal cases.

161. See U.S. Const. §8, cl. 3 (providing that Congress has the power "[t]o regulate Commerce . . . among the several states. . .").

162. See U.S. Const. Amend. XIV: "No state shall . . . deprive any person of life, liberty, or property, without due process of law. . .".

163. See U.S. Const. art. IV, §1: "Full Faith and Credit shall be given in each State to the public Acts, Records, and judicial Proceedings of every other State. And the Congress may by general Laws prescribe the Manner in which such Acts, Records and Proceedings shall be proved, and the Effect thereof."

164. See Cooley v. board of Wardens, 53 U.S. 299 (1851) (holding that grant of power to Congress forbids some but not all state regulation affecting interstate commerce, and upholding state statute imposing pilotage fee as within state's power).

165. See Posner, supra note 44, at 638–44; Fischel, supra note 46, at 74; Saul Levmore, *Interstate Exploitation and Judicial Intervention*, 69 VA. L. REV. 563, 568–69 (1983).

166. U.S. v. Carolene Products, 304 U.S. 144, 152–53 n.14 (1938); see also South Carolina Highway Dept. v. Barnwell Brothers, 303 U.S. 177, 186 (1938) (holding that Commerce Clause applies to state regulation by which states gain "a local benefit by throwing the attendant burdens on those without the state").

167. The theory is referred to as the "representation-reinforcing" view of the Commerce Clause. See JOHN HART ELY, DEMOCRACY AND DISTRUST 83–84, 91 (1980).

168. Gary Becker has shown that interest group competition may cause laws to be Kaldor-Hicks efficient because some interest groups offset the influence of others. See Gary Becker, *Public Policies, Pressure Groups, and Dead Weight Costs*, 28 J. PUB. ECON. 329 (1985); Becker, supra note 102.

169. See supra text accompanying note 24.

170. Indeed, these factors arguably also provide a public interest justifica-

tion for not enforcing the contract. However, the public interest argument is weak in theory, see supra Part I.B, and is refuted by evidence of different results in federal and state courts. See supra Part IV.F.2.

171. See Julian N. Eule, *Laying the Dormant Commerce Clause to Rest*, 91 YALE L.J. 425, 460–68 (1982).

172. See Fischel, supra note 46, at 76.

173. See Edmund W. Kitch, *Regulation and the American Common Market, in* REGULATION, FEDERALISM, AND INTERSTATE COMMERCE 7-55 (A. Dan Tarlock ed., 1981) (arguing that Commerce Clause is unnecessary for this reason).

174. See Levmore, supra note 165, at 565. The states' ability to retaliate has lead Levmore to suggest that the Court should give special attention to laws that exploit special state advantages, such as natural resources, where such retaliation may not be a realistic constraint.

175. 437 U.S. 117 (1978).

176. See Eule, supra note 171, at 466 n. 221 (noting this point but saying that "bottom line" for legislators were votes).

177. See LAWRENCE H. TRIBE, AMERICAN CONSTITUTIONAL LAW 412 (2d Ed. 1988) (suggesting that the case may be explained by the fact that the consumers were an in-state "surrogate" for Exxon). This is shown by a study of the law's effect on the gasoline retailing market in Maryland. See John M. Barron & John R. Umbeck, *The Effects of Different Contractual Arrangements: The Case of Retail Gasoline Markets*, 27 J.L. & ECON. 313 (1984) (explaining that the legal change, among other things, raised gas prices and reduced hours at affected stations).

178. For commentary discussing this approach under the commerce clause see Brilmayer, supra note 65, at 124; Harold W. Horowitz, *The Commerce Clause as a Limitation on State Choice of Law Doctrine*, 84 HARV. L. REV. 806 (1971).

179. 325 U.S. 761, 767 (1945).

180. See Kassel v. Consolidated Freightways Corp., 450 U.S. 662 (1981); Raymond Motor Transportation, Inc. v. Rice, 434 U.S. 429 (1978).

181. See Bibb v. Navajo Freight Lines, Inc., 359 U.S. 520 (1959).

182. See supra Part II.A.4.

183. See Eule, supra note 171, at 441 (making this point in a discussion of *Bibb*).

184. See Fischel, supra note 46, at 88.

185. For authorities suggesting discrimination as the principal basis of Commerce Clause protection, see CTS Corp. v. Dynamics Corp., 481 U.S. 69, 87 (1987); Fischel, supra note 46, at 82–83; see also Donald H. Regan, *The Supreme Court and State Protectionism: Making Sense of the Dormant Commerce Clause*, 84 MICH. L. REV. 1091 (1986) (suggesting that the Court should merely prevent states from engaging in purposeful economic protectionism).

186. A potentially promising "discrimination" approach to protecting contractual choice of law would be to characterize invalidation of choice-of-law clauses as discriminating against law itself as a product sold in interstate commerce. The concept of law as a product has some support in the literature, as discussed supra text accompanying note 38. This would be

similar in effect to the limited theory of Commerce Clause protection of choice-of-law clauses discussed in the next section, which is essentially based on the need to discipline state courts' discrimination against foreign law. However, unlike a broad discrimination argument, the limited theory discussed below would not mandate enforcement of all choice-of-law clauses, but rather would only apply the Commerce Clause to invalidate state statutes to the extent that they preclude enforcement of choice-of-law clauses. Thus, this theory would target the situations in which nonenforcement is most likely to be based on cost-exporting legislation.

187. See Hall v. Geiger-Jones Co., 242 U.S. 539 (1917).

188. See Jonathan Macey & Geoffrey Miller, *The Origin of the Blue Sky Laws*, 70 Tex. L. Rev. 347 (1991) (explaining state securities legislation as an effort by in-state bankers to preclude competition by out-of-state securities firms).

189. There are related questions whether the law of a firm's formation state should govern rights such as owners' personal liability for the firm's debts of the firm or shareholders' inspection rights turns on what matters the parties have agreed would be governed by the law of the state of incorporation. Compare Valtz v. Penta Investment Corp., 188 Cal. Rptr. 922 (1983) (holding that shareholder inspection rights are not an internal affair and so may be regulated under law other than that of state of incorporation) with De Mott, supra note 205, at 189 (noting planning and operational implications of such rules). In theory, a selected state's law could apply to any matter that might be the subject of contract, and the commerce clause should ensure enforcement of a contract providing for application of that law.

190. Cf. Mon-Shore Management v. Family Media. 584 F. Supp. 186 (S.D.N.Y. 1984) (applying a franchise disclosure law under the law of the state selected in the contract).

191. Congress may have eliminated the possibility of any dormant commerce clause argument by explicitly approving the state regulation in its own securities law. See Levmore, supra note 165, at 620.

An alternative explanation of the Constitutionality of the blue sky laws under a theory of the Commerce Clause different from the one I propose is that blue sky laws directly apply only in the regulating state. By contrast, a state antitakeover statute that applies to firms incorporated outside the enacting state not only affects the acquisition of control of the entire corporation, but cannot be avoided because bidders must buy control shares wherever they are located. See Kozyris, infra note 205, at 529–30. The proposed theory would not necessarily invalidate a law that mandates affirmative disclosure of the applicable law that is imposed by the avoided but not the selected state. For a discussion of why such regulation may be efficient, see supra Part II.B.2. This sort of regulation arguably seeks to improve rather than prevent state competition. In any event, even if the regulation is unnecessary and inefficient, it at least does not uphold particular statutory interest-group deals, and therefore does not implicate the cost-exporting basis of my theory.

192. 457 U.S. 624 (1982).

193. Id. at 640–43.
194. 481 U.S. 69 (1987).
195. CTS is also discussed in Chapter Two, infra text accompanying note 86.
196. Id. at 87–88.
197. Id. at 88–89.
198. Id. at 90–91; see Chapter Three, supra at note 55.
199. Id. at 89.
200. Id. at 87.
201. See infra Part V.A.2.
202. See infra Part V.3.b.
203. See supra Part II.C.
204. Gregory Sidak and Susan Woodward argue that state antitakeover statutes are unconstitutional on the different ground that they impose costs on nonresidents. See J. Gregory Sidak & Susan Woodward, *Corporate Takeovers, The Commerce Clause, and the Efficient Anonymity of Shareholders*, 84 Nw. U. L. Rev. 1092 (1990). There are two problems with this analysis. First, even if the externalization-of-costs analysis may be sound as applied in this particular situation, as discussed above in Section V.A.1, once the Court adopts such a test, it must determine in what other types of cases it should be applied. Second, the Sidak-Wordward analysis does not appropriately distinguish CTS-type statutes that apply only to firms incorporated under the statute, and MITE-type takeover statutes that apply on the basis of transactions in the state. While both types of statutes may, indeed, impose costs on non-residents, the CTS-type statute does so only because it is imposed on existing shareholders rather than on an opt-in basis. This is a Contract Clause, not a Commerce Clause, problem.
205. See Sadler v. NCR Corporation, 928 F.2d 48, 55 (2d Cir. 1991) (noting Court's citation of internal affairs rule but nevertheless holding that Commerce Clause did not require enforcing incorporating state's law as to shareholders' inspection right). For commentary suggesting the internal affairs rule is not constitutionally compelled even after MITE and CTS, see P. John Kozyris, *Some Observations on Stage Regulation of Multistate Tender Offers—Controlling Choice of Law Through the Commerce Clause*, 14 Del. J. Corp. 499, 508 (1989). For authorities suggesting that departing from the internal affairs rule may involve a commerce clause problem, see McDermott Inc. v. Lewis, 531 A. 2d 206 (Del. 1987) (stating that Commerce Clause problem is presented by departure from internal affairs rule because of problem of differing state regulation); Deborah A. DeMott, *Perspectives on Choice of Law for Corporate Internal Affairs*, 48 L. & Contemp. Prob. 161, 186–88 (1985).
206. See Wilson v. Louisiana-Pacific Resources, Inc., 187 Cal. Rptr. 852 (1982) (holding that state law requiring foreign corporation to adopt cumulative voting is not so burdensome as to constitute an impermissible restriction on interstate commerce).
207. See supra text accompanying notes 150–157.
208. Robert H. Jackson, *Full Faith and Credit—The Lawyer's Clause of the*

Constitution, 45 COLUM. L. REV. 1, 17 (1945); see also Allstate Insurance Co. v. Hague, 449 U.S. 302, 332–33 (1981) (Stevens, J., concurring).

209. See Arthur T. von Mehren & Donald T. Trautman, *Constitutional Control of Choice of Law: Some Reflections on Hague,* 10 HOFSTRA L. REV. 35, 49 (1981); Kirgis, *The Roles of Due Process and Full Faith and Credit in Choice of Law,* 62 CORNELL L. REV. 94, 120 (arguing that forum cannot refuse to apply another state's rule where, among other factors, it relies on its own rule which applies in a "discrete class of cases" and is inconsistent with its normal conflict rule). One commentator sees a similar principle operating under the due process clause. See Brilmayer, supra note 65, at 121 (stating that state cannot make pretextual assertion of its interest).

210. See Brainerd Currie, *The Constitution and the Choice of Law: Governmental Interests and the Judicial Function,* 26 U. CHI. L. REV. 9 (1958), SELECTED ESSAYS ON CONFLICT OF LAWS 188 (1963).

211. 449 U.S. 302 (1981).

212. The Court held that a similar approach would be applied under both clauses. See 449 U.S. at 308 n.10.

213. See Russell J. Weintraub, *Who's Afraid of Constitutional Limitations on Choice of Law?* 10 HOFSTRA L. REV. 17 (1981) (arguing that Hague indicates that the Court will not give close Constitutional supervision to conflicts decisions); see also WILLIAM W. CROSSKEY, POLITICS AND THE CONSTITUTION IN THE HISTORY OF THE UNITED STATES 555 (1953) (noting prior Hague that the Court has done under Full Faith and Credit merely what it would have done under the modern due process clause).

214. It is equally true that the weak comity principle does not prevent states from applying a state's law that is made relevant by a choice-of-law clause in a contract. See Edith Friedler, *Party Autonomy Revisited: A Statutory Solution to a Choice-Of-Law Problem,* 37 KAN. L. REV. 471 (1989); Ribstein, *supra* note 99. But see Kirt O'Neill, Note, *Contractual Choice Of Law: The Case For A New Determination Of Full Faith and Credit Limitations,* 71 TEX. L. REV. 1019 (1993) (arguing that statutes providing for enforcement of choice-of-law clauses unconstitutionally infringe state sovereignty).

215. Hague, 449 U.S. at 318 n.24 (noting there was "no element of unfair surprise or frustration of legitimate expectations as a result of Minnesota's choice of its law").

216. Id. at 324.

217. Id. at 328–29.

218. 472 U.S. 797 (1985).

219. Id. at 822.

220. See Order of United Commercial Travelers v. Wolfe, 331 U.S. 586 (1947) (enforcing notice-of-claim provision in association's constitution despite law in member's state of residence invalidating contractual shortening of the limitations period); Sovereign Camp of Woodmen of the World v. Bolin, 305 U.S. 66 (1938) (enforcing bylaw providing that member's obligations would cease after twenty years against claim that bylaw was ultra vires); Modern Woodmen of America v. Mixer, 267 U.S. 544 (1925) (enforcing bylaw

concerning effect of member's prolonged absence rather than presumption-of-death law); Supreme Council of the Royal Arcanum v. Green, 237 U.S. 531 (1915) (enforcing increase in assessment rate pursuant to association's constitution).

221. 237 U.S. 531 (1915).

222. For commentary critical of the fraternal benefit association cases and arguing that they cannot be reconciled with the Court's narrower approach to full faith and credit in other cases, see Currie, supra note 210, at 243–59 (arguing that fraternal benefit cases improperly overemphasize interest of formation state); Robert A. Sedler, *Constitutional Limitations on Choice of Law: The Perspective of Constitutional Generalism*, 10 HOFSTRA L. REV. 59, 99–100 (1981) (asserting that associations usually can function with single rule, so national interest in unity rarely justifies applying single law).

223. See supra Part V.A.2.

224. See supra Part III.B.

225. 267 U.S. 544 (1925).

226. Id. at 551.

227. 331 U.S. 586 (1947).

228. See Sedler, supra note 222, at 99 (making the same point).

229. At some point, however, a single rule is practically necessary. For example, it is difficult to see how voting for directors could be structured so that some shareholders vote cumulatively for directors and straight voting applies to others in the same election. Also, even where differential rights are possible, pricing by state may be impracticable.

230. See Currie, supra note 210, at 243–59.

231. See New York Life Ins. Co. v. Cravens, 178 U.S. 389 (1900); Currie, supra note 210, at 224–25. The Court reasoned that this would give an advantage to foreign companies over domestic ones subject to a different local rule. However, the special fraternal benefit association rule obviously gives an artificial advantage to that form of business.

232. Modern Woodmen of America v. Mixer, 267 U.S. 544, 551 (1925) (Holmes, J.).

233. See Order of United Commercial Travelers v. Wolfe, 331 U.S. 586, 609 (1947).

234. Enforcement of the selected law may be necessary if more than one state has significant contacts. See Kirgis, supra note 209, at 140. However, even in this situation a Court might find that the policies of a state with significant contacts justifies application of that state's laws despite the need for certainty. See id.

235. For an article suggesting a federal conflicts code, see Gottesman, supra note 65.

236. See supra text accompanying note 210.

237. See supra text accompanying note 164.

238. See Richard A. Posner, *The Constitution as an Economic Document*, 56 GEO. WASH. L. REV. 4, 17 (1987).

239. For commentary skeptical of a presumption favoring judicial power

See Elhauge, supra note 121; Posner, supra note 238, at 8 (stating that judges "have weak incentives to be faithful agents").

240. See generally Eskridge, supra note 121.

241. For a support-maximizing theory of federal government action, see Jonathan R. Macey, *State and Federal Regulation of Corporate Takeovers: A View from the Demand Side* 69 Wash. U. L. Q. 383 (1991); Jonathan R. Macey, *Federal Deference to Local Regulators and the Economic Theory of Regulation: Toward a Public Choice Explanation of Federalism*, 76 Va. L. Rev. 265 (1990).

242. See Ernest J. Brown, *The Open Economy: Justice Frankfurter and the Position of the Judiciary*, 67 Yale L.J. 219, 220–21 (1957); Levmore, supra note 165, at 569.

243. For a case even more clearly limiting federal preemption in this context, see Amanda Acquiaition Corp. v. Universal Foods Corp., 877 F.2d 496 (7th Cir.), cert. denied 493 U.S. 955 (1989) (holding that Williams Act does not require the states to adhere to a particular balance between bidders and management).

244. See Santa Fe Industries, Inc. v. Green, 430 U.S. 462, (1977).

Chapter 6: Conclusion

1. See Larry E. Ribstein, "The Constitutional Conception of the Corporation" (ms. 1994).

2. U.S. Const. art. IV, §2 provides: "The Citizens of each State shall be entitled to all Privileges and Immunities of Citizens in the several States." The application of the "privileges and immunities" clause to corporations was rejected in Paul v. Virginia, 75 U.S. (8 Wall.) 168 (1869). Richard Epstein criticizes this case for wrongly distinguishing between the corporation and the individual shareholders of whom it is composed. See Richard A. Epstein, *Bargaining with the State*, 118–20 (1993). However, it follows from our analysis in Chapter 5 that a "foreign corporation" amounts to a contract by the parties to the firm to apply the law of a particular state. A court's refusing to enforce or penalizing this choice of law by imposing burdens on foreign corporations presents a problem of protecting interstate commerce. This problem differs significantly from that of discriminating against people on the basis of state of origin that is addressed by the privileges and immunities clause. The privileges and immunities clause should no more protect a foreign corporation than it should protect, for example, a publishing or franchise contract that has a contractual choice of law clause.

3. See Braswell v. U.S. 487 U.S. 99 (1988).

4. U.S. Const. art. VI, cl. 2.

5. 481 U.S. 69 (1987).

6. See Chapter Five, text at notes 194–207.

7. See Chapter Five, text at notes 187–191.

About the Authors

HENRY N. BUTLER is the Fred and Mary Koch Distinguished Teaching Professor of Law and Economics at the University of Kansas Schools of Business and Law, and he is the director of the school's Law and Organizational Economics Center. He is the author or coauthor of several books and dozens of journal articles concerning corporate governance, economic analysis of law, and the impact of government regulations on business activities.

LARRY E. RIBSTEIN is the GMU Foundation Professor of Law at the George Mason University School of Law, and he is the coordinator and principal developer of the school's Corporate and Securities Law Track. He is the author of numerous casebooks, treatises, and practitioner handbooks and dozens of journal articles concerning partnerships, corporations, corporate governance, and limited liability companies. He is active in numerous professional committees.

A NOTE ON THE BOOK

This book was edited by
Cheryl Weissman
of the staff of the AEI Press.
The text was set in Palatino, a typeface designed by
the twentieth-century Swiss designer Hermann Zapf.
Coghill Composition, of Richmond, Virginia,
set the type, and Data Reproductions Corporation,
of Rochester Hills, Michigan, printed and bound the book,
using permanent acid-free paper.

The AEI Press is the publisher for the American Enterprise Institute for Public Policy Research, 1150 17th Street, N.W., Washington, D.C. 20036; *Christopher C. DeMuth,* publisher; *Dana Lane,* director; *Ann Petty,* editor; *Leigh Tripoli,* editor; *Cheryl Weissman,* editor; *Lisa Roman,* editorial assistant (rights and permissions).